The Life

of

Dr. Orrington

Dr. James Orrington

ISBN: 978-1-965663-04-2

First printing, edition 2024
Orrington publishing
7931 S. King Dr.
Chicago, IL 60619
www.apdminis.com
info@airguardhealth.com

Disclaimer: *This book is a work of creative nonfiction. Names, characters, businesses, places, events, and incidents are either the products of the author's imagination or used in a fictitious manner. Any resemblance to actual persons, living or dead, or events is purely coincidental.*

Dedication

To those who stand firm in their faith and uphold the integrity of their families, even in the face of deceit. This book is dedicated to all who have experienced the betrayal of authority and the misrepresentation of their beliefs. May my stories inspire resilience and foster understanding in a world that often overlooks the truth.

Table of Content

Chapter 1

Dr. James Orrington II stood beside the dental chair, his smile bursting with warmth. The instrument in his hand shone bright under the sterile lights of the office, one of those fixtures now so familiar to anyone who had ever sat in the dentist's chair. To Orrington, however, it was something more.

"Well, hello, friend," he began, his voice smooth and reassuring, as would come from a good friend over coffee. "I am Dr. James Orrington II, a family dentist, second generation. I have practiced since 2001, though my story goes way back, actually to the '80s. I was thirteen, working as a dental assistant for my dad." He chuckled low, his eyes distant for a second, as though he was there, in that old office, breathing in the unmistakable scent of dental antiseptic.

In those few seconds, it flashed before him—years of learning, adjustment, and evolution in his profession. But what was more important, what he really wanted to share with them, was not about being a dentist. No, this was something far more basic. Something that informed every aspect of his work—and his life.

"You know, over the years, one thing I have learned is this," he continued, lowering himself just enough to give the notion of sharing a secret, "good health, just like a good life, starts with water."

He turned away from me and walked toward the sterilization machine, which sat neatly in the equipment room. Putting his hand on it, he almost gestured as if out of respect, with a show of great responsibility. "In my practice, water quality means everything. We don't take any chances—from installing special devices to using only distilled water, we make sure that it's all done right."

His eyes sounded a note of nostalgia as he spoke. He chuckled with a glint in his eye, "Anybody would think at this moment that I am crazy to be talking to myself out loud like this," he chuckled.

"My dad, well, he wasn't so lucky. You see, back then, the sterilizing machine would break down—regularly, as clockwork, every other month. And do you know why?" He didn't wait for the answer but beamed with knowing. "Tap water was the villain. I saw this happen time after time until it became a sort of ritual."

He does not say another word but remembers it just like yesterday. The smell of the old office, the hum of machines, and the sound of his father's frustrated sighs as another sterilization machine got out of order. The look in his father's eyes—the frustration in them—was a constant reminder of how small, minute things could suddenly become big problems.

And then the memory opened, and he was back again, a little boy standing at the door of the office, watching his father frown as the machine went haywire. It had happened often enough that even thirteen-year-old James had begun to understand the patterns.

"Maybe, Dad, it's the water?" he had said one day, standing there with the towel draped like a cape over his shoulder, a pint-sized dentist in training.

He glanced up from the machine, his eyes tired but considerate. He'd sighed, his shoulders sagging just that little bit, as if carrying the weight of every machine failure before this one. "Could be, son. Could be."

It had just been an exchange, but something James remembered all his life.

"So, when I started my own practice," Dr. Orrington said, back in the present, "I drew a conscious decision. I changed over to vapor-distilled water for everything. And do you know what? Two decades later, no breakdowns—except perhaps for the odd door hinge." He chuckled sanguinely to himself, as if sharing an inside joke with the viewer.

The lesson was simple: sometimes it was the smallest things that made all the difference. But it was not just about keeping machines hot. To Dr. Orrington, pure water was more than that. Times more than that. Far surpassing.

He strolled toward a small water feature in the corner of his office, and dipping his fingers into the cool, flowing stream, began to speak. "This distilled water," he started off, "was value thereof." His tone was more reflective suddenly. "It doesn't just keep my equipment going, but it's a reminder—a reminder of the power of pure water, how something so simple can be so basic and have such a profound impact."

He looked down to the water feature, where the soft murmur of running water filled the small room. "I bought this fountain a few years back," he said, with just the shadow of a grin. "And the salesperson told me, 'the pump will fail, it always does.' But here we are, years later, and mine is still going strong."

One eyebrow arched—the message blunt: quality matters. But there was more, much more, behind that look, something deeper, for to Dr. Orrington, water was far more than accommodation or tool about his practice. Water was life. In every sense of the word.

But, he said, his voice turning serious, it wasn't over there.

His manner now serious, more contemplative, as he walked. "In 2020, something happened that really changed everything. I was checking the water collected by a dehumidifier that sat in my office, and well, I found something that wasn't quite normal. Biomolecular magnetic nanomaterials."

It was a discovery that had come to him as a surprise—something so completely unexpected that it opened for him a whole new realm of understanding. This was no longer about dentistry. It was something far bigger.

"This finding," he continued, "it wasn't just about the water of my office. The finger was pointing at something much deeper. It was something that affects us all."

He paused, letting the weight of his utterances set in. Water, he had learned, was so much more than a simple chemical compound. It was an electromagnetic force, a vibration—a carrier of energy. It was the source of life, and it was the medium through which we communicate with our environment.

The scene then shifts to a serene nature environment—a calm river flowing under the midday sun. This crystal clear, pure water stood for something more essential than that of water. One could consider that the river's flow is representative of life, whereby there is an interlink between nature and the human body.

"Agua," his voice continued, soft now and almost reverent, "isn't just something we need—it's life—it's energy—it's how we communicate with the world around us."

Sitting back in the dental chair, as if to sit down and begin a discussion with his imaginary viewers, Dr. Orrington continued in his office.

"Let me share with you a profound fact," he said, leaning forward just a little. "A secret, if you will. Water, left to its purest form, is an unbending, ethereal 'ineluctability.' It uplifts, it protects, and most of all, it enriches our being."

There was something in the way he said it, this quiet conviction that told him this wasn't about medicine, about technology—this was about life.

In the laboratory, Dr. Orrington demonstrated water distillation: how simple tap water became pure, vapor-distilled water. Each step was methodical, precise, as if he were performing an intricate dance with the elements. "I've spent years studying the properties of water," he said, his voice calm but with a deep sense of purpose. "I've experimented with ways of harnessing its potential. And this led me to develop this, which I call the Orrington Technique." The words hung a second in the air, vested in the gravity of years of research and discovery. "It is a method that allows us to deliver light, energy, and frequency directly into the body through water. Pure water becomes a conduit for life."

Dr. Orrington smiled warmly but was filled with the knowledge of a truly historical revelation he was about to share. "So, where do we begin? With you. You are a vessel of water, a conduit of energy and life. And the secret to unlocking your potential lies in understanding the power of pure water."

"When I first came to Vatican City," he said, "I was struck by the beauty of a painting by Michelangelo, *The Creation of Adam*." The scene then cut to a close-up of that famous scene when God extends his hand to Adam—the divine spark of life across their gap. "My attention," Dr. Orrington went on, "was riveted by the clouds around the Heavenly Father. And then it came to me—those clouds, they represent water. The elixir of life."

Chapter 2

Standing literally at the center of Vatican City, Dr. Orrington was taken by the unforgiving glare at Michelangelo's masterpiece, *The Creation of Adam*. The fresco was characteristic of a breathtaking scene of the divine moment when God gave man life, the celestial energy coursing through the space within their outstretched fingers. It was in that moment of quiet contemplation that he realized the profound truth contained within the artwork.

Indeed, he said to himself meditatively, through water, the Heavenly Father speaks directly to the human mind—a thought that stirred an erotic charge in his soul. The outline of the human brain, captured subtly in the fresco's background, lingered in the mind and produced a sense of clarity that had evaded him for so long. It was through water, a universal medium connecting humankind to divinity, he comprehended, that the essence of creation surged.

"It came to me," he said dreamily, his eyes fixed elsewhere, "about water." He continued by saying, "It's as if it were the very sap that courses through each and every life form. Without it, nothing can survive." Indeed, the thought weighed heavy in his mind, and somehow he felt refreshed, almost as if he had received some kind of transcendental insight about the universe.

Stepping out, he found himself on the bustling streets of Rome. There was nothing less than laughter, conversations, and the subtle sound of water plummeting. Fountains speckled the landscape, simple beauties speaking unto the life-giving power of water. The sun flashed off the surface, making a mesmerizing dance of light as it cascaded over in pristine streams.

"While in Rome, I think I must have passed a fountain here, a fountain there, and actually, all of them having water so clean that locals drink directly from them without hesitation," he narrated to himself, wonderstruck by the people's ordinary routines. He watched one of them approach one of these fountains, making sure to cup his hands for a drink right from the flowing water, exuding a semblance of trust and connection that was timeless.

"The Roman Empire was the greatest that ever was known, and I really feel that their access to pure water played an important part in that," he thought aloud, with thoughts swirling in historical overtures. The ancient structures around him whispered stories of glory and ambition, and he could have almost sworn to hearing the echoes of voices from centuries past.

"I know it seems almost too simple," he thought, a smile creeping onto his face, "but sometimes, the simplest answer is the answer." In that instant, he felt a connection to the past. Understanding that the basis of civilization was harnessed from the very core of life itself.

As he walked deeper into the heart of the city, he found his head running archival footage—a clip of Viktor Schauberger, the celebrated Austrian naturalist and inventor. The film ran with detail in his mind: Schauberger working with water, his enthusiasm palpable frame by frame. He could almost hear Schauberger's voice: "Water protects those who protect it." That philosophy was something he had clung to a long time—and lived by, both personally and professionally.

It came to him one morning in a quiet moment of his conscious mind, on a suburban street—nothing of an exception but for how humble it was—made to feel almost extraordinary by his dreamlike visitation. A man in early middle age, absorbed in the miniature glowing rectangle he held in his hand, strolled by. Then, a bird swooped down at him, as if about to alight on his shoulder. The man jerked, startled. Dr. Orrington laughed low, to himself, observing the scene.

"Two incidents with the birds this year confirmed my belief in divine protection," he narrated. He turned everywhere, looking into the bewildering behavior of that bird, and lo, almost instantly for a second their eyes locked into each other.

"One day, as I walked down a street, distracted by my phone, a wild bird tried to land on my shoulder," he said, reliving the feeling. "There was much space around, but somehow, it felt like flying into him in a busy corridor." It was that connection that somehow told them something invisible was happening between them.

A little later, he came upon a gleaming, rented yacht dry-docked at the dock. As he drew near, he saw another bird sitting in the captain's chair inside the boat—an extremely unlikely occurrence. Dr. Orrington wondered how in the world it had managed to find its way in through such a small opening. The bird regarded him with interest, as if considering the impact of this interloper.

"As I drew closer, it flew off," he remembered, his eyes following as the bird filled the sky the brilliant shade of blue. "These occurrences seemed like omens—signs that I was on the correct path. Later, I read that these cross-species encounters indicate divine protection."

His heart had filled with so much gratitude in the middle of this salty air, being wrapped by the ocean breeze. Every day was like a new chapter; there was something around the corner, waiting to be unwrapped.

The next significant moment came two weeks into his journey as he found himself in Mexico. There was an ominous-looking sky ahead as a vicious hurricane was about to arrive, and guests were on top of his hotel, looking with anxious eyes as it neared. Dr. Orrington felt a bad sense of foreboding, but deep inside, he remained hopeful.

"But then the hurricane is coming, and the most amazing thing in the world happens," he recalls. It was this powerful and relentless hurricane that suddenly just stopped. He couldn't believe his eyes as it seemed to stay stopped just five miles away from the bay for hours, after which the direction totally changed.

"When it was just five miles from the bay, the hurricane came to a complete stop. It stayed there for hours in that position before changing direction," he narrated and remembered the reactions of astounded guests around him. They had crowded around the television in the house, where a weatherman spoke in incredulity.

"This is super unusual. Normally that doesn't happen," the weatherman said, with disbelief almost spilling over into his voice.

"In that instant, I realized—our weather was a living thing," mused Dr. Orrington as his sharp mind realized it was being nourished by forces beyond comprehension. "Like us, it feeds off energy and vibration."

Continuing his trip to Greece, he embarked on a business trip that would keep him ever so convinced of the close link between people and water. Before him stood the ancient ruins of Athens, unparalleled in their splendor. Straining his eyes in wonder, he beheld the Parthenon and several other constructions, each testifying to human genius.

"I was most struck," he said, "by the heavy presence of water amongst these ruins." His gaze fell on the pools catching the sunlight. It also seemed to him that the ancient buildings around him were not so high as he had thought them. But it was very plain at least that much water was there. The reflective face of it glimmered, like the reflex of a sheet of polished silver, shiny to the little oncoming winds through all the length of their wagon road.

"Up close, these sites felt more modest than I had envisioned, yet the presence of the water was clear—there to remind me of how water has and will continue to play a part in our world." The connection was palpable, and he felt an urge to dive deeper into the history and the stories of those who had come before him.

It was in thinking through these ancient sites that Dr. Orrington went into what felt like the closing montage of moments. He watched a scene transition: from the Sistine Chapel still wrapped around his mind with *The Creation of Adam*, moving to the ancient ruins of Athens, the flowing rivers and vibrant streets of Rome.

"Water, pure, is little more than a substance," he said aloud, but to himself, every word weighing heavy in utterances. "It is one that conveys, protects, binds life forces together." The knowledge settled into him like a warm hug.

"In understanding its power, we find the key to our existence," he finally said as his heart pounded with excitement. All things being interconnected became his cue or guiding principle in life, making him want to let everyone understand.

"Remember, all you need to survive is energy and frequency; that's the secret, that's the key," he said as the depth of conviction in his voice boomed through the stillness of the kitchen.

Dr. Orrington stood in his kitchen, wearing glasses and holding a jar of sun water. Sunlight streamed through the window and cast a golden glow into the pristine liquid contained within the jar. Soft reggae music played subtly in the background, filling the space with warmth and light.

"This is where it begins—the Kingdom of Light," he muttered to himself, while his eyes reflected deep reverence, placing the jar with tender care onto a mirror tray. The sun sparked a reflection in the water, and he turned the position so that it captured every drop of sun.

"Energy, vibration, frequency—all of it inside this liquid. The power to change everything," he reflected, the words a mantra that vibrated within him. And he stood in silent awe, lost in the profundity of meanings behind that simple jar of sun water.

As he straightened up, his gaze strayed out the window; with it came a rush of urgency—the puzzles of water held secrets to be laid bare, and he would learn the ways of harnessing their power.

He knew still that his journey was far from complete at this moment in time. Each experience, each moment of divine connection with the world surrounding him, had brought him up to this very instance in time—a realization that would mold what was to follow. He could feel it in his bones, this call to plunge even deeper into the mysteries of existence. With

Chapter 3

The chirping of birds and gentle rustling of leaves under the light breeze brought life into the garden. With a serene countenance, Dr. Orrington sat at his desk, reviewing some reports in front of him. Outside, the sun shone brightly, casting golden hues over the lush greenery. The door burst open, slamming into the wall, as Faye—more quick-witted and dynamic than ever—barged in, holding a thick folder full of documents. Her eyes were shining with urgency as she said, "Dr. Orrington," she puffed, urging for breath. "You have to see this."

Dr. Orrington turned slowly, his manner calm, yet with a fresh-awakened curiosity. Rarely did Faye show such enthusiasm over a report. He folded his hands across the desk and waited for her explanation.

"What is it, Faye?" he asked. His voice was steady.

She hurried over, flipping through the pages as if searching for the exact part that would explain her agitation. "We ran the Orrington Technique on the metal-infused water sample again. The contaminants broke down, and it wasn't some gradual process like earlier. The energy shift was almost instant."

For a moment, nothing came from Dr. Orrington as his mind digested the information. Dr. Orrington leaned back into his chair; his eyes drifted to a jar of Sun Water on his windowsill—catching the sunlight, shining through the clear liquid. That water shimmered and sent small rainbows in every direction on his walls.

"The frequencies," he whispered, almost to himself, yet speaking to Faye. "They're responding."

Faye followed his gaze to the jar. She'd seen him stare at it a million times, but now she felt an odd kind of affinity with it—though she wasn't quite sure why. "What is it?" she asked, quieter now, curiosity lacing her tone.

Dr. Orrington leaned forward and picked up the jar with reverent hands, as if it were some sacred thing. "This," he said, holding it for a moment in the light, "is no ordinary water. It's Sun Water. Distilled light. Pure vibration."

Faye stepped closer, still a little skeptical but decidedly curious. "And you believe this can—what? Heal people? Realign their energy?"

He turned to her, his face serious yet composed, as sure of it as he had ever been of anything. "It can change everything, Faye. Our bodies, our minds, everything is connected with the frequencies around us. Water," he said, holding the jar a little higher again, "is the conduit."

The sun cut through the window just so, casting its rays perfectly on the jar, and for one instant, it was practically breathing—the water inside pulsed like life within. Faye could not look away, yet her mind was still shadowed by doubt.

"But how can you be certain?" she asked, her voice low, brow furrowed.

Dr. Orrington gave the jar a slow, deliberate shake, his eye never leaving hers, the spark in it never flickering once. "You'll know soon enough."

In a moment, an odd sensation swept the room, some kind of vibration, at least undeniably barely perceptible. Faye felt it undulate the air, almost as if the very walls hummed. She craned her neck cautiously around the room.

"What was that?" she asked tensely.

Dr. Orrington smiled faintly—he wasn't the least bit surprised. "It's starting," he whispered. "The energy shift."

Faye was taken aback as the enormity of what she was being told started to sink in. She looked at the jar again; it's something else entirely. In a hushed whisper, she asked, "What are you going to do with it?"

Dr. Orrington retained the jar once more, and the sun began to glow stronger through the water. His eyes were practically distant, as if he stared into a future only he could envision. "I'm going to give it to the world," he responded, with the slightest bit of determination in his tone. "One drop at a time."

***

Later that day, Dr. Orrington stood in his dental clinic, adjusting his instruments with the same precision he applied to everything in life. The sterile, modern space was filled with blocks of sunlight streaming through the large windows, casting a warm, almost serene glow over the room. His mind, however, wasn't on the patient in front of him.

"In our line of work," he said to himself, "it is all about precision. Every detail, down to the millimeter, must be exact. May it be the water we use in our 1mm lines—it has to be distilled into its purest form."

But something deeper tugged at him—a find below the surface of his routine. As he worked, his mind wandered to those magnetic nanomaterials he had found concealed in places no one would have ever thought. "Nanomaterials," he mused to himself. "There, yet never seen. The CDC once said the human body had more pathways than anyone had ever imagined."

When the procedure was finished and the patient gone, Dr. Orrington retired to his office, where he sat at his desk once more. On a screen in the corner of the room, complex diagrams showed human vessels, water molecules, and detailed nanotechnology. His eyes flickered over years of compiled research.

"And then one day," he remembered, the research vanished. LIGHT.

His fingers moved almost automatically as he clicked through his files and immediately to the work of Charles M. Lieber, which had once been his yardstick, the key into the difficult inter-relationships between water and nanotechnology. Now, as he scrolled down, he saw an error message flash across his screen: "Document removed." His heart sank a little, although really he should expect this.

"Harvard's files on Lieber's work," he thought, leaning back in his chair. "Gone. But I had seen enough."

Memories flooded in—long sleepless nights spent in the lab peering through the microscope, watching molecular structures of hydrogen tampered with by miniature machines. Fascinating it was, and horror to him, too. "Nanorobots," he whispered, "meddling with hydrogen itself. They pull it off."

A silent tension befalls him as he weighs the implications. He turns again to the water lines running through his clinic, his mind's eye tracing the path of nanobots through them, unseen yet omnipresent. "We use water for everything," he thought, "but what if it's no longer pure? What if the very foundation of life is compromised?"

He recalled the meetings—countless briefings with bureaucrats and state officials, even his peers in the dental society. He had laid out his findings before anyone who would listen. But their faces remained blank; the same responses always came.

"Too far-fetched," they had said. "Too unorthodox."

But Dr. Orrington knew better. For he had seen the connections—all those undeniable links between water and life itself. It wasn't just a resource, but a vessel, a transmitter of signals, a keeper of memory.

Later that evening, as he knelt at his bedside, hands clasped in prayer, he let his eyes slip to the small glass of water on his bedside table. Candlelight beside it rustled aimlessly, incidentally casting a golden aura over the surface of the liquid.

"I prayed on this," he thought. "Sun Water, alive with wisdom, energy, light. It made me wiser. More aware. The world needs to understand." His prayer was simple, but his conviction deep. He rose to his feet and walked over to the window, staring out through it where the stars were dimly twinkling in the sky. He watched for a long while—working his thoughts out—knowing soon the world would have to come to his same judgment. "It's now," he told himself. "The time of silence. The time for the Earth to heal itself. Water must be rested."

The next morning, Dr. Orrington walked through a busy city park, totally aware of a world around him that moved at a completely impossible pace. People were running by him, plugged into phones, unaware of forces at work all around them. He stood still amidst the chaos and took it all in. "The source of everything is water," he thought, "but it is much more than what they understand. It is sacral. And could change it all."

Later still, as he again stood in his clinic regarding the water lines with silent determination, a sense of peace settled over Dr. Orrington. The answers were close now. The time for revelation was at hand. "We shall be repaid," he mused, "our quiet, our faith. Yonder in the pool, yonder in the Play Kingdom." And as the sun began to set behind the mountain peaks, casting long, quivering shadows upon the earth, Dr. Orrington raised a small glass vial of water to the horizon and let the last rays of daylight dance across its surface. "The Kingdom of Light," he whispered, "it's where we're headed, all of us. I know it."

Chapter 4

His eyes traveled across the floor as they locked into each face in the audience, silently measuring the capacity of the gathered audience to absorb the story he was about to unfold. His hands came to rest on the edges of the podium, his fingers tapping lightly in rhythm, a sign that what he was about to say would leave its mark on everyone within the audience.

"You all have heard of Dr. Karen Romano, haven't you?" His voice was calm yet full of weight that won him the favor of the crowd in an instant. "Once, she was a young girl, just like all of you here, fascinated by the prospects of being a dentist. But her story… well, her story took quite a different turn that none of us could ever believe."

The room hushed as death. Everybody moved a little more forward, more interested; several of them had already whispered Karen's name, as if it was some kind of forbidden temptation. Orrington's eyes shined momentarily—he had them right where he wanted them. The tale he was about to share would, for them, forever rewrite the meaning of success, power, and ambition.

"In the beginning," he said, allowing every word to fall with considered deliberation from his lips, "Karen had but one dream. She wanted to become the best dentist in the world. That's all."

***

Standing in her bedroom, twelve-year-old Karen Romano was brushing her teeth with the vigor and detail of a surgeon performing an operation. The childhood trophies of her dreams were framed posters of tooth anatomy and dental hygiene hanging on her walls. Catching her reflection, Karen faked the perfect smile over and over, aping the dentists she idolized.

Ambition shone in her eyes—a gleam that seemed to reflect the iron determination of a will that knew no bounds. Every morning, her routine was more than hygiene; it was training. She knew then, and she does now, that perfection doesn't happen by accident; you make it happen, and Karen did whatever it took.

"Karen was like many of us," Dr. Orrington narrated, the memory of her early days almost a vision through his words. "Eager. Full of hope. Driven by one single desire: to succeed."

Her dreams were simple, based on what she had considered a noble profession. Yet ambition, so well knew Orrington, could be a dangerous thing. Life generally had a way of complicating even the best-laid plans.

***

Karen Romano, in her thirties, stood tall and poised in front of the State Dental Office. Her name, Dr. Karen Romano, Dental Director of Illinois, shone on the door with its gold letters, shining and shimmering in testimony to all those years of hard work. Her black hair cascaded down her shoulder, immaculate. She was a picture of success, every bit the accomplished professional.

Her smile, which was perfect since her childhood, seemed to invite and command all at the same time. An I-know-your-secret kind of smile that disarmed all her peers, charmed the hearts of her patients, and made anyone believe that she reached the pinnacle of her career simply because she worked hard.

"She'd reached the top," Orrington said, with no pomposity, as though he was looking at her climb himself. "Director of Dentistry for the whole of Illinois. Respected, admired... envied."

That was not all, but nobody knew about it.

***

Well into the night, Karen sat in her office. A soft, golden glow emanated from her desk lamp onto stacks of documents neatly arranged, as if chaos could never touch where she was. Outside, the hum of the city was only just audible, drowned out by silence consuming that space. She sat alone, flipping through the reports of patients when, on the desk, her phone vibrated softly, a gentle hum.

She didn't hesitate. The voice on the other end spoke no longer than a few seconds, but Karen's expression changed from cool professionalism to something altogether colder, altogether more sinister in that time. She nodded once, her eyes narrowing, then hung up the phone, setting it down with a sense of finality.

"What no one knew," Orrington's voice dropped to almost a whisper, forcing the room to lean in for more, "was that Karen wasn't just the Dental Director of Illinois. She had another identity. One whispered in the darkest corners of Chicago."

***

La Bella Tigre was a name spoken in shadowed alleys in Chicago, and it belonged to none other than Karen Romano. All in black, she rose from a sleek car in movements deliberately graceful, but with a deadly edge. She was a presence sensed before she could be seen. A few men stood waiting—pale faces, wide eyes, fearful. Their silent acknowledgment of who she was, what she was capable of, was well-founded.

"Karen had her claws deep in Chicago's underworld," Orrington explained, the sharp notes in his words cutting through the growing tension of the room. "Great was her influence, and it reached farther than from just the world of dentistry."

Beneath the facade of respectability, Karen had constructed an empire that reached into both legitimate and criminal worlds. The men before her knew better than to cross her. In the Chicago underworld, the name Karen Romano inspired respect and terror.

***

Karen sat across from the Governor of Illinois in his richly appointed office, confident. Her smile was soft and charming but with a sharpness behind it that only those who knew her true nature would recognize. She was making a point, delivering her lines perfectly, and the Governor, one of the most influential men in the state, laughed in response, completely under her spell. "She had the governor wrapped around her finger," Orrington said, shaking his head in an almost admiring reaction to how she had played both worlds. "The political world and the crime world were two sides of the same coin in Karen's hands."

For Karen, politics and crime were inseparable. One fed into the other, and she used both to consolidate her power. She was not just playing the game—she was running it. She pulled the strings on the governor's decisions as easily as she did with criminal operations on the streets. Nobody ever said no to her. Nobody could.

***

Karen stepped into her brother Antonio's funeral home in the dead of night, the air thick with incense and something a little more sinister. The building was quiet, dimly lit, almost somber. It was a perfect cover for what they were really doing. Her brother Antonio had always been there for her. Since childhood, he'd taken her cue. When she'd paid his way through mortuary science school, that was more than sibling charity. Antonio's funeral home sat at the epicenter of

Chicago's Italian hood. Legit on the surface, it actually served a far more sinister purpose.

"The funeral home didn't need to be a success," Orrington's voice grew darker, revealing another level to Karen's empire. "It contained a cremator—one which Antonio knew very well how to use."

***

Down in the basement of the funeral home, Antonio eyed the cremator with silent intensity that spoke volumes on the thousand times it had been done before.

He hardly looked up as Karen came in, but the flicker of eye contact that passed between them said it all: it was just another day at the office. Antonio was her closest partner, her centuries-long confidant. When Karen wanted something—or someone—to disappear, Antonio would be the one who professionally made it so. The bond that held them together was thicker and more binding than blood. It was forged in secrets, in silences.

"Antonio would do anything for Karen," Orrington said, an almost reverential tone entering his voice. "Together they built something indestructible, something that could never be touched by the law."

***

Back in her office during the day and every inch the professional, Karen sat behind her desk, her face unruffled, her smile polite. Nobody who ever saw her on those days could have imagined the depths of darkness she carried. Her reputation was seamless, and so was the manner with which she handled everything that her particular job threw at her. Underneath it all, however, Karen Romano was considerably more dangerous than anyone knew.

"She was always courteous, always polite," Orrington said dryly. "Until she wasn't."

***

Karen stood over the lifeless body that had lain in the darkened warehouse. The man at her feet had once been prosperous, powerful, but in Karen's world, nobody was allowed to remain above if they crossed her. Her eyes were cold, emotionless, as she lowered the gun.

Nothing showed in her facial expression in the way of regret, no faltering in her actions. The job done, she had turned and walked away, the smile again spreading on her face as though nothing had happened.

"Karen could kill as easily as she could fill a cavity," Orrington said, and the room stiffened with the thought. "And she did. More than once."

***

The quiet of the funeral home and the bonding effect of wine made the two sit together, sharing a rare moment of peace. Karen and Antonio were inseparable—their bond unbreakable, their loyalty to each other absolute. They had built an empire together, and nothing—not the law, not the rival crime families, not even the threat of exposure— could shake what they had. "In the end, it was always family for Karen," Orrington said. His voice seemed to fade for a moment, almost as though recalling a bittersweet memory. "Antonio was her protector, her partner. The one person she trusted."

***

The lights of Chicago glowed in the night, a vast city filled with secrets. Somewhere, in the shadows, Karen Romano continued her reign—untouchable, her perfect smile concealing the darkness of an empire that had become her. No one dared to challenge her. No one could. "And so," Orrington concluded, his voice slow and deliberate,

Chapter 5

Dr. Orrington's words hung in the air like a heavy fog as he continued to describe Karen's pivotal moment with Frankie DeLuca. The audience was silent, captivated by the tale of a once-innocent girl from the suburbs who would soon find herself entangled in a web of power and danger.

"It was in that small clinic," Orrington said, his tone somber, "that Karen was forced to make a choice. A choice that would change the course of her life forever."

***

Karen sat in her office, staring at Frankie. The weight of his offer pressed down on her like a storm cloud, dark and full of potential devastation. She knew the stakes. Refusing a man like Frankie wasn't an option, not really. And the thought of becoming tied to a criminal empire—an empire that operated in the shadows, far beyond the boundaries of the law— made her stomach churn.

But at the same time, the promise of power, wealth, and influence was intoxicating. Frankie had laid it all out for her: protection, money, and the chance to be part of something bigger than just a small dental practice. It wasn't about fixing teeth anymore. It was about fixing people's futures, controlling their destinies.

Frankie took another drag from his cigar, watching her closely, waiting for her decision. His smirk never wavered, his confidence unnerving. He knew she couldn't say no.

"You don't have to answer right now, Doc," Frankie finally said, his voice smooth like silk, but with an undercurrent of menace. "Take some time. Think about it. But don't take too long. Specter doesn't like to wait."

With that, Frankie stood up, brushing a stray bit of cigar ash from his tailored suit. He extended his hand to Karen, who hesitated for only a moment before shaking it. His grip was firm, almost too firm, as though he was making sure she understood just how serious this was.

"I'll be in touch," Frankie said, his eyes gleaming as he turned and walked out of the clinic, leaving Karen alone with her thoughts.

***

Later that night, Karen found herself unable to sleep. She paced the floor of her small apartment, her mind racing. Every time she closed her eyes, she could see Frankie's smirk, could hear the veiled threat in his words. She knew that once she stepped into the world of Specter, there would be no going back. But the lure of what Frankie had promised was undeniable. She had worked so hard to get to where she was, but now, it seemed like the only way to truly secure her place was to take the deal.

She poured herself a glass of wine and sat down at her kitchen table, staring at the dark liquid swirling in the glass. Her reflection in the window caught her attention, and for the first time, she wasn't sure she recognized the woman staring back at her. Was she really about to throw everything away for power and money? Or was she simply stepping into the role she had always been destined for?

"Karen wrestled with her conscience that night," Dr. Orrington explained, his voice now more introspective. "But in the end, her ambition won out. She had spent her whole life fighting for success, for dominance. And this... this was just another way to win."

***

The next morning, Karen stood in front of her clinic, the decision already made. She knew what she had to do. There was no other option. As much as she hated to admit it, Frankie had been right: this was bigger than just dentistry. This was about survival, about thriving in a world that didn't play by the rules.

Karen picked up the phone and dialed the number Frankie had left her. It rang only once before he answered.

"Dr. Romano," Frankie's voice was cool, confident. "I was hoping I'd hear from you."

"I'm in," Karen said, her voice steady, betraying none of the turmoil she had felt the night before. "I'll do it."

Frankie chuckled softly on the other end. "I knew you'd make the right choice, Doc. Welcome to the family."

The line went dead, and Karen slowly lowered the phone, her heart pounding in her chest. She had crossed a line, one that she could never uncross. And as she stood there, alone in her office, the weight of that decision settled over her like a heavy cloak.

***

From that moment on, Karen's life changed. She was no longer just a dentist in a small clinic. She became something else entirely—La Bella Tigre, the Beautiful Tiger. It started small at first. Frankie would send her a few clients—people who needed more than just dental work. They needed documents forged, secrets hidden, or sometimes, bodies disposed of. And Karen, with her pristine clinic and her brother Antonio's funeral home at her disposal, was perfectly positioned to help them.

"At first, it was simple," Orrington continued, his voice measured. "Karen handled the small jobs—money laundering, covering tracks, forging documents. But soon, Specter saw her potential. They saw that Karen could handle much more than that."

Karen's reputation within Specter grew quickly. She was efficient, ruthless, and above all, discreet. She never asked questions, never hesitated, and never made a mistake. And as her influence grew, so did her power. She became Frankie's go-to person for anything that needed handling in Chicago. And soon, she wasn't just a part of Specter. She was running it.

***

One night, Karen sat in a dimly lit restaurant, the kind where powerful people met to make deals that never appeared in the headlines. Across from her sat Frankie, his usual smug grin plastered across his face.

"You've done good work, Doc," Frankie said, taking a sip of his whiskey. "Real good. Specter's impressed."

Karen didn't respond right away. She had heard the compliments before, had seen the looks of admiration and fear from the men she worked with. But tonight, something felt different. She wasn't just another cog in Specter's machine. She was the machine.

Frankie leaned in closer, his voice dropping to a conspiratorial whisper. "Specter wants to give you more responsibility. More control. They think you're ready for it."

Karen raised an eyebrow. "What kind of responsibility?"

Frankie's grin widened. "Chicago. All of it. You'll be in charge. Every operation, every deal—it'll go through you."

Karen's heart skipped a beat, but she remained calm, her face betraying none of the excitement she felt. This was what she had been working for, what she had been building towards ever since she first shook Frankie's hand in her clinic.

"Are you ready for that, Doc?" Frankie asked, his eyes gleaming.

Karen took a sip of her wine, her gaze steady as she looked Frankie dead in the eye. "I've been ready."

***

And so, Karen Romano—now known to the underworld as La Bella Tigre—became the most powerful woman in Chicago. She controlled every aspect of Specter's operations in the city, from money laundering to drug trafficking to political bribery. Nothing happened without her approval. And with each passing day, her power grew.

But with that power came enemies. Rival families, jealous associates, even law enforcement—everyone wanted a piece of what Karen had built. And they were willing to do whatever it took to bring her down.

"Karen had always been strong," Orrington said, his voice now tinged with a note of warning. "But the higher she climbed, the more dangerous the game became. And in Chicago, no one stays on top forever."

***

It was a cold winter night when Karen received the first real threat to her empire. She was sitting in her office, reviewing some paperwork, when the phone rang. She answered, her expression unreadable as she listened to the voice on the other end.

"They're coming for you," the voice said. "The DeLuca family. They think you've gotten too big, too powerful."

Karen's jaw tightened, but she remained calm. "Let them come," she said, her voice cold and steady. "They'll regret it."

She hung up the phone and leaned back in her chair, her mind already working. The DeLuca family was one of the oldest crime families in Chicago. They had been around long before Specter, and they didn't like the idea of someone else running the show.

But Karen wasn't afraid. She had faced bigger threats before, and she had always come out on top. This would be no different.

***

The next morning, Karen met with Antonio at the funeral home. The air was thick with the scent of flowers and incense, a stark contrast to the cold, calculating conversation they were about to have.

"They're going to come after you," Antonio said, his voice low. "The DeLucas don't play games."

Karen nodded. "I know. But we've dealt with worse."

Antonio's eyes darkened. "This is different, Karen. They've got the city's top politicians in their pocket. If they want you gone, they'll make it happen."

Karen stood up, her expression hard. "Then we'll make sure they can't."

Antonio nodded, his loyalty to his sister unwavering. They had been through too much together to let anyone tear them down now.

"We'll hit them first," Karen said, her mind already formulating a plan. "And we'll hit them hard."

* * *

As the DeLuca family prepared their attack, Karen moved quickly, using every resource at her disposal. She called in favors, made deals, and ensured that when the time came, she would be ready.

The night of the attack, Karen stood in her office, her eyes cold as she watched the city below. The streets

Chapter 6

Karen sat behind her desk, eyes scanning the dimly lit room of her dental clinic. The patient she had just seen left moments ago, smiling, oblivious to the storm of thoughts swirling in her mind. Her hands gripped the arms of her chair tightly as she leaned back, her face betraying no emotion. The ticking of the clock on the wall seemed louder than usual, each second stretching into eternity.

Her phone buzzed on the desk. She reached for it slowly, as if already knowing what awaited her. The name on the screen made her heart race for a brief moment, but she quickly tamped it down, reminding herself of who she had become. Karen answered, her voice calm, calculated.

"It's done," a man said on the other end, his tone as flat as hers.

Karen nodded, though the man couldn't see her. "Good. Make sure it doesn't trace back to me."

"Never does."

She hung up without another word and stared at the phone in her hand for a long moment, her reflection looking back at her from the dark screen. This was who she was now—untouchable, powerful. But with that power came a weight that threatened to crush her.

Karen stood and walked to the window, peering out into the Chicago night. The streets were quiet, but she knew that beneath the surface, a world of chaos swirled. And at the center of it all was Specter, the organization that had wrapped its tendrils around every facet of her life.

Her phone buzzed again, and this time, the message was from Antonio.

"We need to talk. It's about Specter."

Her hand hovered over the screen. She hesitated, then put the phone back down. Antonio had always been the voice of reason, the anchor that kept her grounded, but lately, his messages were filled with more fear than wisdom. He didn't understand. He couldn't. She had sacrificed too much to turn back now.

Karen poured herself a glass of whiskey from the small bar in the corner of the office. The amber liquid swirled in the glass as she took a long sip, her gaze distant. She thought back to the last time she and Antonio had spoken face to face. It had been at his funeral home, the place where he ran a legitimate business by day—and helped her clean up Specter's messes by night.

Antonio had always looked at her with worry and admiration, but that night, there had been something else in his eyes. Fear. Not just for himself, but for her.

"You're in too deep, Karen," he had said, his voice low as they stood in the dimly lit basement of the funeral home. The hum of the cremator had been the only sound in the room. "Specter isn't just another mob. They're something else."

She had brushed him off then, like she always did. "I know what they are, Antonio. And I know what I'm doing."

But now, as she stood alone in the dark, Karen wasn't so sure anymore.

The door to her office creaked open, and she spun around, her hand instinctively moving toward the drawer where she kept a small handgun. But it was only Frankie, his silhouette filling the doorway. He sauntered in, his ever-present smirk firmly in place, a cigar dangling from his lips.

"Can't stay away from your favorite dentist, huh?" Karen said, her voice dripping with sarcasm as she relaxed, though her eyes remained sharp, watching his every move.

"Can't help myself," Frankie replied, taking a long drag from his cigar. "You've built quite the empire here, Karen. Almost makes me jealous."

"What do you want, Frankie?" she asked, her tone flat. She wasn't in the mood for his games tonight.

Frankie's grin widened as he stepped closer, blowing smoke into the room. "Specter's got a new assignment. Something big. They need you to handle it."

Karen crossed her arms, her brow furrowing slightly. "I'm listening."

"A senator's been snooping around places he shouldn't. Specter wants him gone. Quietly."

She felt the weight of his words settle over her, but her face remained impassive. "I'm not an assassin, Frankie. I'm a dentist."

Frankie chuckled, taking another puff from his cigar before leaning in closer. "You're whatever Specter needs you to be. We've all got our roles to play."

The silence between them stretched, thick and suffocating. Karen stared at him, her mind racing. She knew there was no saying no to Specter. Not if she wanted to stay alive. But the thought of taking a life—even someone as corrupt as the senator—made her stomach churn.

"I'll think about it," she finally said, her voice tight.

Frankie tapped the ash from his cigar onto the floor and turned to leave. "You don't have much time to think," he said over his shoulder. "Clock's ticking."

As the door clicked shut behind him, Karen sat back down at her desk, her hands trembling slightly as she reached for the whiskey. She took another long sip, but it did little to calm her nerves. The life she had built—the power, the money, the control—was slipping through her fingers, and she wasn't sure how much longer she could hold on.

Her phone buzzed again. This time, she picked it up without hesitation. Another message from Antonio. *"We need to meet. Now."*

49

Karen's jaw clenched. She had been avoiding him for days, knowing that whatever he had to say wouldn't change anything. But she also knew she couldn't keep running from him forever.

With a resigned sigh, Karen grabbed her coat and headed out into the night.

***

Antonio paced back and forth in the basement of the funeral home, his hands shaking as he clutched a piece of paper in his fist. The dim light cast long shadows on the walls, making the already grim atmosphere even darker. He looked up when Karen walked in, her face as unreadable as ever.

"Thanks for meeting me," Antonio said, though his voice was laced with frustration. "I've been trying to warn you for weeks."

Karen leaned against the cold metal of the cremator, crossing her arms. "You've made your concerns clear, Antonio. I'm handling it."

"Handling it?" Antonio snapped, waving the crumpled paper in the air. "This isn't just another job, Karen. They want me to—" He paused, his voice faltering.

"They want you to what?" Karen's voice was cold, though a flicker of dread stirred in her chest.

Antonio hesitated before tossing the paper at her. She caught it and unfolded it slowly, her eyes scanning the name written on it. Her heart stopped.

It was her name.

"Karen," Antonio whispered, his voice breaking. "They want me to take care of you."

Karen's blood ran cold as the weight of the situation crashed down on her. Specter didn't trust her anymore. They wanted her gone. And now they were using her own brother to do it.

"We need to disappear," Antonio said urgently, stepping closer. "I know people—people who can help us get out, go somewhere far away where Specter can't reach us."

Karen's mind raced. She had always known this day might come, but she had never truly believed it would. She had been so careful, so precise. But in the end, Specter was always one step ahead.

For a moment, she considered it—running, leaving everything behind, starting over. But then she thought of the power she had fought so hard to gain, the empire she had built. Could she really walk away from it all?

"No," Karen said, her voice hardening. "I'm not running, Antonio. I'm not afraid of Specter. If they want me gone, they'll have to come for me themselves."

Antonio stared at her, his face filled with fear and disbelief. "Karen, you don't understand—"

"I understand perfectly," she interrupted, stepping away from the cremator and heading toward the door. "I'll take care of this. Just like I always do."

As she left the funeral home, the cold night air hit her like a slap to the face, but she didn't flinch. She was no longer the woman who once feared Specter. She was their Beautiful Tiger. And she wasn't going down without a fight.

Chapter 7

Karen leaned against the cold metal table in the dimly lit meeting room, her sharp features illuminated only by the soft glow of a single overhead light. The air was thick with tension as a small group of mobsters gathered around, their voices a low murmur of caution and camaraderie. She caught Gus's eye, his imposing figure a contrast to her own, and nodded, signaling for him to start.

"I've got what you need," Karen said, her voice steady as she slid the falsified dental records across the table. "These will keep your associates off the grid while the heat's on."

Gus picked up the papers, his brows furrowing as he scanned the details. "You sure these will hold up?" he asked, skepticism lacing his tone. "The heat's getting closer, Karen."

Karen's lips curled into a confident smile. "You know I've never let you down. These records will keep them busy while we handle the real issues."

Gus chuckled, a deep sound that resonated in the room. "Yeah, well, I've got a family to think about.

Just make sure your end's tight. We can't afford any slip-ups."

"I'm too deep into this to mess it up now," she replied, her voice firm. She could feel the weight of his scrutiny, but she had built a reputation for being reliable.

The other mobsters exchanged glances, their expressions shifting from skepticism to intrigue. Karen had earned her place in this world, blending charm with shrewdness.

As the conversation shifted, Karen felt the adrenaline surge in her veins.

Later, Karen stood in her sleek dental office, the familiar smell of antiseptic filling her senses. Vinny, a high-ranking mob associate, reclined in the plush dental chair, a gold chain glimmering against his chest.

"Doc, you really outdid yourself," Vinny said, gazing at himself in the mirror. "I look like a damn movie star!"

Karen feigned modesty, a playful grin tugging at her lips. "Well, you're in the business of appearances.

Can't have you looking anything less than perfect, especially not in front of the bosses."

Vinny's expression darkened slightly, and he leaned closer. "You know, they say you're the one to watch in this city. Keep doing what you're doing, and you might just outshine us all."

Karen felt the weight of his words, but she shrugged it off. "I'm not trying to steal anyone's spotlight. Just doing my part to keep things running smoothly."

As Vinny grinned, Karen's thoughts raced. She had carved a niche for herself, yet the stakes were rising.

The atmosphere shifted as Karen entered her family's funeral home, the scent of lilies heavy in the air. Her brother Antonio sat hunched over a desk, papers scattered around him, his brow furrowed in concentration.

"Hey, Antonio," Karen greeted, leaning over the desk. "How's everything going?"

Antonio looked up, exhaustion etched on his face. "Just another night of coordinating. We've got sensitive operations coming in, and they're all riding on you."

Stepping closer, Karen felt her heart race. "I know. I'm working hard to keep everything on track."

Antonio studied her for a moment, admiration and concern in his eyes. "You're playing a dangerous game, Karen. These people aren't just average criminals. They expect loyalty, and when they don't get it…"

"I can handle myself," she interjected, her voice steady. "You taught me that. Besides, I've got you watching my back."

"Just promise me you'll be careful," he said, his tone serious.

Karen nodded, the bond between them palpable in the air.

The next evening, Karen stood in a dimly lit warehouse, the sounds of clinking bottles and hushed voices surrounding her. Gus was deep in conversation with another associate, their tones low and urgent.

"Karen!" Gus called, gesturing for her to join them. She approached, the gravity of the moment settling in.

"What's going on?" she asked, glancing at the nervous energy that filled the room.

"Rumor has it, the Feds are sniffing around," Gus said, his jaw tight. "We need a distraction, something big to keep them off our backs."

"I can get you some records," she suggested, her mind racing with possibilities. "But I need time."

"Time is not a luxury we have," he replied, frustration evident in his voice. "We need something now."

Karen took a breath, weighing her options. "What if I staged a minor incident? Something that'll draw their attention away?"

Gus raised an eyebrow. "Like what?"

"I could arrange for a truck to get hijacked, something that looks big but is really just smoke and mirrors. It'll buy us time."

Gus rubbed his chin, considering her idea. "That could work. But it better not blow up in our faces."

"It won't," Karen assured him, determination flooding her veins. "Trust me."

In the solitude of her dental office, Karen meticulously crafted the details of her plan. Her phone buzzed, breaking her concentration. It was Antonio.

"Hey, how's it going?" he asked, his voice laced with concern.

"Busy," she replied, her fingers dancing over the keyboard. "But I think I've got a way to keep the heat off us for a while."

"What are you planning?" he inquired, his tone wary.

"I'm staging a distraction—making it look like a big deal," she explained, choosing her words carefully. "A truck hijacking. It'll pull their focus away from us."

Antonio paused. "Karen, that's risky. What if it goes wrong?"

"Nothing will go wrong," she reassured him. "I've got it all figured out."

"Just be careful, okay? You know how these guys can be," he cautioned, his voice tinged with brotherly concern.

"I will. I promise," she said, though her heart raced with uncertainty.

As night fell, Karen drove through the city, her mind racing with the intricacies of her plan. The streets were slick with rain, reflections of neon lights dancing across the pavement. She felt the weight of the decision pressing down on her, a reminder of the stakes she was playing for.

Arriving at the designated spot, she parked and took a moment to gather her thoughts. A few moments later, she spotted a familiar figure approaching—a tall man with a confident stride, his eyes sharp and assessing.

"Ready for this?" Gus asked, a hint of skepticism in his voice.

"As ready as I'll ever be," she replied, trying to steady her nerves.

"Just remember, we're in this together. If it goes south, we all go down," he warned, his expression serious.

"I know," she said, meeting his gaze. "But it won't go wrong. I've planned every detail."

Gus nodded, though doubt lingered in his eyes.

The atmosphere was charged as the crew gathered at a hidden location, the air thick with anticipation. They discussed the finer points of the operation, the excitement mingling with apprehension.

"Alright, everyone knows their roles?" Gus asked, scanning the group.

Karen raised her hand, breaking in. "I'll take care of the logistics. Just make sure everyone stays in their lanes."

The others nodded, their focus shifting back to the task at hand. The energy was palpable, and Karen felt the adrenaline surge within her. This was her moment to shine.

The time came, and Karen positioned herself at a vantage point, watching as the truck approached. She could feel her heart pounding in her chest, the anticipation electric in the air.

As the truck neared, she signaled to the crew, and they sprang into action. The hijacking unfolded seamlessly, chaos erupting as they executed the plan.

"Go, go, go!" she shouted, adrenaline fueling her every move.

The operation unfolded like clockwork, the distraction drawing attention away from their true activities. Karen felt a rush of exhilaration, a sense of empowerment as she played her part.

After the dust settled, the crew reconvened at their hideout, the atmosphere buzzing with excitement and relief.

"That was incredible!" one of the men exclaimed, slapping Gus on the back.

Karen basked in the glow of their approval, her confidence soaring.

"See? I told you it would work," she said, her voice steady.

Gus looked at her, a newfound respect in his eyes. "You've got a knack for this, Karen. You might just be the best asset we've got."

Her heart swelled with pride, but a nagging feeling lingered in the back of her mind. She was in too deep, straddling the line between her two worlds.

Later, back in the sanctuary of her family's funeral home, Karen found Antonio waiting for her, worry etched on his face.

"Are you okay?" he asked, his voice low.

"I'm fine," she replied, though her heart raced. "The operation went off without a hitch."

He studied her, concern clouding his eyes. "You don't look fine. You're playing a dangerous game, Karen."

"I know," she admitted, the weight of his words settling in. "But I can handle this."

Chapter 8

Karen leaned back in her chair, a confident smile spreading across her face as she surveyed the room. The polished mahogany table gleamed under the fluorescent lights, reflecting the seriousness of the meeting at hand. Executives from the major insurance company surrounded her, their expressions admiration and wariness.

"Dr. Romano," began MR. HAWKINS, the lead executive, adjusting his tie as he cleared his throat. "We appreciate your presence today. Your reputation precedes you."

Karen leaned forward, her tone smooth and persuasive. "Thank you, Mr. Hawkins. I believe we can forge a partnership that not only benefits our organizations but also reshapes the dental insurance landscape in this state."

A murmur of agreement rippled through the room, but Karen noticed the skeptical glance exchanged between a few executives. She pressed on, her eyes narrowing slightly as she sensed their hesitation.

"I understand that some of you may have concerns," she continued, her voice steady. "But consider this:

with my expertise in dentistry and your resources, we can streamline processes, reduce costs, and ultimately increase patient satisfaction."

MR. GRAHAM, a burly man with a grizzled beard, leaned back in his chair. "That sounds promising, Karen, but let's not kid ourselves. We know the state of the industry—it's riddled with inefficiencies. How do we know you can deliver?"

Karen's smile remained intact, but her eyes sparked with determination. "I've already begun to analyze the current system, and the findings are alarming. Incompetence is rampant, and the public is suffering for it. Together, we can eradicate these inefficiencies."

"And how do you propose we start?" another executive interjected, folding his arms defensively.

Karen's lips curled into a knowing smile. "We establish a pilot program that prioritizes preventive care. It'll require an upfront investment, but I assure you, the returns will be substantial."

The executives exchanged glances, weighing her proposal. Karen seized the moment, leaning into the tension. "You know that I have connections within the labor unions and political circles. With my backing, we can secure this deal and ensure its success."

Suddenly, the door swung open, and a flustered assistant rushed in, her eyes wide. "Dr. Romano, the governor wants to see you immediately. It's urgent."

Karen's heart raced. She glanced at the executives, her mind racing through possible implications. "Excuse me for a moment," she said smoothly, rising from her chair. "I'll return shortly."

As she stepped into the hallway, she dialed her brother, Antonio. "I need you to find out what's going on with the governor. Now."

"Got it, Karen. I'll dig into it," Antonio replied, his voice steady. "You think it's serious?"

"I don't know, but it's never good when he calls on short notice." Karen hung up, her mind racing with possibilities as she headed toward the governor's office.

The governor's office door stood ajar, and Karen could see him pacing back and forth, his usually composed demeanor visibly shaken. She knocked lightly, and he looked up, his expression turning serious.

"Karen," he said, rubbing the back of his neck, "I'm glad you're here. We have a situation."

"What happened?" Karen asked, her heart pounding. "Is it about the event?"

He nodded gravely. "Yes. The authorities are starting to ask questions. They want to investigate what happened to… to the man who died."

Karen's mind raced as she processed the implications. "We need to shut this down before it escalates. What's your plan?"

The governor sighed, running his hands through his hair. "I've already talked to the chief of police, but I need you to help me convince them that it was just a tragic accident. We can't let them dig too deep."

"I can handle it," Karen replied, her tone firm. "We'll gather the right people, and I'll make sure the narrative stays controlled. Just trust me."

"Alright," the governor said, his voice filled with uncertainty. "But we need to move fast."

As they strategized, Karen felt the familiar thrill of power wash over her. She relished the control she had over the situation and the governor. "Let's call a meeting with the police chief and the key witnesses. I'll make sure everyone's on the same page."

"Good. You're the best at this, Karen," the governor said, his voice tinged with desperation. "Just make it happen."

Once they finalized their plans, Karen stepped back into her office, her mind swirling with the intricacies of manipulation and deceit. She sat behind her desk, glancing at the newspaper headline about her recent appointment as Dental Director of the State. The weight of the role pressed down on her, but it also fueled her ambition.

As she continued to juggle her growing power within the dental field and her covert activities with Specter, her phone buzzed. It was Antonio.

"Karen," he said, his tone serious, "I dug up some information on the governor's meetings. It looks like some of his closest allies are getting nervous about the investigation."

"Are they questioning my involvement?" Karen asked, her voice sharp.

"No, but they're worried about their own reputations," Antonio replied. "If they feel threatened, they could turn against you."

Karen clenched her jaw, a dangerous glint in her eyes. "Then we need to ensure they feel secure. I'll arrange a gathering at my place—an exclusive dinner to reassure them."

"I'll help with the arrangements," Antonio offered. "We can make it look like a celebration of your recent successes."

"Exactly," Karen replied, her confidence surging. "Let's show them that crossing me would be a mistake."

As the days passed, Karen's influence continued to expand, but so did the risks. She became a master at managing her image, balancing her public persona as a dedicated dental professional with the dark undercurrents of her dealings.

Karen worked late, her office illuminated only by the soft glow of her desk lamp. The clutter of dental reports was intermingled with files detailing her rivals' weaknesses. She made a call to a contact within the police department, ensuring the ongoing investigation would remain superficial.

"Make sure the focus stays on the accident," she insisted, her voice cool and collected. "I don't want any more questions about my involvement or that night."

"Understood, Dr. Romano," the officer replied. "We'll keep it quiet."

Satisfied, she hung up and leaned back in her chair, a smile creeping across her face. Just then, her phone buzzed again. It was the governor.

"Karen, I need to see you," he said urgently.

"Is it about the dinner?" she asked, sensing the tension in his voice.

"No, it's bigger than that. We have a problem."

"What kind of problem?" Karen demanded, her heart racing.

"The police are getting pressure from higher-ups. They want to dig deeper into the circumstances surrounding the death," he said, his voice low and anxious.

Karen felt her stomach drop. "We need to control this. If they start uncovering things, it could all fall apart."

"I'm trying to manage it, but you know how these things go. The media is sniffing around, and they won't stop until they find something juicy."

"I'll handle it," Karen said, her mind already racing with ideas. "I can set up a distraction. Something that will take the media's focus away from us."

"Just be careful," the governor warned. "We can't afford any mistakes."

"Trust me," Karen replied, her voice steady. "I always have a plan."

As she hung up, she glanced at the case files strewn across her desk, her enemies and rivals mapped out before her like pieces on a chessboard. She knew she needed to act fast. Her mind raced through possibilities, each more elaborate than the last.

Later that evening, Karen gathered with a select group of influential figures from the community at her home. The room was adorned with lavish decorations, and the air buzzed with the sound of clinking glasses and laughter.

"Karen, this is quite the gathering," said a high-profile businesswoman, adjusting her diamond earrings as she surveyed the scene. "I can see your influence is growing."

"Thank you, Margaret," Karen replied, pouring herself a glass of wine. "I believe it's important to celebrate our successes together."

As the night unfolded, Karen made sure to engage her guests in meaningful conversations, subtly reinforcing her position and power within their circles.

"Have you heard about the upcoming changes in the dental insurance policies?" asked a local politician, intrigued.

"I have," Karen said, her eyes sparkling with ambition. "I believe we have a unique opportunity to advocate for better access to dental care. It's essential that we bring attention to the inequalities that many face."

"Absolutely," the politician agreed, impressed. "I like the way you think."

As they spoke, Karen kept an ear tuned to the gossip swirling around the room. She noted the subtle exchanges between her guests, always calculating how each piece of information could be leveraged in her favor.

In a quieter corner, Antonio leaned against the wall, observing the interactions with a keen eye. He approached Karen with a concerned expression. "You're drawing a lot of attention tonight, sis. Just make sure you don't attract the wrong kind."

"Relax, Antonio," Karen replied, dismissing his concern with a wave of her hand. "I can handle it."

As the evening progressed, a flicker of unease settled in the pit of her stomach. The more she gathered influence, the more she felt the weight of her actions. But with each conversation, she also felt the thrill of power.

Chapter 9

The evening light filtered through the windows as Dr. Orrington leaned closer to the dehumidifier, his gloved hand hovering just above the collection bin. Lisa, his assistant, stood nearby, tidying up the instruments. She glanced over at him, her brow furrowed in curiosity.

"Dr. Orrington, is everything alright? You've been staring at that thing for a while now," Lisa said, her voice gentle but tinged with concern.

Without looking up, Dr. Orrington replied, "Lisa, do you ever think about how simple processes, like water condensation, might mimic the way our bodies work? How the air we breathe, the water we drink... it's all connected."

Lisa hesitated, unsure of where he was going with this. "I mean, I've thought about how everything is connected in some way. But... what do you mean exactly?"

He finally glanced at her, his eyes thoughtful. "This," he said, pointing at the dehumidifier. "It pulls in air, extracts moisture, and converts it back to liquid. It's a basic process, but what if the same thing is happening inside us? What if there's more to the water in our bodies than we realize?"

Frowning slightly, Lisa moved a little closer. "Are you saying the water we produce... could be more than just moisture?"

"Exactly," Dr. Orrington said, nodding. "Think about it. We breathe, we perspire, we collect moisture within us just like this machine. But lately, I've noticed something strange with certain patients. The texture of the fluids in their mouths, the way it coagulates when exposed to hydrogen peroxide—there's something more going on."

Lisa's face grew serious. "You think it's related to what's happening with the nanobots?"

Dr. Orrington paused, considering her words. "I'm not sure... yet. But I do believe there's a connection. The body's response to external stimuli, the way fluids behave—" He trailed off, his mind clearly racing with ideas.

Lisa stepped even closer, her eyes searching his face. "What are you going to do about it?"

"I need more data," he said, almost as if talking to himself. "I need to see if this is a recurring pattern or if it's isolated to specific patients. And I need to understand how hydrogen factors into all of this."

The office was quiet now, the hum of the dehumidifier the only sound breaking the silence. Dr. Orrington moved to the patient files, pulling out charts from the past few months. Lisa stood behind him, watching closely.

"Unvaccinated patients," he muttered, flipping through the files. "That's the common thread. 2020, the year when all of this began. Their bodies are reacting differently—fluids thickening, strange sensations in the mouth. It's not just dental; it's systemic."

Lisa stepped closer, her voice soft but urgent. "So what does that mean? Is it the nanobots or something else?"

Dr. Orrington shook his head, his eyes still scanning the files. "I don't know yet. But it's something we can't ignore. There's a pattern here. And hydrogen... it plays a key role."

Lisa frowned, confused. "Hydrogen? How does that fit in?"

"Hydrogen is the fundamental building block for water," Dr. Orrington explained, finally closing the last file and looking up at her. "It's in every molecule of water we drink, every breath we take. And I think it's interacting with the nanoparticles in ways we haven't fully understood yet."

Lisa stared at him for a moment before speaking. "So... what now?"

Dr. Orrington set the files down and leaned against the counter, his face thoughtful. "I need to conduct more tests. We need to track the patients more closely, analyze their fluids, see how they react to different stimuli. And if I'm right, we may be looking at something much bigger than we initially thought."

Lisa nodded, her concern deepening. "This sounds dangerous, Dr. Orrington. Should we even be doing this alone?"

"We don't have a choice," he said firmly. "If we don't figure this out, no one will."

Lisa stepped back slightly, taking in the weight of his words. "So you think it's the hydrogen interacting with something inside them... like the nanobots? You've always been cautious about those things."

Dr. Orrington nodded, his mind racing as he pieced together the fragments of his observations. "I've always suspected they were too unpredictable, too unregulated. But it's not just them—it's how they react to elements in the body, like hydrogen. When combined, they could change the properties of the fluids inside us. Maybe even alter the way cells function."

Lisa looked shaken, her eyes wide. "You're talking about... a whole new level of biological interference. If the government or any large corporation is involved, they wouldn't let this come to light. Not if they're controlling these... experiments."

Dr. Orrington let out a heavy sigh. "Exactly. That's why we need to be discreet. We can't let anyone know we're onto something—at least not yet. We need proof, undeniable proof."

Lisa bit her lip, nodding in agreement. "So, how do we get it? Are you going to test more patients?"

"I'll start with the ones who've already shown these symptoms. But we have to be careful. If anyone suspects we're looking too closely, it could jeopardize everything. The patients, our work... even our lives."

The room grew silent again, the air thick with tension. Lisa stepped closer to Dr. Orrington, her voice soft but determined. "I'm with you. Whatever you need, I'm here to help."

Dr. Orrington gave her a grateful nod. "Thank you, Lisa. We're going to need all the help we can get."

They both stood there for a moment, the weight of the situation settling in. Finally, Dr. Orrington broke the silence.

"We'll start tomorrow. I'll run some tests on the collected samples and compare them with what we know about hydrogen's behavior. There has to be something we're missing."

Lisa nodded, then glanced at the door. "Do you think anyone's watching us? I mean... if we're onto something this big, they must already know, right?"

Dr. Orrington stiffened, his eyes narrowing as he looked around the room. "I wouldn't be surprised if someone's keeping tabs on us. But we can't let that stop us. We'll just have to be careful."

Lisa's hand rested on the counter as she steadied herself. "What if they come after us, Dr. Orrington? What if—"

He cut her off gently. "We'll cross that bridge when we get to it. For now, we stay under the radar. No one knows except us."

Lisa nodded, her resolve hardening. "Alright. Let's get started."

Dr. Orrington turned his attention back to the dehumidifier, watching the water swirl inside the collection bin, his thoughts racing faster than ever before. He knew they were on the verge of something monumental—something that could change everything they thought they knew about the human body, science, and perhaps even the world itself. But the danger of being so close to the truth was just as clear.

Chapter 10

Karen sat at her sleek desk, the glow from the security monitor illuminating her focused expression. The room was filled with the weight of confidential documents, each one a puzzle piece in the elaborate game she was playing. She leaned back in her chair, her mind racing as she reviewed the footage from the recent dental trade show. The chaos of the event, with its swirling crowd of professionals and shady figures, had always fascinated her.

"Unbelievable," she muttered to herself, shaking her head at the faces of potential allies and enemies. "They have no idea what's really at stake."

Her phone buzzed, interrupting her thoughts. It was a message from Antonio, her brother.

"Hey, Have you seen the latest report on the nanobots? They're raising concerns," from Antonio.

Karen typed back quickly.

"I'm looking into it. Meet me at the usual spot. We need to discuss this."

She stood, smoothing out her fitted blazer as she prepared to leave. The weight of her ambitions settled on her shoulders, but she was undeterred. The secrets she held gave her power, and she knew how to use it.

***

A dimly lit bar in a back alley served as the perfect meeting point. Antonio was already there, nursing a drink. His brow furrowed with concern as Karen slid into the booth opposite him.

"Karen," he began, lowering his voice. "I'm worried about these nanobots. If they're as dangerous as some say, we could have a real problem on our hands."

She leaned forward, her eyes narrowing. "We've always known they were a double-edged sword. They can be used for good or ill. It's all about who controls them."

Antonio sighed, running a hand through his hair. "But if they fall into the wrong hands—"

"They already have, Antonio," she interrupted, her tone firm. "Specter is well aware of their potential. That's why we need to keep our eyes open."

"Did you see the way those scientists were acting at the trade show?" he asked. "They were nervous, like they knew something was coming."

Karen nodded, recalling the tension in the air. "I did. That's why I want to meet with Dr. Orrington. He might have insights we haven't considered yet."

"You trust him?" Antonio asked, raising an eyebrow.

"I trust him to be useful," she replied, a hint of a smirk playing on her lips. "In this world, usefulness is the currency that matters."

Back in her office, Karen poured over the confidential report detailing the advancements in scientific technologies. She wanted to know everything, to be ahead of the curve.

"Dr. Orrington," she spoke into her phone, her tone professional yet laced with a hint of challenge. "I need to discuss the implications of the latest nanobot developments. Can you meet me tomorrow?"

"Of course, Karen," he replied. "I'll make time. This is something we cannot afford to overlook."

"Good," she said, feeling a sense of satisfaction. "I'll see you then."

The following day, in the heart of the university, the atmosphere buzzed with anticipation. Karen walked alongside Dr. Orrington, who was explaining the latest advancements in nanotechnology.

"Imagine the possibilities," he said, his eyes alight with enthusiasm. "Nanobots that can target specific cells in the body, revolutionizing medicine as we know it."

"Or weaponizing them," Karen interjected, her voice steady. "The potential for abuse is immense. We must consider every angle."

Dr. Orrington paused, looking at her with a mixture of admiration and caution. "You always think two steps ahead, don't you?"

"It's how I survive," she replied, a hint of a smile on her lips.

As they entered the laboratory, the sight of scientists meticulously working with cutting-edge equipment was both impressive and intimidating. Karen's heart raced; this was where innovation met ambition.

Meanwhile, in a dimly lit room, Specter agents gathered around a table strewn with blueprints and reports. A tall man, sharp-featured and intimidating, presided over the meeting.

"Listen up," he began, his voice low and commanding. "The nanobots we've secured are our key to power. We can control water sources, agricultural outputs—everything."

An agent piped up, "But what about the risks? If they're detected—"

"They won't be," he snapped. "Not if we control the narrative. We need to eliminate anyone who poses a threat to our plans."

***

Back at the university, Karen and Dr. Orrington reviewed the latest findings on a large screen. Data flickered as they analyzed the potential impacts of the nanobots.

"Here," Karen pointed at a graph showing rapid replication rates. "If these bots replicate in the wrong environment, we could have an uncontrollable situation on our hands."

"Exactly," Dr. Orrington agreed, his brow furrowed. "And we have to ensure they don't end up in the wrong hands. We need to find a way to contain them."

Karen crossed her arms, contemplating. "What if we introduced a fail-safe mechanism? Something that would neutralize them if they stray from their intended purpose."

"That could work," he mused. "But we'd need funding and approval from the higher-ups. That could be tricky."

"Leave that to me," she replied, her voice laced with confidence. "I have a few connections who might help us secure the necessary backing."

***

Later, in a high-end restaurant, Karen met with a wealthy investor who had a penchant for funding innovative technologies. They sat in a secluded booth, the dim light creating an intimate atmosphere.

"Dr. Romano," he said, leaning back with an air of superiority. "I've heard whispers about your latest project. Nanobots, you say? Quite the cutting-edge venture."

She smiled, her charm disarming. "Indeed, Mr. Thompson. But it's not just about the technology. It's about the implications—medical breakthroughs, agricultural advancements. Imagine the impact we could have."

Thompson raised an eyebrow, intrigued. "And what do you need from me?"

"Funding," she replied, her voice steady. "With your backing, we can make this a reality. But more importantly, we can ensure it's done ethically."

He chuckled, a glint of skepticism in his eyes. "Ethics in science? A rare commodity these days."

"Perhaps," Karen acknowledged, her smile unwavering. "But if we're to lead the charge, we must set an example."

***

Meanwhile, back in the underground lab, the atmosphere was tense. Agents were monitoring the progress of the nanobots as they began to multiply.

"Are they ready?" one agent asked nervously, glancing at the screen displaying rapid replication rates.

"They're close," another responded. "But we need to ensure they're contained before we proceed."

"Containment is key," the lead agent asserted. "We cannot afford any leaks or failures."

***

As the days passed, Karen's influence grew stronger. Meetings with Dr. Orrington became more frequent, and her connections with investors blossomed. However, the shadow of Specter loomed large, its grip tightening around the burgeoning technology.

Karen leaned back in her office chair, reviewing her growing list of contacts. The excitement of new possibilities swirled in her mind. "This is just the beginning," she whispered to herself, determination igniting her spirit.

She picked up her phone and dialed Antonio. "We need to discuss our next steps. The nanobots have potential, but we must tread carefully. I need your eyes on the ground."

"On it," he replied, his voice steady. "I'll gather intel and report back."

***

Later that evening, Karen found herself at another upscale event, mingling with influential figures. The air was thick with ambition and the promise of power. She approached a group discussing the future of healthcare.

"Dr. Romano!" one of the executives greeted her. "What an honor to have you here. Your insights are invaluable."

"Thank you," she replied, exuding confidence. "Healthcare is evolving, and we must adapt to these changes. That includes embracing innovations like nanotechnology."

A man stepped forward, skepticism etched on his face. "But what about the ethical implications? Can we really trust these advancements?"

Karen met his gaze, her smile unwavering. "Innovation always comes with risks. But if we approach it responsibly, we can mitigate those risks and pave the way for a better future."

***

The next day, as she walked through the university hallways, Karen couldn't shake the feeling that she was on the verge of something monumental. Her meetings with Dr. Orrington had solidified her understanding of the technology, but it was the potential for power that truly excited her.

Antonio caught up with her, his expression serious. "Karen, we've got a problem. I've heard whispers that Specter is planning to move on the nanobots soon. They want to control the narrative."

Her heart raced at the news. "We can't let that happen. We need to act fast."

"What's the plan?" he asked, his brow furrowed.

"We have to secure the technology before they do. I'll leverage my connections to push for expedited research and development."

Antonio nodded. "I'll keep my ear to the ground and see what I can find out about Specter's movements."

Chapter 11

The atmosphere in the courtroom was thick with tension as Dr. Romano stood before the jury, her icy demeanor a sharp contrast to the warm wood tones of the room. The Moolinyans sat at the defendant's table, their expressions a mixture of defiance and fear. Whispers rippled through the spectators, who were drawn into the drama unfolding before them.

Dr. Orrington's voice echoed in the back of the courtroom. "Dr. Romano took express pleasure in falsely accusing the Moolinyans. She wanted all of them in jail. I, the narrator, had the unpleasant experience of dealing with this woman. Thank God I survived her machinations." The irony of his words hung in the air, a reminder of how entangled their lives had become.

Dr. Orrington sat in his small, dimly lit apartment, surrounded by piles of documents. The weight of his situation pressed down on him as he sifted through a file labeled "KIDNAPPING ACCUSATION." Each page he turned felt like a dagger, revealing the falsehoods Dr. Romano had spread to protect her interests and eliminate anyone who stood in her way.

"Every accusation is a weapon," he murmured, his voice barely above a whisper. "And I refuse to be a casualty."

He clenched the file tightly, determination flooding his veins. "I stood strong against her lies." The night deepened around him, but his resolve only strengthened. He had to expose her for who she truly was.

Meanwhile, in a sleek corporate office, Dr. Romano met with several utility company executives. Their smiles were tight, their exchanges careful. As they handed over briefcases stuffed with cash and signed agreements, the air crackled with unspoken deals.

"Remember," one executive warned, glancing nervously at the door. "We have to keep this discreet. If the public finds out—"

"Relax," Karen replied smoothly, her confidence unwavering. "These transactions are all perfectly legal... on paper. Besides, who would question the utility companies when they're filling the state's coffers? Power is about perception."

Dr. Orrington's voice filled the room again. "Karen leveraged her political connections to exert influence over the state's utility companies. These companies, generating substantial profits, often engaged in undisclosed unethical activities for political appointees and government officials."

Later that evening, alone in her office, Karen stared out of the window, the city lights twinkling below like stars fallen to Earth. She reflected on her actions, the alliances she had forged, and the power she wielded.

"Is this what it means to be powerful?" she wondered, a hint of uncertainty creeping into her thoughts. She had walked a fine line between right and wrong, and tonight, it felt more precarious than ever.

Dr. Orrington's voice continued, "Dr. Karen Romano realized that her unique position between two worlds could be a powerful force for good or evil." The reflection of her own face in the glass mirrored the duality of her existence. She had the ability to change lives, but at what cost?

The scene shifted to Dr. Orrington's dental office, bright and meticulously organized. He worked diligently on a patient with braces, a young woman whose smile radiated optimism, a stark contrast to the darkness surrounding his recent encounters with Dr. Romano.

"Everything alright?" he asked, glancing up from his work.

"Yes, Dr. Orrington! I love the new colors!" she replied, her eyes sparkling with excitement.

"Great," he said, adjusting the brace's colors with care, but his mind wandered.

"Sometimes, I wonder if I'm doing enough," he thought, as he meticulously adjusted the braces, each click echoing in the stillness. "This chapter is based on my personal experience in the dental office at the beginning of 2020."

Dr. Orrington's face was half-hidden behind his protective gear. His eyes revealed a storm of emotions—intense concentration mixed with worry and resolve. The vulnerability of his exposed forehead contrasted sharply with the carefully constructed façade he presented to the world.

He was not just a dentist; he was a man grappling with the repercussions of a war waged in shadows and deceit.

"Sometimes, it feels like I'm the only one fighting for the truth," he mused, his thoughts racing. "But I won't give up. Not now."

The dental office buzzed with the sounds of machinery and chatter, but in that moment, Dr. Orrington was isolated in his thoughts. The battle lines were drawn, and he was determined to reclaim his narrative from the clutches of Dr. Romano's lies.

As he finished the procedure, he glanced at the young woman, her bright smile a reminder of what was at stake. He had to stand up for the innocent, for those who couldn't fight for themselves. The weight of responsibility settled on his shoulders, but it felt like a mantle he was finally ready to bear.

The next chapter of his life was unfolding, and he could feel the tension of the impending clash. It would be a fight not just for his own innocence but for the truth buried beneath layers of corruption and deceit. And he was ready to confront whatever lay ahead.

As he removed his gloves and washed his hands, he caught a glimpse of his reflection in the mirror. The determination etched on his face solidified his resolve. "I will not be silenced," he vowed silently, as the world outside continued to spin, blissfully unaware of the storm brewing within the walls of power.

Chapter 12

The atmosphere in the courtroom was thick with tension as Dr. Romano stood before the jury, her icy demeanor a sharp contrast to the warm wood tones of the room. The Moolinyans sat at the defendant's table, their expressions a mixture of defiance and fear. Whispers rippled through the spectators, who were drawn into the drama unfolding before them.

Dr. Orrington's voice echoed in the back of the courtroom. "Dr. Romano took express pleasure in falsely accusing the Moolinyans. She wanted all of them in jail. I, the narrator, had the unpleasant experience of dealing with this woman. Thank God I survived her machinations." The irony of his words hung in the air, a reminder of how entangled their lives had become.

Dr. Orrington sat in his small, dimly lit apartment, surrounded by piles of documents. The weight of his situation pressed down on him as he sifted through a file labeled "KIDNAPPING ACCUSATION." Each page he turned felt like a dagger, revealing the falsehoods Dr. Romano had spread to protect her interests and eliminate anyone who stood in her way.

"Every accusation is a weapon," he murmured, his voice barely above a whisper. "And I refuse to be a casualty."

He clenched the file tightly, determination flooding his veins. "I stood strong against her lies." The night deepened around him, but his resolve only strengthened. He had to expose her for who she truly was.

Meanwhile, in a sleek corporate office, Dr. Romano met with several utility company executives. Their smiles were tight, their exchanges careful. As they handed over briefcases stuffed with cash and signed agreements, the air crackled with unspoken deals.

"Remember," one executive warned, glancing nervously at the door. "We have to keep this discreet. If the public finds out—"

"Relax," Karen replied smoothly, her confidence unwavering. "These transactions are all perfectly legal... on paper. Besides, who would question the utility companies when they're filling the state's coffers? Power is about perception."

Dr. Orrington's voice filled the room again. "Karen leveraged her political connections to exert influence over the state's utility companies. These companies, generating substantial profits, often engaged in undisclosed unethical activities for political appointees and government officials."

Later that evening, alone in her office, Karen stared out of the window, the city lights twinkling below like stars fallen to Earth. She reflected on her actions, the alliances she had forged, and the power she wielded.

"Is this what it means to be powerful?" she wondered, a hint of uncertainty creeping into her thoughts. She had walked a fine line between right and wrong, and tonight, it felt more precarious than ever.

Dr. Orrington's voice continued, "Dr. Karen Romano realized that her unique position between two worlds could be a powerful force for good or evil." The reflection of her own face in the glass mirrored the duality of her existence. She had the ability to change lives, but at what cost?

The scene shifted to Dr. Orrington's dental office, bright and meticulously organized. He worked diligently on a patient with braces, a young woman whose smile radiated optimism, a stark contrast to the darkness surrounding his recent encounters with Dr. Romano.

"Everything alright?" he asked, glancing up from his work.

"Yes, Dr. Orrington! I love the new colors!" she replied, her eyes sparkling with excitement.

"Great," he said, adjusting the brace's colors with care, but his mind wandered.

"Sometimes, I wonder if I'm doing enough," he thought, as he meticulously adjusted the braces, each click echoing in the stillness. "This chapter is based on my personal experience in the dental office at the beginning of 2020."

The focus narrowed on Dr. Orrington's face, half-hidden behind his protective gear. His eyes revealed a storm of emotions—intense concentration mixed with worry and resolve. The vulnerability of his exposed forehead contrasted sharply with the carefully constructed façade he presented to the world.

He was not just a dentist; he was a man grappling with the repercussions of a war waged in shadows and deceit.

"Sometimes, it feels like I'm the only one fighting for the truth," he mused, his thoughts racing. "But I won't give up. Not now."

The dental office buzzed with the sounds of machinery and chatter, but in that moment, Dr. Orrington was isolated in his thoughts. The battle lines were drawn, and he was determined to reclaim his narrative from the clutches of Dr. Romano's lies.

As he finished the procedure, he glanced at the young woman, her bright smile a reminder of what was at stake. He had to stand up for the innocent, for those who couldn't fight for themselves. The weight of responsibility settled on his shoulders, but it felt like a mantle he was finally ready to bear.

The next chapter of his life was unfolding, and he could feel the tension of the impending clash. It would be a fight not just for his own innocence but for the truth buried beneath layers of corruption and deceit. And he was ready to confront whatever lay ahead.

As he removed his gloves and washed his hands, he caught a glimpse of his reflection in the mirror. The determination etched on his face solidified his resolve. "I will not be silenced," he vowed silently, as the world outside continued to spin, blissfully unaware of the storm brewing within the walls of power.

Chapter 13

Dr. Orrington stood still, his gloved hands gripping the hydrogen peroxide bottle. The sharp pain from his head persisted, but the sight before him demanded his full attention. His assistant, usually calm and composed, had her eyes wide open, frozen as she stared at the strange coagulation forming in the patient's mouth.

"Doctor, what... what is that?" his assistant finally asked, her voice trembling.

Dr. Orrington didn't respond immediately, too mesmerized by the cotton-like mass accumulating. The patient, still seated in the chair, could only look at him with confusion. Her eyes darted between the peroxide-soaked cotton mass and the dentist, who was now visibly unsettled.

"I don't know," he said finally, stepping back slightly, his voice low. "But I've never seen anything like it. This shouldn't be happening."

The patient shifted in her seat, starting to panic. "Is something wrong? What's in my mouth, Doctor?"

Dr. Orrington's hands were shaking slightly as he placed the peroxide bottle down on the counter. He had experienced many bizarre things in his career, but this was unlike anything he had encountered before.

"No need to panic," he said, though the words felt hollow even to him. "It's just... a reaction. Let me take a closer look."

He leaned in again, carefully removing the strange cotton-like formation with tweezers. His assistant stood by, holding her breath as she observed him at work. The formation didn't resist being removed, but it felt unnatural in his hands, almost like it had a life of its own.

"How are you feeling?" Dr. Orrington asked the patient, keeping his tone as neutral as possible.

"I'm fine... I think," she replied hesitantly. "But... why is this happening? Did I do something wrong?"

Dr. Orrington shook his head. "No, this isn't your fault. It's nothing you're doing. I'll get to the bottom of this. Just try to relax for a moment."

The patient took a deep breath, though she was clearly unnerved. Dr. Orrington turned to his assistant, lowering his voice.

"Get me the patient's file," he ordered. "I need to check her history."

The assistant nodded and quickly exited the room. Dr. Orrington leaned against the counter, staring at the cotton-like mass in the tweezers. His mind raced through every possibility, but none made sense. Nanobots, cancer cells, chemical reactions—none could explain this phenomenon.

He took off his gloves, rubbing his temples, trying to make sense of the strange sensation still lingering on his scalp. He felt a jolt of realization as his thoughts returned to that moment earlier—when the patient lowered her mask, and the sound of tiny pebbles hitting his face shield had begun. He had dismissed it then, but now... now it felt connected.

Before he could ponder further, his assistant returned, holding the patient's file.

"Here it is, Doctor," she said, handing him the documents. "Everything looks normal in her history.

No known allergies, no unusual reactions to medications."

Dr. Orrington skimmed through the papers, growing more frustrated with every passing second. The patient's history was pristine. There was no reason for this reaction.

"I don't get it," he muttered, flipping through the pages. "There's nothing here that would explain—"

He stopped mid-sentence as his eyes caught something near the bottom of the file. A single note scribbled in the margins of her last dental visit:

Patient reported slight metallic taste in mouth during last checkup. No further investigation done.

"Metallic taste?" he repeated aloud, his brow furrowed.

"Doctor?" His assistant looked at him, concerned. "Is something wrong?"

"She mentioned a metallic taste before," Dr. Orrington explained. "But why didn't anyone follow up on it? That could be a sign of something... different."

He glanced up at the patient, who was still sitting patiently, watching their exchange with nervous curiosity.

"Do you remember having a metallic taste in your mouth recently?" he asked her directly.

The patient nodded slowly. "Yeah, it's been happening for a while. I thought it was nothing serious, so I didn't mention it again. Why?"

Dr. Orrington's mind worked quickly, trying to piece together the puzzle. A metallic taste, the sound of pebbles, and now this strange reaction to hydrogen peroxide... There had to be a connection.

"Have you had any dental work done recently?" he asked. "Anything involving metals or implants?"

The patient shook her head. "No, just my braces. Nothing else."

He frowned, feeling the weight of confusion press down on him. None of this added up. The nanobot theory resurfaced in his mind, but he quickly dismissed it. That was speculative at best, something he had only heard about in scientific whispers. Could it really be related to that?

Just as he was about to speak again, the sensation in his scalp intensified. He grimaced, reaching up to touch his head, his fingers brushing over the tender spot where the pain had originated earlier.

"Doctor, are you okay?" his assistant asked, noticing his discomfort.

"I'm fine," he lied, though his head felt anything but. The prickling sensation had returned, and with it, a sense of unease that he couldn't shake.

"We need to run more tests," Dr. Orrington said, turning to the patient. "This... reaction you're having isn't normal. I'll refer you to a specialist for a full examination."

The patient's eyes widened in alarm. "A specialist? Is it that bad?"

"I don't want to take any chances," he replied, trying to calm her down. "It's probably nothing serious, but I want to be thorough."

As he spoke, his mind wandered back to the strange, inexplicable occurrences over the past few days. Dr. Karen Romano, Specter's involvement, the nanobot technology... Could this be connected to the greater conspiracy he had stumbled upon?

He clenched his jaw, realizing that he might be in far deeper than he had initially thought.

"We'll figure this out," he said, though the words were as much for himself as for the patient.

The assistant began preparing the referral paperwork, while Dr. Orrington stared at the cotton-like formation on the tray. His thoughts spun wildly. Was this just a coincidence, or had he inadvertently become part of something much larger? Something dangerous?

The sensation in his head persisted, and as the minutes passed, it became harder to ignore. Whatever was happening, it wasn't going to stop here.

Chapter 14

Dr. Orrington stood over the patient, his brows knit together as she shifted uncomfortably in the chair. Her tongue tingled, and though he had conducted a thorough examination, he found no physical explanation for her complaint.

"Doctor, it feels... strange, like my tongue is going numb," the patient mumbled, her voice thick as if she were slurring. "Is this normal?"

Dr. Orrington's gloved hand hovered just above her mouth as he scrutinized her tongue again. There was no swelling, no discoloration, no sign of trauma.

"I haven't administered any anesthetic," he said, more to himself than to her. "This isn't normal."

The assistant, standing by with a concerned expression, watched closely. "Should I grab a different tool or run a diagnostic, Doctor?"

"No, no need," Orrington replied, pulling away from the patient's mouth and removing his gloves with a sharp snap. "Let's give her a moment. Maybe the sensation will subside on its own."

The patient gave a slight nod, though the discomfort was clear in her eyes. She rubbed her tongue against the roof of her mouth, frowning.

"Just breathe normally. We'll keep an eye on it," he said softly, though his mind was already miles away, trying to piece together the strange incidents that had been happening more frequently in his practice.

The assistant spoke up after a moment of awkward silence, her voice hesitant. "This isn't the first time something like this has happened, right? Didn't that man last week say something similar?"

Dr. Orrington glanced at her sharply. "Yes... yes, you're right."

He turned back toward the patient, offering a placating smile. "I'll let you rest for a bit. If the sensation persists, we'll take further steps."

The patient nodded, though her anxiety was evident. She pressed her lips together, rubbing her tingling tongue with uncertainty. Orrington and his assistant stepped out of the examination room, leaving her alone.

In the hallway, Orrington leaned against the counter, rubbing his forehead. "This is becoming too frequent," he muttered under his breath. "That man last week, and now her. There's a pattern emerging, and I don't like it."

His assistant looked at him, concern deepening in her eyes. "Doctor, do you think it's something... more than just a coincidence?"

Orrington didn't answer immediately. His mind drifted to his earlier experiences—particularly the string of unexplained incidents that had started back in early 2020. It wasn't just the tingling tongues, or the odd sensations; something deeper was at play.

"I don't believe in coincidences, not when things happen this often," he finally said, his tone firm. "I need to take another look at the records."

The assistant followed him as he strode back to his office. Inside, the walls were lined with medical journals, research papers, and case files, all meticulously organized. He walked straight to the filing cabinet, pulling open the drawer with a practiced hand. He flipped through the files with a sense of urgency until he found what he was looking for.

"Here," he said, yanking a file out and tossing it onto his desk. "It's not just the man from last week, or today's patient. There were others. Look—patients all reporting similar symptoms. Tongue tingling, numbness, strange sensations with no apparent cause."

His assistant leaned over the desk, scanning the pages. "But... Doctor, none of these patients had any major medical conditions, right? Nothing that could explain it?"

"Exactly." Orrington sat down heavily in his chair, pulling another file out and comparing it with the first. "It's not random. There has to be a connection, something we're missing."

He flipped through more of the records, his expression growing more troubled by the second. His assistant remained silent, allowing him to focus as he pieced together the timeline in his mind.

"This all started around 2020," he muttered, almost to himself. "Right at the beginning of the pandemic. Unvaccinated patients, mostly."

His assistant's eyes widened. "Do you think it has something to do with that? With the virus?"

"I don't know," Orrington replied, shaking his head. "But the timing is too perfect to ignore."

The room fell silent as the two of them contemplated the possible implications. Orrington's mind wandered further back—back to the early days of his career. Something tugged at the edges of his memory, a fragment of a long-forgotten research project.

He stood abruptly and walked over to the bookshelf, scanning the rows of old textbooks and research papers. His assistant looked puzzled as he began rifling through the volumes.

"Doctor... what are you looking for?"

"In 1994," he murmured, "I was part of a research project. We were studying nanoparticles—specifically, how they could be cultivated inside mammalian subjects. It was cutting-edge back then, something I thought had been shelved for good."

He pulled a dusty binder off the shelf and flipped through its yellowed pages. His assistant leaned in, her curiosity piqued.

"And you think this is related?"

"I don't know for sure," Orrington replied, his fingers pausing on a particular page. "But I remember we hypothesized that certain elements—particularly hydrogen—could be manipulated in ways we didn't fully understand."

He held up the page, showing a diagram of a nanoparticle structure. His assistant squinted at the tiny print.

"Hydrogen?" she asked, confused.

"It's the most fundamental element," Orrington explained, pointing to the periodic table on the wall. "The building block of water, the essence of life itself. But it's also incredibly reactive. Under certain conditions, it can behave unpredictably."

His assistant still looked puzzled. "But what does that have to do with your patients?"

Orrington set the binder down and rubbed his chin. "I'm not entirely sure yet. But when I was working on that project, we observed some strange phenomena—particularly in the way nanoparticles interacted with hydrogen in the body. If something similar is happening now, it could explain what we're seeing."

He turned back to the periodic table on the wall, his eyes resting on the symbol for hydrogen. The assistant followed his gaze, her brow furrowed.

"You really think this could all be connected to something from that long ago?" she asked.

"Maybe," he said, his voice distant. "Or maybe it's just a coincidence. But either way, I need to dig deeper. These patients, these symptoms... they don't make sense on the surface, but if we look closer—"

He was interrupted by a soft knock on the door. The patient from earlier stood in the doorway, looking apprehensive.

"Doctor? I don't mean to interrupt, but... my tongue still feels weird," she said quietly. "It hasn't gone away."

Orrington's expression hardened, his focus sharpening. "Come back in," he said, motioning her toward the chair. "We're going to run some more tests."

As the patient took her seat, Orrington reached for his tools again, his thoughts racing. Whatever this was, he was determined to get to the bottom of it. Too many unanswered questions hung in the air, and he wouldn't stop until he had answers.

The sensation at the crown of his head returned, a sharp, electric prickle that made him wince. He ignored it for now. There was work to be done.

Chapter 15

The evening light filtered through the windows as Dr. Orrington leaned closer to the dehumidifier, his gloved hand hovering just above the collection bin. Lisa, his assistant, stood nearby, tidying up the instruments. She glanced over at him, her brow furrowed in curiosity.

"Dr. Orrington, is everything alright? You've been staring at that thing for a while now," Lisa said, her voice gentle but tinged with concern.

Without looking up, Dr. Orrington replied, "Lisa, do you ever think about how simple processes, like water condensation, might mimic the way our bodies work? How the air we breathe, the water we drink... it's all connected."

Lisa hesitated, unsure of where he was going with this. "I mean, I've thought about how everything is connected in some way. But... what do you mean exactly?"

He finally glanced at her, his eyes thoughtful. "This," he said, pointing at the dehumidifier. "It pulls in air, extracts moisture, and converts it back to liquid. It's a basic process, but what if the same thing is happening inside us? What if there's more to the water in our bodies than we realize?"

Frowning slightly, Lisa moved a little closer. "Are you saying the water we produce... could be more than just moisture?"

"Exactly," Dr. Orrington said, nodding. "Think about it. We breathe, we perspire, we collect moisture within us just like this machine. But lately, I've noticed something strange with certain patients. The texture of the fluids in their mouths, the way it coagulates when exposed to hydrogen peroxide— there's something more going on."

Lisa's face grew serious. "You think it's related to what's happening with the nanobots?"

Dr. Orrington paused, considering her words. "I'm not sure... yet. But I do believe there's a connection. The body's response to external stimuli, the way fluids behave—" He trailed off, his mind clearly racing with ideas.

Lisa stepped even closer, her eyes searching his face. "What are you going to do about it?"

"I need more data," he said, almost as if talking to himself. "I need to see if this is a recurring pattern or if it's isolated to specific patients. And I need to understand how hydrogen factors into all of this."

The office was quiet now, the hum of the dehumidifier the only sound breaking the silence. Dr. Orrington moved to the patient files, pulling out charts from the past few months. Lisa stood behind him, watching closely.

"Unvaccinated patients," he muttered, flipping through the files. "That's the common thread. 2020, the year when all of this began. Their bodies are reacting differently—fluids thickening, strange sensations in the mouth. It's not just dental; it's systemic."

Lisa stepped closer, her voice soft but urgent. "So what does that mean? Is it the nanobots or something else?"

Dr. Orrington shook his head, his eyes still scanning the files. "I don't know yet. But it's something we can't ignore. There's a pattern here. And hydrogen... it plays a key role."

Lisa frowned, confused. "Hydrogen? How does that fit in?"

"Hydrogen is the fundamental building block for water," Dr. Orrington explained, finally closing the last file and looking up at her. "It's in every molecule of water we drink, every breath we take. And I think it's interacting with the nanoparticles in ways we haven't fully understood yet."

Lisa stared at him for a moment before speaking. "So... what now?"

Dr. Orrington set the files down and leaned against the counter, his face thoughtful. "I need to conduct more tests. We need to track the patients more closely, analyze their fluids, see how they react to different stimuli. And if I'm right, we may be looking at something much bigger than we initially thought."

Lisa nodded, her concern deepening. "This sounds dangerous, Dr. Orrington. Should we even be doing this alone?"

"We don't have a choice," he said firmly. "If we don't figure this out, no one will."

Chapter 16

Dr. Orrington's fingers moved rapidly across the keyboard, the clacking sound filling the otherwise silent room. He leaned forward, his eyes narrowing as he concentrated on crafting his report. His desk was cluttered with papers, medical journals, and a coffee cup, now cold and abandoned. Every word he typed carried the weight of the urgency he felt. His discoveries weren't just a minor concern—they were a potential threat to public health, and he needed to get this information out before it was too late.

As he paused to reread the last sentence, his thoughts raced. His internal voice narrated, "I notified my board of directors and government officials about these findings, hoping to address the issue." He hit the final keystroke with a sense of determination, saving the document and preparing to deliver it in person.

A few hours later, Dr. Orrington found himself standing in front of a large government building. The midday sun was blinding as he shielded his eyes, squinting at the towering structure. Clutching the report tightly under his arm, he walked through the revolving doors, his mind set on delivering the warning. The building's interior was cold, sterile even, with its white walls and the faint scent of disinfectant lingering in the air.

Inside the government office, he faced a stern-looking official sitting behind a wide desk. The man barely glanced up as Dr. Orrington approached, handing over the carefully prepared report. The official accepted it with an almost robotic motion, flipping through the pages with quick, dismissive glances. His face showed no signs of the urgency Dr. Orrington felt. After a brief silence, the official nodded, though his expression remained cold and distant.

"Thank you for bringing this to our attention, Dr. Orrington," the official said, his voice flat and void of any real concern. He put the report down as if it were just another routine file.

Dr. Orrington watched closely, his heart sinking. The official's skepticism was written all over his face. He knew that look well. He had seen it before, every time he tried to push forward with groundbreaking findings or propose an initiative that challenged the status quo. The government's complacency, their inability to see the urgency of the situation, was infuriating.

Despite his calm outward appearance, Dr. Orrington's thoughts were racing. "Despite my efforts, I faced retaliation," his internal voice echoed. "My warnings were met with disbelief, and I became a target for those who wished to silence me."

The official cleared his throat, pulling Dr. Orrington out of his thoughts. "We'll review the report and get back to you." The statement was delivered with a bureaucratic tone that Dr. Orrington had come to loathe.

He nodded, muttering a quick "thank you" before turning on his heel and leaving the office. The walk back to his car was a blur. All he could think about was how the gravity of the situation had been downplayed, how his report had been shuffled into the never-ending pile of government paperwork.

Later that night, he found himself back in his office, the air thick with tension. The overhead light cast long shadows across the room, making the space feel even more isolated. Dr. Orrington sat at his desk once again, but this time his posture was slumped, his hands resting idly in his lap. The exhaustion was catching up to him, both physical and emotional. His laptop was open, the screen illuminating his tired face, but he couldn't bring himself to type another word.

He stared at the blinking cursor on the screen. Every keystroke from earlier played back in his mind, as though mocking him for thinking he could make a difference. His thoughts began to spiral. He had given everything—years of research, countless sleepless nights, and now, even his reputation was on the line. All for what?

The room was silent except for the faint hum of his computer. Dr. Orrington let out a long sigh, running a hand through his disheveled hair. He knew that by stepping into the spotlight with his findings, he had attracted the wrong kind of attention. People with influence, people who didn't want the truth exposed, were now turning their eyes toward him. There were rumors—rumors that people like him were silenced, their careers dismantled before they could cause any real change.

But there was no turning back now. He had seen too much, knew too much. The implications of ignoring this crisis were too great. His fingers hovered over the keyboard, ready to start a new document, another letter, another plea to someone who might listen. But the weight of the world seemed to bear down on his shoulders.

For the first time in a long while, Dr. Orrington allowed himself to feel the depth of his isolation. The loneliness in his dimly lit office was suffocating. The shadows on the walls felt like they were closing in on him, as if the very space around him was trying to choke out his resolve.

Leaning back in his chair, he closed his eyes, letting his mind wander for just a moment. He thought about the faces of the people who would suffer if this issue wasn't addressed, the lives that hung in the balance. No matter what resistance he faced, he couldn't stop now.

Chapter 17

Dr. Orrington shifted in his seat, his eyes drifting toward the window as the last remnants of daylight faded. The city skyline stretched out before him, a mixture of glowing buildings and distant shadows. His reflection stared back at him through the glass, a face marked by exhaustion, the lines around his eyes deeper than they had been just months ago. The weight of his dilemma seemed to pull him deeper into the leather chair. He'd risked everything by coming forward with his findings, but now, he found himself wondering what the next move should be.

"My situation grew increasingly perilous as I faced mounting opposition," his internal voice echoed, the words lingering in his mind like a distant warning. Each day brought more resistance from powerful forces, all bent on discrediting him, silencing his work. "I researched figures like Charles M. Lieber," he thought, recalling the renowned scientist who had faced similar scrutiny, "whose experiences offered some insight into my own predicament." Orrington couldn't help but draw parallels between their stories—the pushback, the isolation, the veiled threats.

He had often read about whistleblowers, about those who had spoken up against powerful institutions, only to find themselves abandoned and vilified. Now, he was living that reality, unsure of who to trust. His gaze remained fixed on the darkened horizon, but his mind was miles away, spinning through possibilities. What if he had already gone too far? What if there was no coming back?

Across the city, outside a pristine, high-end dental clinic, Dr. Karen Romano stepped out into the daylight. The clinic's polished glass doors slid shut behind her as she made her way across the street. Her crisp white coat fluttered slightly in the breeze, but her expression remained composed, her movements deliberate. She appeared unbothered, yet a palpable tension hung in the air.

The sleek, black SUV parked just a few feet away didn't go unnoticed by her. It had been there every day for the past week, its tinted windows hiding the faces of the SPECTER operatives waiting inside. They weren't there to intimidate her, not directly at least. Their presence was more a reminder, a constant shadow cast over her decisions.

As she approached the vehicle, one of the back doors opened with a soft click. A man in a tailored black suit stepped out, his eyes shielded by dark sunglasses that reflected the city streets back at her. He nodded once, a gesture that felt more like a command than a greeting.

Dr. Romano stopped in front of him, her calm demeanor betraying none of the internal conflict raging within her. She was no stranger to these encounters, having worked closely with SPECTER for years. But something had changed recently. There was a growing divide between her obligations to the organization and her own moral compass.

"I found myself at a crossroads," her internal voice narrated, the words playing over in her mind as she met the operative's gaze. "My loyalty to SPECTER was tested against my desire to help the people of my State."

The agent said nothing, simply gesturing toward the open door of the SUV. She hesitated for just a moment, her fingers lightly tapping the strap of her leather bag as she considered her next move. Was she truly ready to step back into the darkness, to fully commit to the path SPECTER had laid out for her? Or had she reached her breaking point?

Her mind flashed back to the countless patients she had treated over the years, the faces of those who had come to her clinic seeking help. She had always prided herself on her ability to heal, to offer solace and comfort through her medical expertise. But SPECTER demanded more than just her professional skills. They wanted her allegiance, her silence, her complicity in something far larger than she had ever imagined.

She took a slow breath, her eyes flicking back to the SUV. It would be so easy to get in, to continue down the path she had walked for so long. But that path had grown darker, more dangerous with every step.

Her internal voice spoke once again, quieter this time, more resolved. "Ultimately, I chose to help myself."

Without another word, Dr. Romano stepped forward, her decision made. The operative moved aside, allowing her to enter the vehicle. The door closed softly behind her, sealing her fate for better or worse. As the SUV pulled away from the clinic, blending seamlessly into the city traffic, Dr. Romano gazed out the window, her calm expression betraying none of the turmoil swirling inside her.

Chapter 18

Dr. Romano reclined on the plush, velvet sofa of her high-end apartment, her fingers tracing the delicate embroidery on one of the many decorative cushions. The luxurious space around her gleamed under the soft glow of ambient lighting—gold accents, marble countertops, and abstract art pieces that adorned the walls. It was the kind of apartment that screamed success, the kind reserved for those who had made it to the top of their profession. And Dr. Romano had certainly made it, though her route was far from traditional.

Her phone buzzed on the glass coffee table, interrupting the serene quiet of the room. She glanced at it, a knowing smirk pulling at the corner of her lips. With a leisurely motion, she picked up the device and answered the call.

"Yes?" she said, her tone smooth and dripping with a hint of satisfaction.

On the other end, a voice spoke, confirming details that only she needed to hear. She let the caller ramble on, her eyes drifting toward the floor-to-ceiling windows that provided an unobstructed view of the city below. Lights from the buildings flickered like stars, illuminating the night with an almost calming sense of order.

As she listened, her mind wandered. Her internal monologue was clear, confident. "I continued to discreetly further my own agenda," she thought. "Leveraging my position for personal gain while carefully maintaining my dual role." It was a balancing act—one she had mastered over time. SPECTER might have believed they controlled her, but Dr. Romano knew better. Every move she made was calculated, each decision serving her long-term goals. She thrived in the gray areas, navigating between her public persona as a respected doctor and the clandestine activities she engaged in behind the scenes.

After a few more moments of perfunctory conversation, she ended the call, her smile widening. Things were falling into place just as she had anticipated. Leaning back into the cushions, she allowed herself a moment of quiet triumph before deciding her next steps.

Across town, in stark contrast, Dr. Orrington sat in the sterile confines of his small office, the fluorescent lights casting a harsh glow over his desk. Papers were strewn everywhere—notes, reports, and diagrams of intricate systems involving nanorobots and their potential effects on the human body. His fingers trembled slightly as he sifted through the documents, eyes scanning the same lines over and over again as if the answer he sought would suddenly jump out at him.

His mind was a whirlwind of anxiety and determination. The findings he'd uncovered were more terrifying than anything he had ever worked on before. These nanoparticles—they had the power to reshape everything, and yet the world remained ignorant, blissfully unaware of the storm that was brewing. His stomach churned at the thought of what was at stake.

Suddenly, his phone rang, jolting him from his thoughts. He fumbled to pick it up, his voice taut with urgency as he answered.

"Hello?"

On the other end, a voice spoke hurriedly, though it seemed distant in Dr. Orrington's fog of stress. His heart pounded in his chest as he listened, every muscle in his body tensing as though expecting the worst.

Dr. Orrington's inner thoughts raced once again, his conviction burning through his growing fear. "Despite the threats, I remained committed to uncovering the truth," he told himself, repeating the mantra that had kept him going through sleepless nights and relentless pressure. His investigation into the effects of nanoparticles was far from over, and he knew that walking away was not an option. He had seen too much, understood too much. His sense of responsibility weighed heavily on him, urging him to continue, no matter the personal cost.

The voice on the phone continued, but Dr. Orrington's thoughts drifted. He stared at the notes in front of him, focusing on the intricate diagrams of nanorobots, their tiny forms capable of monumental changes at a cellular level. His discoveries had revealed both promising and deeply concerning possibilities—he knew that these microscopic technologies could revolutionize medicine, but they could also be weaponized in ways that were too horrifying to contemplate.

His sense of urgency grew stronger. Time was slipping through his fingers. If he didn't act now, there would be no turning back. The implications of what he had uncovered were too great to ignore. He set the phone down, his hand hovering over the receiver for a moment before he snapped back into action, reaching for his laptop.

His internal voice rang out, firm and resolute. "My investigation into the effects of nanoparticles continued, driven by a sense of responsibility and urgency." The dangers were becoming clearer, but so was his purpose. Even as threats loomed on the horizon, his moral compass pointed him toward the truth.

Chapter 19

Dr. Romano stepped into the dimly lit room, the sound of her heels clicking on the polished marble floor. The space was narrow, dark, and unsettling. The walls were lined with heavy drapes that muffled the noise, giving the room an almost suffocating atmosphere. Several members of SPECTER were seated around a large, circular table in the center, their faces partially obscured by shadows. Only the faint glow of a low-hanging lamp illuminated the room, casting an eerie light over the proceedings.

Dressed in a sleek black suit that fit her perfectly, Romano's sharp figure exuded confidence and control. Her eyes, cold and calculating, scanned the room as she approached the table. These meetings had become a routine for her, yet the tension always lingered—danger lurking in every conversation, every unspoken word. Tonight was no different.

The briefcase sat prominently on the table in front of her, its presence a stark reminder of the deals being struck in the shadows. No one spoke as she reached the table. One of the operatives, a tall man with a strong jaw and a scar running down his cheek, gave her a slow, deliberate nod. His eyes never left hers, watching every move she made. She could feel their eyes on her, studying her, assessing whether she was still playing her part.

Romano met his gaze for a moment, her expression neutral, before her hand extended toward the briefcase. As her fingers curled around the handle, she could feel the weight of what it represented— power, influence, and her continued survival in this dangerous game. Lifting the briefcase, she gave a slight nod in return, a silent acknowledgment that she understood her role in this exchange.

"Is everything in order?" a low, gravelly voice asked from the opposite end of the table. It belonged to an older man, a senior figure in SPECTER, his face hidden in the shadows.

Romano didn't look up. "Yes," she replied, her voice smooth and unwavering. "Everything has been handled as expected."

Her calm demeanor masked the ever-present undercurrent of danger that flowed through these meetings. She knew the stakes. Failure or hesitation could mean the end for her. There was no room for doubt, no margin for error. She had come too far to falter now.

One of the operatives leaned forward, his elbows resting on the table as his steely gaze locked onto hers. "You've been quite effective, Dr. Romano," he said, his tone laced with something that almost resembled approval. "But make no mistake, if things go sideways, you'll be held responsible. You understand that, don't you?"

Romano's lips curled into a faint, knowing smile. "I wouldn't expect anything less."

Her inner monologue took over for a moment, a quiet reflection as she faced down the silent stares of the SPECTER members. "In the shadows, I navigated dangerous alliances," she thought, her mind sharp. "Every decision I make keeps me alive, keeps me at the top. I balance my commitments to SPECTER, ensuring my survival and advancement. But the moment I lose focus, they'll tear me down."

Her thoughts drifted to the countless meetings like this one—the hidden deals, the whispered threats, and the carefully orchestrated manipulations. This world had no room for weakness. Romano had spent years perfecting her ability to walk this tightrope, using her intelligence and cunning to ensure her place among these dangerous men and women.

One of the younger members of SPECTER, seated to her left, finally broke the silence. He was newer to the organization, still learning the ropes, and his arrogance showed in the way he spoke. "You may have gotten this far, Doctor," he said, his tone condescending. "But you're still only as good as your last success. Don't forget that."

Romano turned her head slowly, her eyes narrowing as they locked onto his. "I haven't forgotten anything," she replied coolly. "But perhaps you should be more concerned with your own position."

There was a moment of palpable tension as the young operative shifted uncomfortably in his seat, clearly unnerved by her response. The older members of the group exchanged knowing glances but said nothing. They knew better than to challenge Romano—she had earned her place at the table, and her track record spoke for itself.

The man with the scar on his cheek leaned back in his chair, his fingers tapping idly on the table. "We expect continued results, Dr. Romano. Specter doesn't pay for complacency. The briefcase is just the beginning."

"I understand," she said evenly, though her mind was already elsewhere. She had far more to gain than just what was in the briefcase. These men, as powerful as they were, didn't know half of what she was truly capable of. Her alliances, her knowledge, extended far beyond the walls of this room. And soon, they would see just how deep her influence ran.

There was a long pause before the man with the scar stood up. "This meeting is over," he declared, his tone final.

Romano took that as her cue. Without another word, she lifted the briefcase and turned toward the door, her steps measured and deliberate. Her heels clicked against the floor once more, echoing in the near-silent room as she made her way out.

As she exited the room and stepped into the cool night air outside, her thoughts raced. The briefcase in her hand was only a small piece of the puzzle. "I'm in control," she thought, her internal voice echoing with a steely determination. "I always have been."

Romano let out a slow breath, her grip tightening on the briefcase as she descended the steps and walked toward the sleek black car that awaited her at the curb. The city lights glittered in the distance, a reminder of the world she navigated—one where power was gained in whispers and shadows, not in boardrooms or public displays.

As the car door opened and she slipped inside, Romano's thoughts turned once more to her long game. She had played her part well tonight, but there were more moves to be made. And soon, even SPECTER would see that she was more than just a player in their dangerous game.

Chapter 20

Dr. Romano gazed at the view of the sprawling city from her office window, the night sky punctuated by glistening lights. It was a breathtaking sight, but to her, it symbolized more than just a bustling metropolis. Every glittering light was a reflection of power plays, of hidden agendas, of people manipulating others for personal gain. She understood that better than most—after all, she had mastered the art herself.

Her mind buzzed with thoughts, carefully calculating her next move. She leaned back in her plush chair, a cool expression on her face as her fingers tapped rhythmically on the armrest.

"The choices I made," she thought to herself, "were driven by necessity and ambition. In a world where power and influence intertwine with darkness, survival demands both cunning and discretion." Her inner monologue echoed her relentless drive, the knowledge that her dual roles, as a respected professional and a key player within SPECTER, had made her life far more precarious than she could ever show.

Romano had long accepted that every decision came with a cost. There was no room for missteps. As she swiveled her chair back toward her desk, her gaze fell on the numerous confidential files spread out before her. Each one contained names, profiles, and records of people who, like her, lived dangerous double lives. But unlike her, many had already stumbled. The difference between survival and failure in this world was often razor-thin, and Romano wasn't about to let herself fall.

She picked up one of the files, its contents chronicling the behavior of an unstable dentist she had recently been monitoring. A dangerous liability to both her and the organization. If anything went wrong, the fallout would ripple back to her. She opened the file, skimming through the details, her sharp eyes catching the discrepancies and alarming behaviors that had gone unchecked for too long.

She glanced at her phone. It sat silently beside the files, though she could feel the weight of the unread messages waiting for her. With a calculating look, she picked it up and unlocked the screen, scrolling through the names of her contacts, each one representing another carefully maintained connection in her network. Each one was a chess piece in her game, and she had to decide how to move them.

Her thoughts drifted to the narrator's growing influence, a looming threat that had started to creep into her dealings. Though she had been able to stay one step ahead, neutralizing this force had become a pressing concern. She couldn't afford to be careless. "The influence of the narrator..." she mused, "it's growing beyond what I can control."

Dr. Romano's hand hovered over her phone for a moment as she contemplated her options. The strategies that had worked before needed adjustment. She couldn't rely on the same old tactics when the stakes were this high.

"I'll need to devise something new," she thought. Her mind flickered back to police retaliation tactics she had studied—techniques that worked quickly and with finality. Yes, those methods could be adapted to fit her needs. She had always been skilled at taking inspiration from unlikely places. The rules didn't apply to her in the same way they did to others.

She put down her phone and opened another file, her focus sharpened. Neutralizing the narrator's influence wouldn't be easy, but it was necessary. And necessary was what drove her. Just like every time she sat across from those SPECTER operatives, feigning loyalty while advancing her own agenda.

She knew how to play both sides, and she played them well.

Her office, modern and sterile, contrasted sharply with the dark, dangerous undercurrents of her world. The view outside her window was of a city that represented success, but the truth was far more complex. The city, much like her, was a façade. Behind every polished surface, there was a deeper, more sinister reality at play.

Her phone buzzed again, and this time, she answered. The voice on the other end was tense, anxious. "Dr. Romano, we need your assistance. The situation is escalating."

She listened carefully, her expression never betraying the storm of thoughts racing through her mind. "I'll handle it," she replied curtly before ending the call. Whatever issue had arisen, it was just another complication in her already tangled web of responsibilities. But she was used to it. Handling crises was part of her skill set.

As she leaned forward and began to type on her computer, drafting yet another report that masked her true intentions, she knew one thing for sure—there was no going back. The lines between her life as Dr.

Karen Romano, respected dentist, and her life as a covert operative for SPECTER had blurred beyond recognition. And yet, she felt no regret. Regret was for those who had lost control.

Her fingers moved rapidly across the keyboard, the hum of the city outside blending with the click of her typing. She had always been quick to adapt, and this time would be no different. Neutralizing the narrator would just be the latest in a long list of challenges she had overcome.

Her thoughts once again turned inward, her ambition burning brightly. "If I neutralize this threat," she thought, "it'll cement my place further. But I need to be careful—one wrong move, and everything I've built could crumble."

The weight of her decisions pressed heavily on her shoulders, but she welcomed it. This was the price of power, and she had been paying it for years. Survival wasn't guaranteed, but she would fight for it every step of the way. After all, in her world, there were only two options—stay ahead or fall behind.

As she finished typing, she sat back, letting out a slow breath. The office around her felt colder than usual, the sterile air a stark contrast to the turmoil in her mind. But Karen Romano thrived in turmoil. It was where she did her best work.

Outside, the city lights continued to glisten, unaware of the shadowy figures pulling the strings behind closed doors. Unaware of the power struggles and dangerous games that unfolded in places far removed from the shiny surface of everyday life.

Dr. Romano smiled to herself, a small, satisfied smile. She would win this round, just as she had won so many others. Because in the end, she always knew how to play the game.

Chapter 21

Dr. Romano sat behind her polished desk, the phone pressed lightly to her ear, her expression calm and collected. On the other end, the state official listened intently, though his face betrayed a certain unease. His pen hovered above his notepad as her voice filled the line, dictating the next phase of her plan with precision.

"The process must be subtle," Dr. Romano's voice, smooth and controlled, echoed through the receiver. "There can be no direct involvement from our side. Inform the dentists that their licenses are at risk, and make it clear that the narrator is working with the state to enforce this."

The official nodded, even though she couldn't see him. "I understand," he replied, his voice wavering slightly. He scribbled down her instructions, each word carefully recorded. The weight of what she was asking seemed to settle in the room, but there was no turning back now. He knew better than to question her methods. Dr. Romano's influence extended far beyond the professional world, and those who crossed her rarely did so twice.

"I trust you'll handle this with the utmost discretion," Dr. Romano continued. Her tone was a delicate balance of assurance and threat. "The goal is to provoke. We want them to react. Violently, if necessary. That will justify the steps we need to take."

The official's pen moved faster now, driven by the urgency in her voice. He was uncomfortable, but there was no choice but to comply. Dr. Romano had a way of compelling people to follow her lead, whether they wanted to or not. He cleared his throat, trying to suppress the growing tension in his chest. "Understood, Doctor," he said finally. "I'll make sure it's done."

Dr. Romano's lips curled into a faint smile. "Good," she replied, her voice laced with satisfaction. "Keep me informed." Without another word, she ended the call, placing the phone gently on her desk before leaning back in her chair.

The plan was simple, effective, and brutal. The dentists in question were already on edge, their careers hanging in the balance due to their unstable practices. All it would take was the right nudge—the right misinformation—to push them over the edge.

And Dr. Romano was nothing if not an expert at pulling the right strings.

As she stared out the window, the city skyline once again in her view, her thoughts drifted to the narrator. They had become an obstacle, a problem that needed to be dealt with. By inciting the dentists to act violently, she would create the perfect storm, a situation where the narrator would be seen as the source of their downfall. Once the chaos unfolded, it would be far easier to move in and neutralize the threat without raising suspicion.

"I instructed state officials to discreetly inform multiple unstable dentists that the narrator was collaborating with the state to potentially revoke their licenses," Dr. Romano thought to herself. The plan was already in motion, and she felt a familiar thrill at the thought of what was to come. "The goal was to incite a violent reaction."

It was a tactic she had perfected over the years— using fear and desperation to her advantage. She knew that once these dentists believed their livelihoods were being threatened by someone working behind the scenes, they would lash out. And when they did, the resulting chaos would only serve to further her goals.

She stood up and walked over to the large window, her hands clasped behind her back as she gazed down at the city below. From this height, everything seemed so small, so insignificant. It was easy to forget that real lives were being manipulated and destroyed. But for Dr. Romano, this was just another day in the life of someone who had learned to play the game better than anyone else.

In the distance, the sun was beginning to set, casting long shadows across the streets. The world kept turning, unaware of the machinations unfolding in the dark corners of power. People went about their lives, oblivious to the forces at play, to the dangerous moves being made by those who held their fates in their hands.

Dr. Romano smiled to herself. Soon, the dentists would act out of fear, and the state would have the perfect excuse to clamp down on them. And the narrator, seen as the one pulling the strings, would be caught in the crossfire. It was a flawless strategy, one that would ensure her own survival while eliminating the growing threat.

Her phone buzzed on the desk, and she turned away from the window to check the message. It was from the same state official she had spoken to earlier. "The information has been passed along," the message read. "We're monitoring their reactions."

Dr. Romano allowed herself a small moment of satisfaction. Everything was falling into place. She knew she would have to remain vigilant—there were still many moving pieces to this puzzle—but for now, she could afford to relax, just a little. The pressure was mounting, but so was her control over the situation. The dentists would do exactly what she expected them to do, and when they did, she would be ready.

With a contented sigh, she sat back down at her desk, her fingers tracing the edge of one of the confidential files that still lay open. The stakes were higher than ever, but that was exactly how she liked it. There was no thrill in easy victories, no satisfaction in winning without a challenge. Dr. Romano thrived in situations like this—where every decision, every move, had to be calculated with precision. And this time, as always, she intended to win.

The sun dipped lower on the horizon, and the office was bathed in the soft glow of twilight. Dr. Romano closed her eyes for a moment, her mind already moving ahead to the next phase of her plan. The pieces were in motion, and soon, the consequences would begin to unfold.

And when they did, she would be ready.

Chapter 22

Dr. Jones stood behind his desk, pacing in tight circles as he held the phone to his ear. His knuckles turned white as his grip tightened, and his face flushed an even deeper shade of red. The voice on the other end of the line, calm and composed, relayed the news that had set him off. He had always been on edge, but this—this was the final straw.

"What?!" Dr. Jones bellowed, his voice echoing off the sterile white walls of his dental office. "That's outrageous! Who does he think he is? I'll make sure he pays for this!"

The state official remained silent, letting Dr. Jones rant. He had done his job; the information had been delivered, and now it was only a matter of waiting for the reaction Dr. Romano had so meticulously planned. The unstable dentist was like a fuse, and it had just been lit.

Dr. Jones slammed the phone down, his heart pounding in his chest. He could feel the anger rising, consuming every rational thought he might have had. It was bad enough that his practice had been scrutinized lately, with whispers about his methods and rumors spreading among colleagues. But now, to hear that the narrator—someone he barely knew—was allegedly working with the state to have his license revoked? It was unthinkable.

"They think they can get rid of me?" Dr. Jones muttered to himself, his fists clenched by his sides. "I've been doing this for years. No one can tell me how to run my practice!"

He stormed across the room, knocking over a stack of patient files in his path. His mind raced with thoughts of revenge, each one more irrational than the last. He wasn't about to let anyone ruin him. Not the state, not the narrator, not anyone.

***

Dr. Romano watched the city unfold below her, the late afternoon light casting long shadows across the skyline. She had expected Dr. Jones to react this way. It was all part of her plan. She had seen it play out in her mind long before she gave the orders to the state officials. Unstable people were always the easiest to manipulate. It didn't take much to push them over the edge, and once they were there, chaos followed.

"In the same way the police would lie on the streets, waiting for violence to erupt," Dr. Romano thought to herself, "I aimed to ignite a fire through these unstable individuals."

She could picture Dr. Jones now, probably shouting into the phone, his blood pressure spiking as the thought of losing everything sank in. That anger would simmer for a while, but soon enough, it would boil over, just as she intended.

The narrator, unknowingly caught in the crossfire, would become the perfect scapegoat. And once the dentists acted out of desperation, her hands would remain clean. It was a flawless tactic, honed through years of watching how fear and misinformation could be weaponized.

***

Dr. Jones tore through the drawers of his desk, searching for something, anything, to distract him from the rage building inside. His fingers brushed against a half-empty bottle of whiskey, and without hesitation, he grabbed it. He unscrewed the cap and took a long, burning swig, the alcohol doing little to soothe his agitation.

"This can't be happening," he mumbled, wiping his mouth with the back of his hand. "They can't take this away from me."

His mind spun with wild thoughts. Maybe he could confront the narrator directly. Maybe he could stop this before it spiraled further. But the more he thought about it, the less sense it made. He didn't know who to trust anymore. For all he knew, the narrator had been plotting this from the beginning, slowly undermining his credibility until now, when they had the state on their side.

Dr. Jones slammed his fist on the desk, the sharp pain jolting him back to reality. He needed to act. Sitting here, letting the fear gnaw away at him, wasn't going to help. His career, his reputation—everything was on the line. And if the narrator was working with the state to bring him down, then it was time to fight back. He didn't know how, but he'd make sure they regretted it.

The phone rang again, startling him. He hesitated for a moment before answering, his voice shaky with anger.

"Jones here."

"Dr. Jones," came the familiar voice of a colleague on the other end. "I just got word from a patient—someone's been asking questions about your practice. Do you know anything about this?"

Jones's grip on the phone tightened. More whispers. More plotting. His mind began to race again, piecing together the threads of what he believed was a conspiracy against him.

"They think they can pull this off," he whispered to himself, barely able to focus on the conversation. "Well, they're dead wrong."

He hung up without another word, his eyes wild with fury. He had always been a man of action, someone who fought back when backed into a corner. And now, with everything he had built being threatened, he felt that familiar fire rise up in him once again. He wouldn't go down quietly.

***

Dr. Romano smiled faintly as she imagined the chaos beginning to take shape. She could almost hear the tension building from across the city. The dentists, already teetering on the edge, would soon be engulfed in a wave of paranoia and fear. And when they finally lashed out, it would be the narrator caught in the storm.

It was a dangerous game, but one Dr. Romano had played many times before. She had spent years perfecting the art of manipulation, of turning other people's weaknesses into her strengths. And this time would be no different. She would watch it all unfold from a distance, her hands untouched, while the others burned.

"Let them fight among themselves," she thought, her gaze never leaving the skyline. "By the time they realize what's happened, it will be too late."

The phone on her desk buzzed with a new message, but she didn't bother to check it right away. Instead, she leaned back in her chair, feeling the weight of her plan beginning to fall into place. The pieces were moving, the game was in motion, and soon, the results would speak for themselves.

The narrator wouldn't see it coming. And that was exactly how Dr. Romano liked it.

Chapter 23

Dr. Romano sat in a plush conference room, the dim lighting casting a soft glow on the faces of the executives around her. The atmosphere was thick with tension, underscored by the urgency of their conversation. A large mahogany table separated her from the men in tailored suits, all of whom exuded an air of power and authority. Each one had a vested interest in the outcomes of their discussion.

"Let's be clear about our objectives," said one executive, a tall man with graying hair and a sharp suit. "We need to ensure that any information the narrator may disclose about Specter's nanorobots is met with immediate skepticism. The last thing we want is for the public to rally behind him."

Dr. Romano nodded, her expression measured. "I agree. If we can plant the idea that he's involved in fraudulent activity, it will discredit him and detract attention from our operations."

She leaned forward slightly, her fingers steepled. "The plan is straightforward: we alter federal records to imply that the narrator has been manipulating data related to the nanorobots. It will paint him as someone who cannot be trusted, someone whose credibility is in question."

The executives exchanged glances, weighing the potential repercussions of such a plan. The atmosphere shifted as the stakes became clear.

"Are you sure this is a move we want to make?" asked another executive, a younger man with a nervous tic. "If it gets out—"

"It won't get out," Dr. Romano interrupted, her tone firm. "I have connections who will make sure this stays contained. The beauty of it is that the information will be there, but it will be buried in layers of bureaucracy. It's about creating a narrative that people will believe."

The first executive leaned back in his chair, clearly intrigued. "And what if the narrator tries to fight back? If he goes to the press or—"

"Then we'll have our rebuttals ready," Dr. Romano replied confidently. "Once we make the changes to the records, we can craft a story that places him as the villain in this narrative. We'll provide evidence that suggests he's been attempting to defraud the insurance company. By the time he realizes what's happening, it'll be too late for him to defend himself."

Silence fell over the room as the executives considered the implications. The risk was significant, but the rewards could be even greater. With the right manipulations, they could effectively neutralize the narrator and keep their own operations safe from scrutiny.

"Let's say we proceed," said the younger executive, his tone hesitant. "How do we go about altering those records? What's our next step?"

Dr. Romano smiled slightly, relishing the moment. "I have a contact who specializes in this type of work. He knows how to navigate the system without raising any red flags. I'll arrange for a meeting with him, and we can lay the groundwork for what we need."

"Good," the first executive said, nodding. "I want to see this done swiftly. If we can discredit him before he makes any noise, we'll save ourselves a lot of trouble down the line."

"Exactly," Dr. Romano agreed, her voice low and steady. "This is about securing our position and eliminating a threat. We're not just protecting our interests; we're preserving our entire operation."

As the conversation shifted toward the logistics of their plan, Dr. Romano's mind raced with possibilities. Each step they took was calculated, a move in a game where the stakes were life and death. She knew that manipulating federal records was a dangerous game, but it was a risk she was willing to take. The narrator had to be silenced, and this was the way to do it.

***

Dr. Jones paced back and forth in his office, still simmering with rage over the news he had received. He could barely focus on the patients in the waiting room; his mind was consumed with thoughts of revenge against the narrator and anyone else who dared to threaten his practice.

"Excuse me, Dr. Jones?" one of his dental assistants interrupted, peeking her head into his office. "We have a patient ready for you in room two."

He waved her off dismissively. "I'll be there in a minute," he snapped, barely able to contain his agitation.

Dr. Jones stopped and took a deep breath, trying to calm himself. He needed to keep it together, at least for the sake of his practice. But as he looked at the walls adorned with certificates and accolades, all he felt was a sense of impending doom. How could they do this to him?

Suddenly, his phone buzzed on the desk, breaking the silence. He grabbed it, his heart racing as he glanced at the caller ID. It was an unknown number, but desperation drove him to answer.

"Hello?" he said, trying to keep his voice steady.

"Dr. Jones," a smooth voice on the other end said. "I have information that might interest you. It's about the narrator."

Dr. Jones felt a jolt of excitement mixed with apprehension. "What do you know?"

"I know that he's been digging into something he shouldn't be. And I know you're not the only one who's been feeling the heat from him. There are others out there who want him silenced just as much as you do."

"What do you mean?" Dr. Jones asked, his curiosity piqued.

"Let's just say that if you're willing to take matters into your own hands, you might find some allies who feel the same way. The narrator is a threat to many, not just you."

Dr. Jones's mind raced. This could be the opportunity he had been looking for. He felt a surge of adrenaline at the thought of not just defending himself, but going on the offensive. "Who are you?" he pressed, his voice low.

"Someone who knows how the game is played," the voice replied cryptically. "If you're interested, I can set up a meeting. But you need to be prepared to act quickly."

Dr. Jones hesitated for a moment, weighing the risks. But he was already in too deep. The state was closing in on him, and he could feel the walls closing in. "I'm in," he said firmly. "Set it up."

"Good. I'll be in touch," the voice said before hanging up.

***

Back in the conference room, Dr. Romano wrapped up the meeting with the executives. She felt a sense of satisfaction wash over her. They had laid the groundwork for a plan that could eliminate their biggest threat and secure their positions within the industry.

"Let's keep this tight-lipped," she said, her tone leaving no room for argument. "We cannot afford any leaks."

As the executives nodded in agreement, Dr. Romano couldn't shake the feeling that they were on the verge of something monumental. With the narrator discredited, her position at Specter would solidify, and she could continue her work without the threat of exposure.

As she left the building, the night air was cool and crisp against her skin. She relished the quiet, knowing that soon enough, the chaos would begin. And she would be watching from the sidelines, orchestrating it all with precision.

***

Dr. Romano pulled out her phone and glanced at the screen. There was a new message from her contact regarding the federal records. The details were sketchy, but they confirmed that everything was falling into place. She smirked, feeling a rush of adrenaline. The pieces were aligning, and it wouldn't be long before the narrator was taken down.

"Time to set the plan in motion," she thought, already anticipating the chaos that would follow.

Chapter 24

Dr. Romano oversees a meeting with utility company representatives in a dimly lit office, the atmosphere tense with urgency. As she addresses them, her voice is firm and commanding, ensuring that her authority is felt in every word.

"I need you to ensure compliance with the new state regulations," she instructs, her gaze penetrating as she scans the room. "These inspections will serve a dual purpose: we'll gather valuable data while creating a significant disruption in the dental community."

The representatives exchange uneasy glances, their expressions apprehension and intrigue. They're aware that her plans are ambitious, bordering on the reckless. However, they also recognize the benefits that could come from aligning with her.

One of the representatives, a nervous-looking man with glasses, hesitates before speaking up. "What if these inspections lead to findings that expose us? We could face serious backlash if we're caught manipulating the situation."

Dr. Romano raises an eyebrow, her confidence unwavering. "That's a risk we must take. The stakes are high, but so are the potential rewards. Just think about the leverage we'll gain over the unstable dentists. If they believe they're under scrutiny, they'll act impulsively."

As she continues to elaborate on her plan, the atmosphere in the room shifts from tension to determination. The utility representatives nod along, slowly becoming more convinced of her vision. Dr. Romano presents her strategy with meticulous detail, outlining how they'll implement the power cuts and inspections systematically.

"We'll coordinate with the state to conduct surprise inspections during peak hours. The disruption will be chaotic—dentists won't know what hit them," she explains, her enthusiasm igniting a spark of interest among the representatives.

In her mind, Dr. Romano envisions the chaos that will ensue once her plan is in motion. She imagines the instability among the dentists, the panic setting in as they scramble to protect their livelihoods. Her thoughts drift back to her ultimate goal: to neutralize the narrator's influence while ensuring her own ascent within Specter.

As the meeting progresses, the discussion becomes increasingly animated. The representatives begin to throw out ideas, their initial hesitations melting away in the face of Dr. Romano's bold leadership. They brainstorm how to handle potential fallout, the best times for inspections, and methods to ensure their own safety.

The conversation takes a strategic turn when one of the representatives proposes leveraging media coverage. "What if we frame the inspections as part of a state-wide initiative to improve public health standards?" he suggests. "It could provide a smokescreen, making it harder for anyone to connect the dots back to us."

Dr. Romano nods appreciatively. "Exactly. If we can control the narrative, we'll keep ourselves insulated from scrutiny while achieving our objectives."

The plan unfolds further, with Dr. Romano at the center, orchestrating every detail. She envisions the chaos resulting from the combination of power cuts and surprise inspections, all while the state publicly champions the initiative as a progressive step forward.

Meanwhile, her phone buzzes on the table, a message from an unknown number flashing on the screen. She glances at it, curiosity piquing her interest but chooses to ignore it for now, knowing that this meeting demands her full attention.

The representatives finalize the details of their collaboration, and Dr. Romano feels a surge of triumph. She's skillfully maneuvering through the intricate web of alliances, carefully ensuring that her personal ambitions remain intact while pushing forward with Specter's agenda.

As they conclude the meeting, Dr. Romano stands up, her demeanor resolute. "Let's move quickly. The sooner we implement this, the better positioned we'll be to take advantage of the ensuing chaos."

The representatives file out of the office, a newfound sense of purpose igniting their steps. Dr. Romano watches them go, a satisfied smile creeping onto her lips as she contemplates the power she's amassed and the lengths she's willing to go to ensure her success.

Later, in her office, she takes a moment to reflect on the risks and rewards of her actions. The path she's chosen is fraught with danger, but the potential for personal gain drives her forward. She understands that in a world where power plays and hidden agendas reign, the stakes are always high.

With a deep breath, she picks up her phone and finally opens the message that had interrupted her earlier thoughts. The message is cryptic, hinting at new developments regarding the narrator. Her heart races as she reads it, the implications weighing heavily on her mind.

"Looks like things are heating up," she mutters to herself, her determination solidifying. "I need to stay one step ahead."

The city outside her window twinkles with the glow of countless lights, a stark contrast to the darkness of her machinations. She feels the weight of her choices, but within that weight lies a fierce resolve. In a world where ambition often clashes with morality, she is prepared to embrace the shadows, using them to her advantage.

As night falls over the city, Dr. Romano leans back in her chair, plotting her next move in this high-stakes game. She knows the power she wields can easily slip away if she isn't careful. Her mind races with possibilities, strategies, and the ever-present threat of betrayal lurking around every corner.

In her pursuit of success, she's willing to sacrifice everything, including her own moral compass. The choices she's made will ripple through the lives of many, and she remains undeterred. With the right moves, she believes she can reshape her world to reflect her ambitions—no matter the cost.

The clock ticks steadily, each second a reminder that time is of the essence. Dr. Romano picks up her pen, ready to draft the next chapter of her story, one that intertwines power, manipulation, and the pursuit of a vision that only she can see.

Chapter 25

Utility trucks line the streets, their headlights cutting through the night as maintenance workers scramble to execute Dr. Romano's plan. The once-bustling cityscape begins to dim, lights flickering ominously as power is cut in various neighborhoods. Shadows stretch across the streets, and the hum of everyday life gives way to an unsettling silence, punctuated only by the sound of generators and the distant murmurs of confused residents.

As the chaos unfolds, Dr. Romano observes from her office, her expression one of satisfaction. The city she once navigated with ease is now a battleground of her own design. She watches the flickering lights from her window, a twisted sense of triumph washing over her as she considers the implications of her actions.

The utility companies, eager to please, have mobilized quickly. They understand the stakes: align with government interests, and they'll be rewarded; falter, and they risk losing everything. The workers, instructed to act without hesitation, cut the power to several key locations, including dental offices that had been identified as crucial to the narrator's operations.

"Good," she murmurs to herself, satisfaction creeping into her voice. "Let's see how they react to this disruption."

A notification pops up on her phone, and she glances down to see a message from one of her contacts at the utility company. "All systems go. Power outages initiated. Areas affected: downtown, West End, and the dental district," it reads.

Dr. Romano leans back in her chair, absorbing the magnitude of her strategy. The chaos that ensues is precisely what she envisioned: a carefully orchestrated disruption designed to shatter the stability of her adversaries. She knows the narrator will be caught off guard, scrambling to manage the fallout while she stays one step ahead.

As the city plunges into darkness, frantic voices fill the air. Residents emerge from their homes, bewildered and angry, as they try to make sense of the sudden power outages. In the distance, sirens wail, a chorus of confusion signaling the start of a night filled with unrest.

Dr. Romano's phone buzzes again. This time, it's a call from Dr. Jones, one of the unstable dentists targeted by her plan. She answers with feigned concern, knowing full well what kind of reaction she will elicit.

"Dr. Jones, are you okay?" she asks, her tone syrupy sweet. "I heard about the power cuts. It must be incredibly frustrating for you."

Dr. Jones's voice erupts from the speaker, filled with fury. "Frustrating? That's an understatement! I can't believe they would do this! Do they think they can intimidate us? This is outrageous!"

Dr. Romano lets the anger wash over her, pretending to be sympathetic. "I understand your frustration. I think it's crucial that we rally together and show them we won't be silenced."

"Rally together?" Dr. Jones scoffs. "How can we when we can't even keep our practices running? This will ruin us! And if they think we'll just sit back and take it, they're wrong!"

"Exactly," she encourages, keeping her voice steady. "But you need to focus. This isn't just about power; it's about fighting back against the forces that want to control us. We can't let them win."

In her mind, she's calculating how to use his rage to her advantage. His instability, combined with the power outage, could provoke a violent response, one that would further destabilize the dental community and divert attention away from her own machinations.

"What do you suggest?" he asks, his voice lowering slightly as the anger transforms into desperation. "What can we do?"

Dr. Romano leans in, her voice dropping to a conspiratorial whisper. "You gather your colleagues, create a show of force. Make them see that you're united, that you won't back down. Use this outrage to your advantage. Let them know you're not afraid."

As they continue to speak, Dr. Romano carefully plants the seeds of rebellion. She feeds into his fears, stoking the fire of unrest among the unstable dentists, knowing that chaos will serve her purpose.

Meanwhile, she can't help but revel in the strategic positioning she has achieved. She's managed to isolate the narrator, putting him in a precarious situation while also setting the stage for the dentists to turn against him. Each word she utters is a calculated move, every suggestion a step deeper into the intricate web she weaves.

When the call ends, she takes a moment to collect herself, feeling the adrenaline surge through her veins. She knows that the consequences of her actions are far-reaching, and yet, there's an exhilaration that comes with wielding such power.

Her phone buzzes again, this time with an alert about social media posts erupting with outrage from the dental community. "Power outages lead to chaos for local dentists," one headline blares, accompanied by a video of Dr. Jones passionately rallying his peers outside his darkened office.

"Perfect," Dr. Romano whispers, a smile spreading across her face as she watches the chaos unfold in real time. She understands that the narrative is already shifting, and she is at the helm of this storm.

As the night wears on, the city remains shrouded in darkness, a canvas for her ambitions. The power cuts serve as both a distraction and a weapon, turning the dental community against itself while she quietly continues her work, maneuvering through the shadows.

Dr. Romano knows the night is still young, and there are more moves to be made in this game of power and influence. She has set the stage for the upheaval she craves, and with each passing moment, she becomes more convinced that she's on the right path.

"Let them fight," she murmurs, looking out over the cityscape. "In the end, only the strongest will survive."

Chapter 26

Dr. Orrington stares at the blank page before him, his mind racing as he tries to find the right words. The room is dimly lit, the only illumination coming from a flickering desk lamp that casts shadows across the piles of research papers scattered around. The weight of the world seems to rest on his shoulders as he contemplates the implications of his findings. He takes a deep breath, attempting to steady his nerves before he continues writing.

His hand trembles slightly as he pens the words, a testament to his anxiety. "To Whom It May Concern," he begins, then hesitates, re-reading it before continuing. "I must bring to your attention the grave situation regarding the manipulation of water sources across our state. My recent investigations into nanorobots used in water treatment have revealed alarming data that cannot be ignored."

Dr. Orrington pauses, his heart racing as he recalls the clandestine meetings he attended, the hushed conversations that hinted at a larger conspiracy. He remembers the faces of his colleagues, some supportive and others skeptical, their expressions betraying their doubts and fears. He recalls the threats that have loomed over him since he started uncovering the truth, and the feeling of isolation that has grown as he delves deeper into this dangerous territory.

He continues to write, the words flowing more freely now. "The use of these nanorobots is not merely a scientific advancement; it is a method of control, a means to influence populations by manipulating their most vital resource. I have witnessed firsthand the changes in water quality, the unusual symptoms in those who have been exposed, and the subsequent cover-up by those in power."

His voiceover underscores the urgency of his message. "I cannot remain silent. My conscience demands action, and I urge you to investigate this matter further. Failure to do so may result in devastating consequences for public health."

As he finishes the letter, he runs a hand through his disheveled hair, taking a moment to reflect on the risks he is about to take. There is a part of him that fears for his safety, aware of the powerful entities he is up against. But there is also a sense of duty that drives him forward, a belief that he must fight for the truth, no matter the cost.

He signs the letter with a shaky hand, his signature almost illegible in his rush. "Sincerely, Dr. Nathan Orrington." With a heavy sigh, he folds the letter and places it in an envelope, sealing it tightly.

His phone buzzes on the desk, breaking the silence of the room. He picks it up, his heart sinking as he sees the caller ID. It's a number he recognizes all too well, one that has brought nothing but trouble in the past. Hesitating for a moment, he finally answers, his voice steady despite the dread creeping in.

"Hello?"

"Dr. Orrington, we need to talk," a deep voice on the other end states, each word deliberate and commanding. "You've been asking too many questions."

Dr. Orrington's heart races as he grips the phone tighter. "I have a right to know what's happening. This isn't just about research; it's about the health of our community."

The voice chuckles, but there's no humor in it, only menace. "You're treading dangerous waters. You think you're the only one who cares about the truth?

You're out of your depth, and it's time you understood the consequences of your actions."

"I won't be intimidated," Dr. Orrington responds, his voice firmer now, the weight of his convictions bolstering his resolve. "The people deserve to know what's going on. I won't stop until this is exposed."

There's a brief silence, and Dr. Orrington can almost hear the other person weighing their options. "You're a smart man, Dr. Orrington. You know the stakes. But just remember, those who dig too deep often find themselves buried."

The call ends abruptly, leaving Dr. Orrington staring at the phone in disbelief, his heart pounding in his chest. He's shaken, but there's no going back now. He has to act quickly. He knows he can't rely on traditional channels anymore; he needs allies who understand the gravity of the situation.

He stands up from his desk, pacing the small confines of his office as he strategizes. "Who can I trust?" he murmurs to himself, the tension coiling in his stomach. He thinks of his colleagues, those who have supported him in the past, but he knows their fear of retribution may keep them silent.

Suddenly, an idea strikes him. There's one person who might be willing to listen, someone who has always been drawn to the truth: Dr. Karen Romano. They had collaborated on several projects before, and she had always displayed an unyielding commitment to ethical practices in their field. He grabs his phone, quickly dialing her number, hope surging within him as he waits for her to pick up.

"Karen? It's Nathan," he says as soon as she answers, urgency seeping into his voice. "I need to meet. It's about the nanorobots and the water supply. There's something you need to know."

"Is this about your latest findings?" she asks, her tone shifting to one of concern. "You sounded serious in your last email. What's going on?"

Dr. Orrington glances at the clock on the wall, the minutes slipping away faster than he'd like. "It's worse than I thought. Can we meet somewhere private? I need to show you some documents and share what I've uncovered."

"Sure, where do you want to meet?" she replies, her voice steady despite the growing tension.

"Let's meet at the café on Pine Street, in an hour. It's quiet there," he suggests, relief washing over him as she agrees.

"Okay, I'll see you there," she says before hanging up.

As Dr. Orrington prepares to leave his office, he feels a renewed sense of purpose. He knows the path ahead will be fraught with danger, but he cannot ignore the responsibility that weighs heavily on his shoulders. He must convince Dr. Romano of the severity of the situation, and together, they may be able to uncover the truth and stop the looming threat.

With a final glance at his desk, he takes a deep breath, steeling himself for the challenges that lie ahead. He knows time is of the essence; he has to act before it's too late. Grabbing his coat, he heads out the door, determination propelling him forward as he steps into the unknown, ready to confront whatever awaits him.

Chapter 27

Workers at the water treatment facility inspect the complex network of pipes and equipment, their expressions serious and focused. They move quickly, discussing potential issues and assessing the integrity of the systems that ensure clean water flows to the community. The atmosphere is charged with urgency, underscoring the gravity of their tasks.

Dr. Romano's voice resonates in the background, her tone calm yet tinged with foreboding. "Specter's focus on targeting water pipes reveals their broader strategy. Nanorobots disrupt water formation, exacerbating climate-related damage, especially in regions with low COVID-19 vaccination rates." Her words linger, illustrating the dire consequences of tampering with such a vital resource.

As Dr. Romano's voiceover continues, the scene shifts to a control room filled with monitors displaying various data feeds. Operators keep a watchful eye on the information scrolling across the screens, highlighting fluctuations in water quality. Tension fills the room as they exchange glances, clearly concerned about the potential fallout from any disruptions.

In a corner of the control room, a technician points to a monitor, his brow furrowed in worry. "Look at these levels; they're spiking!" he exclaims, drawing the attention of his colleagues. "We need to investigate the source of this contamination immediately!"

Another operator nods, urgency in her voice. "I'll alert the team to check the filtration systems. If there's an issue with the water supply, we could be looking at a public health crisis."

Dr. Orrington, still at his desk, feels the weight of the impending disaster pressing down on him. He has been piecing together the connections between the nanorobots and the disruptions in the water supply. With each new revelation, his concern grows. He knows he must act quickly before the situation spirals out of control.

He takes a deep breath and picks up his pen again, writing fervently. "I must make this public," he declares, determination filling his voice. "The health of our community is at stake, and I refuse to let this injustice continue unchecked." His heart races as he considers the potential consequences of his actions, but he understands that silence is not an option.

The scene transitions back to Dr. Romano, who stands in her sleek office, overlooking the city skyline. She feels a sense of triumph as she reflects on her plans. Her phone buzzes, interrupting her thoughts. It's a message from one of her contacts at the water treatment facility.

She opens the message and reads, "We're monitoring fluctuations in water quality. There's a possibility of contamination, but we're not sure of the source yet." A smirk crosses her face. She knows that chaos is exactly what she needs to solidify her position.

In the shadows of her office, she whispers to herself, "This is just the beginning." Her mind races with ideas on how to exploit the situation further. She knows she must maintain her facade while executing her plans with precision. Dr. Romano's ambition drives her forward, regardless of the cost to others.

Back at the water treatment facility, alarms suddenly blare, cutting through the tension. Workers rush to their stations, adrenaline surging as they scramble to address the unfolding crisis. Dr. Romano's voice echoes in the background, articulating the gravity of the situation. "The disruption is not just a minor setback; it's part of a larger game."

Dr. Orrington, still writing, glances at the clock on the wall, anxiety bubbling within him. He can sense that time is running out. He picks up the phone and dials the local news station, his voice steady as he speaks to the producer. "You need to listen to me. I have critical information regarding the water supply and the potential health risks associated with it."

The producer's voice is skeptical, asking for proof. "We need something concrete before we can air this," she responds, her tone dismissive.

"Just give me a chance to present my findings. I can show you the data that proves my claims," Dr. Orrington pleads, his urgency evident.

As he hangs up, his heart sinks. He knows that without immediate action, lives could be at risk. He considers his next steps, contemplating whether to reach out to the authorities or risk going public in a more aggressive way.

Meanwhile, Dr. Romano is busy orchestrating her next move, knowing that the chaos in the water treatment facility will provide a perfect distraction. She sends a text to her allies, informing them of the situation. "The time has come to initiate phase two of our plan. Make sure the narrator is kept in check while we manipulate the narrative."

As she puts down her phone, she feels a sense of satisfaction. Everything is falling into place. Dr. Romano's ambition is unwavering, and she is determined to see her plans through, no matter the cost.

Dr. Orrington, sitting in the dim light of his office, looks out the window, contemplating the potential fallout from his next decision. He understands that he is risking everything, but the stakes have never been higher. "The truth must come to light," he mutters to himself, resolve hardening within him.

Outside, the city begins to unravel as the lights flicker ominously.

Chapter 28

Dr. Romano sits alone in her office, the glow of the city lights streaming through the large windows casting shadows across her desk. Papers are strewn about, some marked with urgent notes and highlighted sections, evidence of her frantic thinking. Her face shows signs of strain, the weight of her choices evident in the lines etched across her forehead. She leans back in her chair, the leather creaking softly beneath her as she closes her eyes for a moment, allowing herself a brief escape from the chaos surrounding her.

In the silence, her mind races with thoughts of the decisions that have brought her to this point. Each choice she made was deliberate, a calculated step towards securing her position within Specter, yet the repercussions of those decisions loom large in her mind.

"Ultimately, I faced a reckoning decision that would affect not only myself but those I cared about," she reflects, her voice steady but laced with uncertainty. "Every action has consequences, and the path I chose was fraught with risks." She opens her eyes, gazing at the city below, contemplating the lives intertwined with her own. Each flickering light represents a story, a person whose future might be altered by her machinations.

Dr. Romano's phone buzzes on the desk, snapping her out of her thoughts. She picks it up, glancing at the screen. It's a message from a contact within the utility company. "The power outages have started, and we're receiving reports of chaos. Are you ready for the next phase?"

Her heart races at the implications of the message. "Ready as I'll ever be," she replies, her fingers trembling slightly as she types. She knows that the events set in motion will not only benefit her but also serve to eliminate threats that could jeopardize her plans. Yet, the nagging feeling of moral conflict continues to gnaw at her, a reminder of the line she is walking.

As she hits send, she leans back in her chair, breathing deeply. The stakes are higher than ever. She remembers her early days in medicine, filled with dreams of helping others, of making a difference. How had she ended up here, plotting and scheming in the shadows? The thought of those early aspirations feels like a distant memory, overshadowed by the weight of her current reality.

"Am I really helping anyone?" she whispers to herself, her voice barely audible. She shakes her head, dismissing the thought. She reminds herself that in this line of work, sacrifices must be made. The world is not black and white; it's a complicated web of grays, and she's merely playing her part in the grand scheme of things.

A knock on the door interrupts her thoughts. It's one of her assistants, a young woman named Lisa, who enters with a stack of files in her hands. "Dr. Romano, I have the latest reports from the dental offices. Some dentists are starting to express concern over the state's recent warnings."

"Let them," Dr. Romano replies, her tone sharp but controlled. "They need to understand that this is bigger than them. Their compliance is crucial to our plans."

Lisa hesitates, sensing the tension in the air. "But what if they decide to fight back? If they're cornered, they might expose everything."

Dr. Romano's eyes narrow, irritation flashing across her face. "They won't. They have too much to lose, just like we do. Fear is a powerful motivator. Use that to our advantage."

As Lisa nods and steps back, Dr. Romano reflects on the risks involved. She understands the fragility of their situation, the fine line between control and chaos. The unstable dentists they had threatened were a wild card, and she couldn't shake the feeling that their reactions could spiral out of control.

Taking a deep breath, she forces herself to focus on the task at hand. "We need to prepare for any backlash. Make sure our story is tight, and everyone involved knows their role. If we're going to navigate this storm, we must present a united front."

"Yes, Dr. Romano," Lisa replies, her voice steady, yet there's a hint of concern in her eyes. She leaves the office, leaving Dr. Romano alone once again with her thoughts.

She opens the window slightly, letting in the cool night air, hoping to clear her mind. The city buzzes below, alive with energy and uncertainty, and she can feel the weight of the world pressing down on her shoulders.

Her phone buzzes again, this time with a message from Dr. Orrington. "We need to talk. This situation is escalating, and I have evidence that could change everything."

Dr. Romano's heart sinks. She knows that Dr. Orrington has been digging deeper into the issues surrounding the water supply, and his persistence poses a threat to her carefully laid plans. "This is precisely what I was afraid of," she mutters under her breath, frustration boiling within her.

She quickly types a response. "Meet me at the usual place. We need to discuss how to handle this."

Setting her phone down, she stands up, her mind racing. The consequences of her actions are becoming more tangible by the minute. If Dr. Orrington reveals his findings, it could jeopardize everything she has worked for.

As she straightens her blazer, preparing to leave, she feels a surge of determination. She will not let anyone stand in her way. Dr. Romano knows that she must confront Dr. Orrington and neutralize the threat he poses. The clock is ticking, and every moment counts.

Leaving her office, she strides down the hallway with purpose. The stakes have never been higher, and as she heads toward the meeting, she reminds herself of the greater good she is pursuing, despite the moral implications. In a world fraught with danger and betrayal, survival depends on her ability to control the narrative and manipulate those around her.

Dr. Romano steps out into the night, her resolve strengthening with each passing moment. She understands that the choices she makes now will echo through the lives of many, and she is ready to face whatever consequences await her. The reckoning has begun, and she is determined to emerge victorious.

Chapter 29

A crowd gathers around a public notice board, the air filled with murmurs of curiosity and concern. Brightly colored flyers are pinned haphazardly, one in particular catching the eye of passersby. It reads: "Protect Our Water: Understand the Threats!" The bold letters demand attention, and the message resonates deeply with those who stop to read.

Dr. Orrington's voice echoes in the minds of those present, his urgency palpable even in his absence. "You, the listener, also face a reckoning. Water is essential to all species. We need a period of inactivity to replenish our resources and confront the reality of our situation." The weight of his words hangs in the air, stirring emotions and igniting conversations among the crowd.

People gather in small groups, sharing their thoughts and fears. Parents hold their children close, educators discuss potential impacts on schools, and activists begin organizing a response to what they perceive as a growing crisis. The flyer has become a catalyst, sparking a sense of urgency and collective responsibility.

Among the crowd, a young woman named Mia holds the flyer tightly in her hands, her brow furrowed in thought. She had come to the park for a peaceful afternoon but found herself drawn into this unexpected gathering. The message resonates with her, a reminder of her own struggles with water scarcity in her community.

"We can't just stand by and let this happen," Mia exclaims to a small group around her. "If we don't take action now, we might lose everything." Her voice rises with passion, capturing the attention of those nearby. They nod in agreement, her conviction fueling their own resolve.

Dr. Orrington's voice continues in the background, weaving through the conversations. "The threats to our water supply are not abstract. They affect our health, our environment, and our future. We must come together to protect this vital resource." His message transcends the paper it was printed on, echoing in the hearts of those who hear it.

As discussions deepen, various individuals share their experiences and ideas. An older man steps forward, his voice steady and authoritative. "We've been fighting for clean water in our neighborhoods for years," he shares. "If we unite our efforts, we can make a difference."

Encouraged by the older man's words, others begin to chime in, sharing their stories of contamination, shortages, and health issues stemming from inadequate water resources. The atmosphere shifts from passive observation to active engagement, the crowd transforming into a community rallying for change.

In the midst of the gathering, Mia looks around, her heart swelling with hope. This was the kind of action she had dreamed of—a movement fueled by awareness and driven by shared experiences. She realizes they must take their fight beyond this moment, organizing to demand accountability from those in power.

"Let's create a petition," Mia suggests, her enthusiasm infectious. "We need to hold our local officials responsible for the state of our water supply. If enough of us sign, they'll have to listen."

The crowd buzzes with excitement at the idea, and a few people quickly volunteer to help organize the petition. They begin strategizing, discussing potential locations for gathering signatures and ways to spread the word. The flyer that once served as a simple warning has now ignited a fire within the community, transforming passive concern into proactive engagement.

Dr. Orrington watches from a distance, his heart filled with a mixture of pride and anxiety. He had hoped for this kind of response, yet he also knows the dangers that lie ahead. The moment he had anticipated—the reckoning—has finally arrived, but it is only the beginning.

Mia stands at the forefront, leading the charge with conviction. She recognizes the magnitude of the task ahead but feels invigorated by the support around her. "Let's not just stop here. We need to educate ourselves and others about the importance of water conservation and the threats we face. Knowledge is power, and we can use it to drive change."

The crowd responds with cheers, a wave of determination washing over them. They begin to chant slogans, their voices rising in unison. "Protect our water! Protect our future!" The power of collective action resonates deeply, filling the public area with an electric energy.

As the gathering continues, the members of the community start to feel a sense of agency, a realization that they are not powerless in the face of adversity. They have the ability to challenge the systems that have neglected their needs for too long.

With each passing moment, Dr. Orrington's voice echoes in their minds, urging them to confront the reality of their situation. The awareness he has sparked is taking root, growing into a movement that could change the course of their lives. The reckoning is not just his; it belongs to everyone who understands the value of water and the fight for its preservation.

As the crowd disperses, Mia feels a renewed sense of purpose. She is ready to rally her community, not just for themselves but for future generations. The fight for clean, safe water is far from over, and she is determined to lead the charge.

The flyer on the public notice board flutters in the breeze, a silent testament to the power of awareness and the strength found in unity. Dr. Orrington's message has become more than just words; it has ignited a movement, awakening a collective consciousness that will not easily be silenced.

Chapter 30

The city struggles under the weight of power outages and water issues, the skyline punctuated by flickering lights and empty reservoirs. Once bustling streets are now filled with tension as residents grapple with the sudden scarcity of vital resources. The atmosphere is thick with uncertainty, each flicker of light and drop of water serving as a stark reminder of the fragility of modern life.

Dr. Orrington's voice resonates in the background, a steady reminder of the stakes involved. "Water is not just a resource; it is the foundation of life itself. The choices we make now will determine our future. The true nature of water and its vital role must be understood and protected." His words linger, reverberating through the hearts of those who hear them, igniting a sense of urgency and responsibility.

In the neighborhoods, families gather around their dining tables, discussing the latest developments with worried expressions. Children drink from plastic bottles, their parents eyeing the dwindling supplies of water. "What are we going to do if this continues?" one mother asks, her voice trembling with concern.

The silence that follows speaks volumes, the fear palpable in the air.

Elsewhere, community leaders convene in church basements and local halls, strategizing on how to address the crisis. Ideas flow freely as residents suggest solutions, their faces illuminated by the dim light of flickering candles. "We need to organize a town hall meeting," a local activist suggests, determination etched on her face. "We must demand accountability from our officials. This can't go on."

Meanwhile, businesses suffer from the outages. Cafés and restaurants sit dark and empty, their owners anxiously calculating their losses. A barista stands outside her shuttered coffee shop, discussing the need for action with a friend. "If we don't stand together, we'll all sink," she insists, her voice firm. "We can't let this crisis divide us."

As the day stretches into evening, the city remains caught in the grip of uncertainty. Streetlights flicker sporadically, casting eerie shadows across deserted streets. News reports fill the airwaves with warnings about water safety and the dangers of contaminated supplies, heightening anxiety among residents.

In the midst of the chaos, Dr. Orrington continues his research, fueled by the desire to uncover the truth behind the water crisis. His office is cluttered with papers and research materials, evidence of countless hours spent poring over data and analysis. The weight of his findings presses down on him; he knows that time is running out.

"I must get this information out to the public," he mutters to himself, determination in his eyes. "People need to understand the real implications of what's happening." He pulls out a map, tracing the routes of water distribution across the city, plotting a course for potential contamination points.

His thoughts drift back to Dr. Romano and the shadowy organization she represents. "What are they really doing?" he wonders, anxiety gnawing at him. The thought of the powerful forces at play fills him with dread, but he knows he cannot back down now. He recalls the conversations he had overheard, snippets of information that suggest a larger agenda—one that threatens not just individual lives but the health of entire communities.

Outside, the sun begins to set, casting a warm glow over the city. But this tranquility belies the turmoil brewing beneath the surface. Dr. Orrington stares out the window, his mind racing with possibilities. "If I can just get a group of concerned citizens together," he thinks, "maybe we can force the authorities to take this seriously." He imagines organizing a coalition, bringing together scientists, health experts, and community members to demand action.

As the evening deepens, the city remains on edge. In homes and community centers alike, residents are discussing the future, their voices fear and resolve. Dr. Orrington knows that the fight is just beginning. He feels a flicker of hope as he recalls the crowd gathered around the public notice board, the energy and determination that had sparked in that moment. "We can't let fear paralyze us," he reminds himself. "We must act."

With a renewed sense of purpose, he begins drafting a letter to the local newspaper, detailing his findings and calling for public awareness. "It's time for the truth to come to light," he writes, each word fueled by the urgency of the moment.

Dr. Romano sits in her luxurious apartment, reflecting on the consequences of her choices. The weight of her decisions bears down on her, and as she watches the city lights flicker ominously, she contemplates the broader implications of her actions.

The power she sought to wield now seems fraught with peril, and she grapples with the reality that she has unleashed forces she cannot easily control.

The city is at a crossroads, its fate hanging in the balance. The conflict between Dr. Orrington's pursuit of truth and Dr. Romano's ambitious machinations sets the stage for a reckoning that could reshape their world. As the darkness deepens, so too does the resolve of those who understand the importance of water and its central role in sustaining life.

Dr. Orrington finishes his letter, sealing it with a sense of finality. "This is just the beginning," he thinks. He knows that the road ahead will be fraught with challenges, but he is determined to navigate it, drawing strength from the community that is beginning to awaken to the urgency of the situation.

As the city wrestles with power outages and water issues, the voices of its inhabitants grow louder, echoing Dr. Orrington's call to action. The choices made in the coming days will not only impact the present but also shape the future of generations to come. In a world where the threads of power and influence are intricately woven, the struggle for water becomes a fight for life itself.

Chapter 31

The study is filled with dim light from a single desk lamp casting shadows across the room. Shelves are lined with books, scientific journals, and equipment. Dr. Orrington sits at his desk, his face serious as he begins to speak, his voice steady but laced with urgency.

"Welcome," he says, looking directly at the viewer. "You may not know me, but I am Dr. Leonard Orrington, a researcher committed to uncovering the truth about the dangerous technologies currently influencing our society. I want to share my journey, which is intertwined with the unsettling realities of our time."

He pauses, glancing at the clutter on his desk: stacks of papers filled with research notes, photographs of water samples, and a laptop displaying data that he's analyzed for hours. The tension in the room feels palpable as he continues, "The issues I've encountered extend beyond the confines of science; they delve into ethics, safety, and ultimately, the well-being of our communities."

As he speaks, flashes of past events swirl in his mind—moments that led him to this point. He recalls the first time he noticed anomalies in the water supply during a routine examination. "It began innocuously," he reflects. "I was reviewing samples from various treatment facilities and stumbled upon some unusual readings. At first, I thought it was a lab error, but repeated tests proved otherwise."

His expression grows graver. "The findings indicated the presence of nanoparticles, specifically nanorobots, designed to alter water properties. These particles were affecting everything from filtration systems to the very essence of the water we rely on daily. I immediately knew this could have catastrophic consequences, not just for public health but for the environment as a whole."

Dr. Orrington leans back in his chair, rubbing his temples as he recounts his struggles. "I took my findings to the board of directors and government officials, hoping to spark action before it was too late. But instead of support, I faced disbelief and hostility. It became clear that my warnings were seen as threats, not truths."

His voice softens, revealing a flicker of vulnerability. "The retaliation I faced was overwhelming. The very people I sought to help turned against me. I became a target, not just for my research but for standing in the way of powerful interests that thrived on secrecy and control. They wanted to silence me, and I could feel the weight of their threats looming over me like a dark cloud."

He shifts in his seat, gathering his thoughts. "During this turmoil, I turned to the experiences of others who had faced similar fates. One individual whose story resonated with me was Charles M. Lieber, whose own battles with authority and the implications of his research provided a stark reminder of the stakes involved. I understood that my fight was not just for myself; it was for everyone who relied on clean water, who trusted the systems meant to protect them."

As he speaks, he becomes animated, his passion igniting as he delves deeper into his mission. "I knew I had to continue my investigation, no matter the cost. My sense of responsibility to uncover the truth and protect public health outweighed my fear of the repercussions. I started connecting the dots between the nanoparticles and their potential implications for health crises—especially in areas with low COVID-19 vaccination rates."

He leans forward, intensity radiating from him. "I could see the bigger picture—the plan to manipulate resources and control populations. It was an insidious strategy, and I felt compelled to act. But to do so, I needed allies, and I turned to the one person I thought might understand: Dr. Karen Romano."

Dr. Orrington recalls his first meeting with Dr. Romano, who sat across from him in her high-tech office, an aura of confidence surrounding her. "She was brilliant, no doubt," he remembers. "But I could sense an undercurrent of ambition that made me wary. I decided to trust her, thinking she could help me navigate the treacherous waters I found myself in."

Their conversations grew increasingly tense as they discussed their findings. Dr. Romano was initially intrigued by the potential implications of the nanorobots, but it quickly became clear that her loyalty lay with Specter, a powerful organization with its own hidden agendas. "As we talked, I realized she was walking a fine line between ambition and morality. She was drawn to the power of knowledge but at the expense of integrity."

Despite the risks, he confided in her, sharing his findings and fears. "But soon, I understood that I had misjudged her motivations. She began to veer into dangerous territory, exploring how to use our discoveries for personal gain rather than for public good."

Dr. Orrington sighs, the weight of his choices settling heavily on his shoulders. "I should have seen the signs. My desire to find allies blinded me to her true nature. As I delved deeper into the implications of the nanorobots, I found myself trapped in a game I didn't fully understand—a game of power and manipulation."

He reflects on the moment he decided to go public with his findings, despite the potential fallout. "I knew I had to inform the public about the dangers we faced. I drafted a letter outlining the situation and sent it to news outlets, hoping to spark a conversation. But what I didn't anticipate was the ferocity of the backlash. They attacked my credibility, labeling me a fearmonger, trying to discredit my research at every turn."

Dr. Orrington pauses, steeling himself against the memories of those dark days. "In the aftermath of my public disclosure, the chaos that ensued was relentless. But even as the storm raged around me, I held on to hope. I believed that the truth would prevail, that people would wake up to the threats lurking in their water supplies."

He takes a deep breath, his resolve strengthening. "But I realized that I couldn't do it alone. I needed a plan, and I needed to expose those who would do anything to maintain their power, including Dr. Romano."

As he sits at his desk, the shadows deepen around him, echoing the gravity of his mission. "This is not just about me anymore. It's about all of us. Water is life. We need to protect it from those who would weaponize it for their gain."

Dr. Orrington leans forward, "I urge you to listen, to understand the stakes. We can't afford to remain silent. We must confront the reality of our situation and fight for our future. The choices we make now will determine the lives of generations to come."

Chapter 32

Dr. Orrington leaned back in his chair, the dim light of the desk lamp casting flickering shadows across his face. His eyes held a glimmer of urgency as he continued, "Tonight, we embark on an exploration of environmental cues and energy phenomena through the lens of the intriguing docu-series *The Secrets of Skinwalker Ranch.* This documentary offers astonishing insights into the interplay between energy, water, and living organisms."

He paused, allowing the gravity of his words to settle in. "Skinwalker Ranch has long been a site of fascination for researchers, paranormal enthusiasts, and skeptics alike. The various phenomena reported there—unexplained lights, electromagnetic fluctuations, and even purported encounters with otherworldly beings—challenge our understanding of reality itself. But beyond the sensational claims lies a deeper inquiry into how environmental factors influence our lives and the world around us."

Dr. Orrington took a moment to collect his thoughts, glancing at the array of scientific journals lining his shelves. "As we delve into this docu-series, I urge you to consider the broader implications. The connection between water and energy is not merely a curiosity; it holds profound consequences for our health, our ecosystems, and our very existence. Water is the fundamental medium through which energy is transferred in nature, and disruptions to this delicate balance can yield unpredictable effects."

He leaned forward, his voice gaining intensity. "In *The Secrets of Skinwalker Ranch,* we witness firsthand how energy fluctuations can impact biological systems. The ranch's unique geography creates a hotspot for unusual activity, leading researchers to explore how the environment itself may be a conduit for these phenomena. It raises critical questions: What if our water sources are similarly affected by unseen forces? What if the very fabric of our reality is intertwined with the energy patterns in our surroundings?"

As he spoke, the flicker of the lamp seemed to echo his passion, illuminating the depths of his conviction. "Imagine a world where our understanding of energy and water informs not just scientific exploration but also our approach to health and environmental conservation. If we can harness the insights from this docu-series, we could reshape our perspective on sustainability and the preservation of our most vital resources."

Dr. Orrington's expression grew more solemn as he addressed the viewers directly. "However, it's essential to approach these revelations with skepticism and critical thinking. While the phenomena at Skinwalker Ranch are captivating, we must differentiate between anecdotal evidence and scientific rigor. Our goal is to seek understanding through a lens of inquiry, not sensationalism."

He shifted in his seat, his demeanor now reflecting a sense of urgency. "In light of the challenges we face today—climate change, pollution, and the exploitation of our natural resources—the lessons from Skinwalker Ranch are particularly relevant. We cannot afford to ignore the interplay of energy and water in our ecosystems. We must actively engage with the knowledge we gather to safeguard our future."

As he concluded, Dr. Orrington's gaze intensified, reflecting the weight of his mission. "Let this exploration serve as a reminder that our world is full of mysteries waiting to be unraveled. The secrets of Skinwalker Ranch may offer a glimpse into the unseen forces shaping our environment, urging us to take action before it's too late. Together, let's commit to understanding the interconnectedness of our existence and protect the vital resources that sustain us all."

Chapter 33

The vast expanse of Skinwalker Ranch lay bathed in the golden light of morning, the sun casting long shadows across the rugged terrain. Researchers were busy setting up their equipment, the air alive with anticipation and curiosity. Tri-field meters were carefully placed on sturdy tripods, while thermal cameras were mounted on stands, their lenses adjusting to capture the first hints of the day's unfolding mysteries. Infrared cameras were meticulously calibrated for optimal angles, ready to capture any anomalies that might appear in the elusive Utah sky.

As the researchers hustled about, Dr. Orrington's voice resonated, overlaying the scene with a sense of purpose. "In Season One, Episode Two, researchers observe a striking phenomenon: E.T.s, UAPs, and energy entities exhibit the ability to drain batteries with ease." His words echoed through the minds of those present, setting the stage for the unusual events about to unfold.

Dr. Orrington's passion for uncovering the unknown was palpable. He continued, describing how, throughout the episode, the team documented instances where equipment inexplicably shut down, their power sources mysteriously drained as if some unseen force siphoned their energy. The footage was compelling, presenting a perplexing puzzle for scientists and enthusiasts alike.

"There's something about the energy dynamics at play here," Dr. Orrington explained, his tone blending excitement with concern. "The implications of these observations stretch far beyond mere curiosity. If entities can manipulate energy in such a manner, it forces us to reevaluate our understanding of physics, consciousness, and the very nature of reality."

As the researchers reviewed footage from previous experiments, the intensity of their focus deepened. They analyzed every flicker and fluctuation, searching for patterns or anomalies that could lend insight into the bizarre occurrences at the ranch. With each passing moment, a palpable tension filled the air—an acknowledgment that they stood on the precipice of discovery, their findings potentially reshaping scientific paradigms.

Dr. Orrington elaborated on the gravity of these encounters. "The draining of batteries isn't merely a nuisance; it represents a profound interaction between the known and the unknown. These phenomena could signify a form of communication or energy exchange, suggesting a level of intelligence behind the observed occurrences. It challenges our preconceived notions about what is possible."

The scene shifted, revealing researchers gathered around a monitor displaying data in real time. Graphs and charts mapped fluctuations in energy levels, each spike and dip stirring curiosity and apprehension. As the team poured over the data, they speculated on the potential causes. Was it a natural anomaly, an unknown physical force, or something more extraordinary?

Dr. Orrington's voice continued, weaving through the unfolding narrative. "As they delved deeper, the implications of their findings expanded. What if these energy entities are not merely passive observers but active participants in an intricate web of existence? The concept of intelligent energy reshapes our understanding of life and consciousness itself, urging us to consider the possibility of a shared reality intertwined with forces beyond our perception."

With the sun reaching its zenith, researchers prepared for their next phase of investigation. They gathered around an area where strange readings had previously been recorded, the ground tinged with an air of expectancy. Dr. Orrington noted the significance of this moment, the convergence of scientific inquiry and the metaphysical.

"We stand at a crossroads between science and the paranormal," he reflected. "The duality of these worlds beckons us to explore the unknown with courage and an open mind. As we venture further into the depths of these mysteries, we must remain vigilant in our pursuit of truth."

The excitement in the air was contagious as researchers activated their equipment. They exchanged knowing glances, a shared understanding that they were on the brink of uncovering something profound. Dr. Orrington urged his team to stay observant, to document every detail meticulously, for each observation could potentially unlock the secrets hidden within Skinwalker Ranch.

As the sun began its descent, painting the sky with hues of orange and pink, Dr. Orrington and the team prepared to embark on a night filled with possibilities. "Tonight, we may witness phenomena that challenge our understanding of reality," he said, his voice imbued with conviction. "We must approach this endeavor with humility, recognizing that knowledge is a journey, not a destination."

The night sky emerged, revealing a tapestry of stars that seemed to pulse with energy. The atmosphere was thick with anticipation, the researchers positioned themselves to capture whatever might unfold. In that moment, the convergence of science and the unexplained felt tangible, an invitation to delve deeper into the mysteries that lay ahead.

Dr. Orrington's heart raced with the thrill of discovery. He knew that within the shadows of Skinwalker Ranch, answers awaited those brave enough to seek them. And as the first flicker of light danced across the horizon, he felt a sense of unity with the universe—a reminder that in the pursuit of knowledge, the boundaries of reality are meant to be pushed, explored, and ultimately redefined.

Chapter 34

As Dr. Orrington's voice resonated, the focus shifted to a battery-powered device nearby. Its display flickered ominously before powering down completely. Researchers exchanged concerned glances, a ripple of unease spreading through the group. This moment underscored a vulnerability shared by all battery-powered devices, a vulnerability that resonated deeper than mere technology.

"Energy exists all around us," Dr. Orrington explained, his gaze steady. "It flows through everything, connecting life in ways we're only beginning to understand. The implications of these energy exchanges are monumental. If water can store energy, then it acts as a conduit, a medium through which these interactions can occur. This is where our investigation leads us next."

The researchers gathered closer, their attention riveted on Dr. Orrington as he laid out the path forward. "We need to analyze water samples from the ranch. By examining their energy signatures, we can determine if there are any anomalies present. This could provide crucial insights into how these entities operate and interact with their environment."

Before they could proceed, a murmur swept through the group as Dr. Orrington continued, his voice low but urgent. "I must also draw your attention to the broader implications of our research. Lockheed Martin has recently demonstrated its Hybrid 5G-Tactical Mesh Network live in a multi-domain environment. This is a significant step toward ensuring that the Department of Defense has seamless access to critical information. It's a reminder of how technology can be wielded, not just for protection, but as a weapon against individuals. I've personally witnessed how organizations associated with the military use 5G cellular phones as weapons, sending nanomaterial weaponry to the cellular phone's location of those targeted. Anyone within five feet of a cellular phone can be affected."

The gravity of his words hung in the air, shifting the atmosphere. "Your cellular phone is now like a laser-guided targeting device for nanotechnology weaponry. You can never truly turn off your phone because it stays connected, always monitoring. It's crucial for us to understand this as we proceed with our investigation, particularly in how these energy entities might be manipulating the very technology we rely on."

The team nodded, their resolve strengthening as they prepared for the next phase of their experiment. They gathered containers and sampling equipment, their focus now directed toward the nearby water source. The excitement in the air was palpable as they recognized the potential significance of their undertaking.

As they moved to the water's edge, Dr. Orrington continued to elucidate the connection between water and energy. "Water has unique properties that allow it to respond to external stimuli, including sound, light, and electromagnetic fields. It is said to have memory, retaining information about its surroundings and the energies it has encountered. Understanding this can reveal how the ranch's water might be influencing the phenomena we've observed."

The researchers set to work, collecting samples with precision. Each container filled with water felt like a vessel of untapped potential, a source of knowledge waiting to be uncovered. Dr. Orrington emphasized the importance of their task, urging the team to maintain a meticulous approach as they prepared to analyze the samples back at their lab.

Once the samples were secured, they returned to their base camp, where a series of testing equipment awaited them. The atmosphere buzzed with anticipation as they prepared to delve deeper into their findings. Dr. Orrington's excitement was infectious, and the team rallied around him, eager to contribute to the groundbreaking research.

"Let's start with energy readings," he suggested, gesturing to the equipment. "We'll measure the electromagnetic frequencies in each sample. Any irregularities could indicate a significant correlation with the energy phenomena we've been documenting."

As the team conducted the tests, the readings began to unfold. Graphs displayed various frequencies, some peaking higher than expected. Dr. Orrington's brow furrowed with concentration as he analyzed the data, piecing together the puzzle before him.

"Look at this," he said, pointing to the screen. "This sample exhibits a frequency spike that corresponds with the times we observed equipment failures and anomalies. This could signify an interaction between the water and the energy entities."

The realization hung in the air, charging the atmosphere with excitement. The researchers exchanged glances, the weight of their discovery settling in. They were not merely observing strange phenomena; they were on the brink of understanding a profound connection that could redefine the parameters of their research.

"Now we must consider the broader implications," Dr. Orrington continued, his voice steady yet fervent. "If these energy entities can manipulate water in such a way, what does that mean for our environment? What impact does this have on the delicate balance of our ecosystems? And more importantly, who is being targeted?"

As they continued their analysis, a sense of urgency began to build. The implications of their findings stretched far beyond the confines of Skinwalker Ranch. Dr. Orrington was acutely aware that their work could have ramifications on a global scale, particularly for communities of African descent who have historically faced targeted oppression.

"We must approach this research responsibly," he urged, rallying the team. "If we uncover knowledge that can enhance our understanding of energy and water dynamics, we have a duty to share that information with the world. This isn't just about answering our questions; it's about safeguarding our planet and the future of all living beings."

As night descended upon the ranch, the team remained steadfast in their pursuit of knowledge. The stars twinkled overhead, a reminder of the vast mysteries still to be uncovered. Dr. Orrington felt a sense of kinship with the universe, aware that their exploration was a small piece of a much larger puzzle.

With the data collected and analyzed, the researchers prepared to document their findings in detail. They understood that their observations could potentially challenge established scientific paradigms, reshaping their understanding of energy and consciousness.

"Tonight, we are not just researchers; we are pioneers," Dr. Orrington declared, his voice resonating with conviction. "Together, we will venture into uncharted territories, unraveling the threads of existence that bind us all."

As they gathered their notes, a renewed sense of purpose surged through the group. They were determined to uncover the truth hidden within the realms of energy, water, and life itself. The mysteries of Skinwalker Ranch beckoned, promising revelations that could alter the course of science and humanity alike.

Chapter 35

The vast expanse of Skinwalker Ranch spread out before the researchers like a canvas of mystery, bathed in the golden light of morning. Shadows danced on the ground as the sun broke through the clouds, illuminating the rugged terrain that had seen countless tales of the unexplained. As the researchers set up their equipment, the air crackled with anticipation, a shared understanding that they were about to delve into the unknown.

They carefully placed Trifield meters on tripods, ensuring each was calibrated to pick up the slightest shifts in energy. Thermal cameras were mounted on stands, their lenses glinting like watchful eyes scanning the horizon. Infrared cameras were adjusted for optimal angles, the team members working in unison as if they were conducting an intricate ballet. A sense of urgency punctuated their movements, as if each piece of equipment held the key to unlock the secrets lurking within the ranch's borders.

The stillness of the air contrasted sharply with the hum of machinery, a reminder of the high-stakes nature of their mission. As they worked, a palpable tension filled the space, each researcher acutely aware of the history that surrounded them. They had come to explore phenomena that defied explanation, to seek answers to questions that had lingered in the air like the dust stirred by their boots.

Dr. Orrington's voice resonated in the minds of the team, echoing the findings of previous investigations. "In Season One, Episode Two," he had stated, "researchers observe a striking phenomenon: E.T.s, UAPs, and energy entities exhibit the ability to drain batteries with ease." The very idea sent shivers down their spines, igniting a sense of curiosity and dread. What forces were at play here? What energy entities could drain the life from their devices as effortlessly as one might sip water from a glass?

Suddenly, the camera zoomed in on a battery-powered device that stood silently on the ground, a sentinel waiting for a signal. Its display flickered ominously before dimming and then powering down completely. An uneasy silence enveloped the group, and they exchanged concerned glances. Had the unknown already begun its work? The tension in the air thickened, and it became clear that they were not just observers in this unfolding drama; they were participants.

"Keep an eye on the other devices," one researcher called out, breaking the silence that had settled over them. "We need to see if this is a malfunction or something more."

As they resumed their tasks, Dr. Orrington's voice continued to echo in their minds. "To understand this, we need to delve into the nature of energy. All living organisms, including us, are composed of energy, vibration, and frequency." The words were more than a reminder; they were a call to action. Each researcher felt a growing sense of purpose, a collective commitment to uncover the truth.

Water, an element often taken for granted, played a critical role in their investigation. It could absorb and store different forms of energy, serving as a conduit between the visible and the unseen. The researchers exchanged thoughts, their voices rising in excitement as they contemplated the implications. "If water can hold energy, what might be hidden within the depths of Skinwalker Ranch?" one theorized, his eyes gleaming with fear and fascination.

As they worked, the sun climbed higher, casting long shadows that stretched across the ranch. The landscape, once vibrant and inviting, now seemed to pulse with an otherworldly energy. It was as if the land itself held its breath, waiting for them to uncover its secrets. With each passing moment, the tension mounted, and the thrill of discovery blended with a sense of foreboding.

With the equipment in place, the team gathered around a central monitor displaying data readings. The soft glow of the screen illuminated their faces, highlighting the determination etched into each expression. "We've got to stay vigilant," another researcher cautioned. "Whatever is out there won't reveal itself easily."

The atmosphere was electric, charged with the possibility of revelations that could alter their understanding of reality. They were no longer just scientists; they were explorers on the frontier of knowledge, standing at the intersection of science and the supernatural. Every flicker of light, every change in frequency, seemed to carry the weight of the unknown, urging them to look deeper.

Dr. Orrington's insights were woven into their minds, guiding them through the labyrinth of questions that lay ahead. As they delved deeper into the mysteries of Skinwalker Ranch, they knew they were part of something much larger than themselves—a quest for understanding that could reshape the narrative of human existence. In that moment, the stakes felt higher than ever, and the weight of their responsibility pressed heavily on their shoulders. The secrets of Skinwalker Ranch awaited, and they were determined to uncover the truth, no matter the cost.

Chapter 36

In the brightly lit laboratory, the sterile white walls and gleaming surfaces reflected the precision of the scientific pursuit taking place within. A beaker of water sat prominently on the lab bench, its contents calm and clear, unaware of the energy swirling around it. Above, a small device hummed softly, emitting a series of energy waves that radiated outward like invisible tendrils reaching for the liquid below. As the waves interacted with the water, something remarkable began to unfold.

The water, once still, started to bubble and swirl, its surface coming alive with movement. Tiny eddies formed and dissipated, creating a mesmerizing dance that captured the researchers' attention. Each ripple seemed to respond to the energy being poured into it, revealing a language of interaction between the unseen forces and the life-sustaining liquid.

Dr. Orrington's voice resonated in the air, a steady reminder of the significance of what they were witnessing. "Water is more than just a vital substance; it's a reservoir of life-sustaining energy. All organic matter derives from water and depends on it for survival." His words hung in the air, echoing the profound connection that existed between water and life itself. The researchers exchanged glances, their faces illuminated by the soft glow of the bubbling water, each of them aware that they were on the brink of uncovering something extraordinary.

One researcher leaned closer, captivated by the phenomenon unfolding before them. "Look at how it reacts," she marveled, her voice barely above a whisper. "It's like it's responding to the energy, almost as if it has a consciousness of its own." Her fascination was palpable, sparking a sense of urgency among the team. They were not merely observing a scientific experiment; they were witnessing the interplay between energy and life in real-time.

As the water continued to bubble, Dr. Orrington stood at the forefront of the experiment, his eyes fixed on the beaker with wonder and determination. "Every drop of water is a conduit of energy, a carrier of information," he explained, his passion igniting the room. "Understanding how it interacts with different energies is key to unlocking the mysteries of our world." The implications of their work weighed heavily on him, as he considered the vast potential for discovery that lay within each droplet.

The device continued to emit energy waves, and the water responded with increasing intensity. A vibrant display of colors began to dance across the surface, hues of blue and green merging and flowing together in a hypnotic rhythm. It was as if the water itself was celebrating the energy it received, showcasing its beauty in a way that transcended mere science.

"Do you think this could have applications beyond our current understanding?" another researcher mused, her brow furrowed in thought. "If water can store and release energy in this way, what does that mean for our approaches to sustainable energy and healing?"

Dr. Orrington nodded, considering her words carefully. "The possibilities are limitless," he replied, a spark of excitement igniting in his eyes. "From renewable energy sources to advancements in medicine, harnessing the energy of water could revolutionize how we interact with our environment." The atmosphere in the lab shifted, the energy from the bubbling water now fueling their imaginations and ambitions.

As the experiment progressed, the bubbling intensified, creating a symphony of sound that filled the laboratory. It was a reminder of the dynamic nature of water, an element often overlooked but crucial to life on Earth. With each passing moment, the researchers felt more connected to their work, as if they were participating in a greater narrative that intertwined science, nature, and the mysteries of existence.

"Imagine a world where we can harness this energy on a larger scale," Dr. Orrington continued, his voice resonating with conviction. "A world where water is not just a resource, but a source of limitless potential." His words sparked a fire within the team, igniting their aspirations as they envisioned a future where their discoveries could change lives and shape the world.

As the bubbling finally began to settle, the researchers turned their attention to the data being collected. Graphs and readings displayed fluctuations in energy, each line and curve telling a story of interaction and response. They were on the precipice of something groundbreaking, and the air buzzed with a sense of anticipation.

In that moment, the laboratory became more than just a workspace; it transformed into a sanctuary of possibility, a place where the boundaries of knowledge were pushed, and the secrets of water began to unfold. As Dr. Orrington and his team looked toward the future, they knew they were not just investigating water; they were unlocking the very essence of life itself, a journey that would lead them to uncharted territories in their quest for understanding and discovery.

Chapter 37

The ranch lay shrouded in darkness, an expanse of mystery illuminated only by the soft glow of infrared cameras that dotted the landscape. These devices captured a reality unseen by the naked eye, revealing the hidden layers of Skinwalker Ranch. As the researchers huddled around their monitors, the atmosphere crackled with anticipation, tension palpable in the cool night air.

Suddenly, strange, ethereal lights began to form above a water source, casting an otherworldly glow that danced across the ground like wisps of smoke. The researchers leaned closer, eyes wide with wonder and disbelief, captivated by the phenomena unfolding before them. It was as if the water itself had come alive, revealing secrets long buried beneath its surface.

Dr. Orrington's voice resonated in the background, drawing them deeper into the enigma. "In this docu-series, you'll witness extraordinary occurrences, such as the emergence of real-life energy forms—sometimes referred to as demigods—from water when a portal opens." His tone was both informative and ominous, a reminder that the forces they were dealing with were beyond their comprehension.

As the lights flickered and pulsed, the researchers exchanged hushed whispers, their hearts racing. The sight was mesmerizing, yet unsettling—a paradox that spoke to the duality of beauty and danger inherent in the unknown. The glow from the water source painted their faces with an eerie light, casting shadows that seemed to dance around them, as if the ranch itself were alive and aware of their presence.

One of the researchers, a young woman named Emily, pointed toward the phenomenon, her voice barely a whisper. "What do you think it is? It looks like something out of a myth." Her eyes sparkled with excitement and fear, a mixture that drove her closer to the unfolding mystery.

"It's not just myth," Dr. Orrington replied, his gaze fixed on the lights. "Many ancient cultures spoke of beings emerging from water, entities capable of great power and wisdom. What we're witnessing may echo those tales." His words hung in the air, imbued with a sense of urgency and reverence.

As the lights above the water pulsed rhythmically, a low hum filled the air, resonating through the very ground they stood on. The researchers felt the vibrations in their bones, a reminder that they were mere spectators to something ancient and profound. The glow intensified, casting a surreal aura over the landscape, transforming the familiar terrain of Skinwalker Ranch into a stage for the extraordinary.

The monitors captured every detail, the infrared cameras revealing movement within the lights—a swirling, shifting mass that suggested sentience, a consciousness that defied explanation. It was a breathtaking sight, yet it carried an undercurrent of foreboding, as if the very fabric of reality was being stretched and tested.

"Keep the cameras rolling," Dr. Orrington commanded, his voice steady despite the awe that filled him. "This could be a pivotal moment in our research. We need to document everything." His instructions were met with nods of understanding and determination, the team aware that they were on the brink of a breakthrough that could redefine their understanding of energy and existence.

As the phenomenon continued, the ethereal lights began to take shape, forming vague outlines that resembled figures emerging from the water. The air grew thick with tension, and an overwhelming sense of the sacred filled the space. It was as if the ranch were a threshold between worlds, a place where the boundaries of the natural and the supernatural blurred.

Dr. Orrington felt a rush of emotion as he watched the lights twist and turn, invoking ancient memories of stories passed down through generations. "We're witnessing something that has eluded humanity for centuries," he said softly, almost to himself. "The connection between water and energy may hold the key to understanding our place in the universe."

The researchers remained transfixed, their hearts pounding in unison with the pulsing lights. With each moment, they felt themselves drawn deeper into the mystery, a powerful pull that beckoned them to explore further, to understand the depths of what lay before them.

As the night wore on, the lights continued to shift and dance above the water, casting shadows that seemed to whisper secrets from ages long past. The researchers stood united, bound by their quest for knowledge, their fears overshadowed by an insatiable curiosity that drove them forward into the unknown. Each heartbeat resonated with the realization that they were participants in a greater narrative, a tale that would transcend time and space—a journey into the very essence of energy, life, and the enigmatic power of water.

Chapter 38

In the dimly lit observation room, the atmosphere buzzed with excitement and tension as researchers crowded around a large monitor. Their faces illuminated by the flickering light, they leaned in closer, captivated by the images unfolding before them. The screen displayed an otherworldly scene captured by the infrared cameras—unusual light forms and movements that defied conventional explanation.

Dr. Orrington's voice echoed in their minds, his steady tone guiding their understanding. "The footage reveals phenomena beyond the normal visual spectrum. Using infrared cameras, we observe mesas—flat-topped rock formations—emitting light beams not visible to the naked eye." His insights resonated through the room, instilling a sense of wonder and urgency in the team.

The researchers exchanged astonished glances, their breaths held in anticipation. On the screen, the mesas transformed into spectral giants, towering silently against the backdrop of the night sky. As the light beams shot forth, they danced and swirled like ethereal ribbons, weaving intricate patterns that seemed to connect the earth to the cosmos. It was a sight that ignited their imaginations, hinting at ancient energies coursing through the landscape.

"Look at that!" Emily exclaimed, pointing at the monitor. "What do you think it means? Are they trying to communicate?" Her voice trembled with excitement and uncertainty, a reflection of the awe that gripped the entire team.

"Perhaps," Dr. Orrington replied, his gaze never leaving the screen. "These formations may serve as conduits for energy—vessels that connect different realms of existence. This light could represent something far more profound than we can grasp at this moment."

As the researchers studied the display, they noted the way the light fluctuated, pulsing in rhythm with an unseen heartbeat. It was as if the land itself was alive, responding to some cosmic call. The room fell into a reverent silence, each member of the team acutely aware of the significance of what they were witnessing.

"Imagine the implications," one of the senior researchers, Dr. Patel, murmured, breaking the silence. "If these formations emit energy in ways we've yet to comprehend, what does that mean for our understanding of the environment? Could they hold the key to energy sustainability?"

Dr. Orrington nodded thoughtfully. "Exactly. This could revolutionize our approach to energy. But we must tread carefully. The interaction between energy and the natural world is delicate, and we must respect the forces at play."

The images on the screen shifted, revealing a swirling mass of light that coalesced into a shape, a figure that seemed to emerge from the very fabric of the energy surrounding the mesas. Gasps filled the room as the researchers leaned closer, their hearts racing at the sight of what appeared to be a humanoid form, shimmering and translucent.

"What is that?" Emily whispered, unable to tear her eyes away.

"It could be a manifestation of energy," Dr. Orrington speculated, his voice steady despite the escalating tension. "Or perhaps a representation of the consciousness tied to this land. The possibilities are endless, and yet we must remain grounded in our scientific inquiry."

The figure flickered, sending waves of energy rippling across the screen, and the researchers felt a collective shiver run through them. It was both captivating and terrifying—an invitation to explore the unknown, coupled with the weight of responsibility that accompanied such discoveries.

As the team continued to analyze the footage, the light forms danced more erratically, illuminating the room with an otherworldly glow. It felt as if they were peering into a portal, a glimpse into realms that existed beyond their comprehension.

"Can we enhance the footage?" another researcher asked, already typing furiously at the keyboard to manipulate the data. "We need to analyze every detail. This could be a breakthrough."

"Do it," Dr. Orrington commanded, his eyes narrowing with focus. "Every second counts. We need to gather as much information as possible before this phenomenon dissipates."

The room pulsed with energy as the monitor flickered, the enhanced footage revealing even more intricate details. The light beams twisted and turned, each movement resonating with a frequency that seemed to echo in the hearts of those who watched. It was a call to understand, to embrace the unknown and seek the truth hidden within the energy that flowed through their world.

With each passing moment, the realization dawned on them that they were not merely observers but participants in a greater narrative—one that intertwined their lives with the mysteries of the universe. As the luminous forms continued to captivate their attention, the researchers felt a profound connection to the land, to the water that nourished it, and to the very essence of life itself.

The footage played on, a relentless reminder of the beauty and chaos that lay beyond the ordinary, beckoning them to venture further into the mysteries of energy, water, and the interconnectedness of all living things. In that darkened room, illuminated by the glow of the monitor, they stood on the precipice of discovery, united in their quest to uncover the secrets that had long remained hidden beneath the surface.

Chapter 39

The rugged mesa stretched beneath the afternoon sun, its flat top casting a long shadow across the arid landscape. Each geological layer told a story, a record of time etched into the earth's surface, revealing secrets buried for millennia. The sunlight accentuated the distinct striations, creating a tapestry of colors—rich reds, earthy browns, and faded greens that spoke of resilience in the face of time. An ancient mystery enveloped the formation, inviting exploration and contemplation.

Dr. Orrington's voice resonated in the minds of those who ventured near. "A mesa is described as having a flat-lying surface with layers of harder rock on top. This geological structure suggests that life could potentially exist within these formations, challenging our understanding of the earth." His words lingered like the dust that danced in the sunbeams, weaving through the air as if carrying the weight of hidden knowledge.

As the researchers approached the base of the mesa, a sense of awe washed over them. They could almost feel the pulse of the earth beneath their feet, an energy that surged with life, beckoning them to uncover its mysteries. The rough texture of the rocks, worn smooth by the elements, told tales of storms weathered and sun scorched, while the hardy vegetation that clung to the edges defied the harsh conditions, thriving in the unforgiving environment.

"This place feels alive," Emily remarked, her eyes scanning the horizon where the mesa met the sky. "Like it's watching us." The whisper of the wind seemed to carry her words, echoing them back as if in agreement.

"Indeed," Dr. Orrington replied, his gaze fixed on the mesa's flat top, where the land met the heavens. "These formations hold more than just rock and soil. They are potentially ancient habitats, reservoirs of biodiversity that we have yet to fully understand. Our mission here is not just to study the phenomenon above but to delve into what lies beneath."

The team began to set up their equipment, their anticipation palpable. Geologists, ecologists, and physicists worked in tandem, preparing to extract samples from the mesa and analyze its unique composition. Each member understood that this endeavor could redefine their comprehension of life and energy, intertwining science with the spiritual essence of the land.

As the sun continued its descent, casting long shadows across the mesa, a stillness enveloped the area. The researchers took a moment to absorb their surroundings, the weight of history pressing down upon them. They could almost hear the whispers of those who had walked this land before, their stories woven into the very fabric of the earth.

"Imagine the ecosystems that might thrive in the shadow of this mesa," Dr. Patel mused, pulling out a small notebook and jotting down observations. "Microorganisms, unique plant species, perhaps even undiscovered creatures. There's so much potential here."

Dr. Orrington nodded in agreement. "And we must be vigilant. The interactions between energy, water, and living organisms are delicate. Any disruption could lead to consequences we can't predict." He gestured toward the horizon, where the setting sun painted the sky in hues of orange and purple. "Just as the light illuminates the landscape, it also highlights the interconnectedness of all life forms."

The researchers fanned out, collecting samples of soil, rock, and water, each step taken with purpose. The mesa loomed above them, a silent sentinel guarding its secrets. As they worked, the atmosphere thickened with anticipation, an electric energy that seemed to resonate from the very ground.

"Check this out!" Emily called, her voice carrying across the expanse. She had discovered a small crevice at the base of the mesa, where a trickle of water flowed, crystal clear and shimmering in the fading light. The sight was both enchanting and perplexing; how could water persist in such a seemingly inhospitable environment?

"Water can find a way," Dr. Orrington responded, moving swiftly to join her. "This may be an indicator of underground aquifers. We need to sample it."

As they collected the water, the researchers couldn't shake the feeling that they were on the brink of a significant discovery. The mesa, with its layers of history, seemed to hold not only geological wonders but also the potential for revelations that could shift their understanding of life on earth.

With their samples gathered, the team reconvened at their base camp, the sky now adorned with stars. Each member shared their findings, their excitement palpable. Dr. Orrington facilitated the discussion, encouraging collaboration and exploration of ideas.

"Let's not forget the stories that come with these formations," he reminded them. "This is not just about what we can measure or quantify; it's about respecting the wisdom of the land. We must honor its presence as we seek to unveil its secrets."

As the night deepened, the team settled around a campfire, the flickering flames casting a warm glow against the cool desert air. They shared stories, laughter, and dreams of what their discoveries might bring. The mesa loomed silently in the background, a constant reminder of the ancient energy it housed and the possibilities that lay ahead.

Dr. Orrington watched his team with a sense of pride. Each member was not just a scientist but a steward of knowledge, ready to embrace the mysteries of the world. Together, they were embarking on a journey that would challenge their perceptions, deepen their connection to the earth, and perhaps illuminate the path forward for future generations.

As they gazed up at the stars, the vastness of the universe mirrored the potential of their expedition— a reminder that they were but a small part of a much larger tapestry, intricately woven together by the threads of energy, water, and life. The mesa stood as a testament to this connection, a silent guardian holding the secrets of the past while whispering promises of the future.

Chapter 40

Dr. Orrington leaned closer to the computer screen, his brow furrowed in concentration as he meticulously analyzed the data before him. The bright glow of the monitor illuminated his face, casting sharp shadows that accentuated the weariness in his eyes. Rows of graphs and charts filled the display, each line representing a complex relationship between the elements that made up the human body and those found in the rocks and soil surrounding the mesa.

With a click of the mouse, he highlighted a particularly compelling chart that illustrated the elemental composition. Carbon, hydrogen, oxygen, nitrogen—these were the building blocks of life, and astonishingly, they mirrored the mineral makeup of the earth itself. The realization washed over him like a wave: the very elements that constituted human life were intricately woven into the fabric of the planet.

"The human body shares fundamental elements with the earth," he murmured to himself, a spark of excitement igniting within him. "The documentary's findings propose that significant rock formations, like mesas, may harbor life, expanding our view of natural ecosystems."

He leaned back in his chair, allowing the weight of this revelation to settle in. The implications were profound. If these rock formations were indeed capable of supporting life, what other mysteries lay hidden within the earth's crust? Could there be undiscovered organisms, perhaps even forms of life that defied conventional understanding? His mind raced with possibilities, each more intriguing than the last.

Dr. Orrington glanced at the clock on the wall; time slipped away unnoticed in the throes of his fascination. He could almost hear the rhythmic hum of the lab, the whir of machinery punctuating the silence. Researchers moved about, immersed in their own tasks, but he felt a compelling urge to share his findings with the team. This was not just data; it was a key to unlocking deeper truths about existence itself.

"Hey, everyone!" he called out, his voice cutting through the ambient noise. The chatter subsided, and his colleagues turned their attention toward him, curiosity piqued. "I've been reviewing the elemental composition of human bodies in comparison to the soil and rocks we've collected. The similarities are staggering."

He gestured toward the screen, where the graphs danced in vibrant colors. "Look at this! Carbon, hydrogen, oxygen, and nitrogen—these elements are not just components of life; they're also fundamental to the earth itself. This suggests a deeper connection between us and the very ground we stand on."

A murmured excitement rippled through the room as his colleagues gathered around the monitor. Emily, her eyes sparkling with intrigue, leaned forward. "So, you're saying that we might share more than just our planet? Could there be forms of life within those mesas that mirror our own biological structures?"

"Exactly!" Dr. Orrington replied, his enthusiasm infectious. "These significant rock formations may not only be geological wonders; they could be ecosystems in their own right. If we can uncover life that exists in such extreme environments, it could redefine our understanding of biology and evolution."

"Think of the implications," Dr. Patel added, her voice tinged with awe. "If life can thrive in the most unlikely places, what does that mean for our understanding of the universe? Could we find similar ecosystems on other planets?"

The team buzzed with excitement, their imaginations ignited by the possibilities. Dr. Orrington felt a surge of hope; this was why he had dedicated his life to research, to unearth the secrets of the world around them. They were on the cusp of something extraordinary.

As the conversation deepened, the group began brainstorming the next steps. They discussed plans for further field studies, sampling different mesas and rock formations, each one a potential window into a hidden world.

"We should focus on areas with the most unique geological features," Emily suggested. "The more diverse the environment, the greater the chance of finding something unexpected."

Dr. Orrington nodded, his mind racing with ideas. "And we must consider the energy dynamics as well. If these formations hold life, we need to understand how energy is transferred within these ecosystems. We could set up sensors to monitor fluctuations in energy patterns."

As they collaborated, the lab transformed into a hive of activity. Papers were scattered across desks, notes exchanged rapidly, and plans took shape with fervor. Dr. Orrington felt a renewed sense of purpose; they were not just scientists in a lab but explorers on the frontier of discovery.

As the day wore on and the sun began to set, casting golden rays through the lab windows, Dr. Orrington paused for a moment to reflect. He felt an unshakeable connection to the earth beneath his feet and a sense of responsibility to protect the delicate balance of life that thrived there.

"Let's remember," he said, gathering the team's attention once more, "as we venture into these unknown territories, we must approach with respect and mindfulness. Each ecosystem we study is a testament to the resilience of life, and we are merely guests in their world."

With the day drawing to a close, the team rallied around their shared mission, energized by the prospect of what lay ahead. They were ready to dive deeper into the mysteries of life, water, and energy, unearthing the connections that bound them all to the earth in ways they had only begun to understand.

Chapter 41

As the portal slowly opened, an eerie glow filled the darkened streets of the neighborhood. The once-familiar landscape was transformed into something otherworldly. Residents stepped out of their homes, peering into the night with fear and curiosity. The soft hum of energy rippled through the air, causing the streetlights to flicker and dim, creating a strobe-like effect that painted the faces of onlookers in shadows.

People gathered in small clusters, whispering to one another, their eyes darting toward the swirling colors emanating from the portal. Children clutched their parents' hands tightly, their wide eyes reflecting the vibrant light as they watched the strange shadows dance across the pavement. Some elders murmured prayers under their breaths, invoking protection against the unknown forces at play.

Dr. Orrington's voice echoed in the background, overlaying the scene with a sense of urgency. "Regrettably, some experiments appear to disrupt energy levels and mental clarity, particularly in black communities." His words carried weight, a reminder of the delicate balance that existed between scientific exploration and the impact it could have on vulnerable populations.

As the portal pulsated, a deep rumble resonated through the ground, sending a shiver through the residents. The atmosphere grew thick with tension, a tangible energy that wrapped around everyone present. They felt it in their bones—a disturbance that went beyond the physical, tapping into something primal and unsettling.

Amidst the crowd, a woman named Clara stood, her brow furrowed with concern. A long-time resident of the neighborhood, she had witnessed many changes over the years but had never encountered anything like this. The portal loomed large, its swirling colors beckoning and repelling all at once. Clara's instincts kicked in, urging her to protect her community from whatever lay beyond.

"Stay close, everyone!" she called out, her voice steady despite the chaos. "We don't know what this is, but we'll face it together."

A young man named Malik, who had grown up in the area, stepped forward. His heart raced as he gazed at the portal, mesmerized by its beauty yet fearful of its potential. "What do you think it means?" he asked Clara, uncertainty clouding his voice.

Clara shook her head, her gaze unwavering. "I don't know, but we need to be prepared. There's something about this that doesn't feel right."

Just then, a flash of light erupted from the portal, illuminating the street in an otherworldly glow. The crowd gasped collectively, some shielding their eyes while others stood transfixed. Shadows twisted and contorted, taking on forms that resembled familiar faces—friends, family members, people from their past.

Dr. Orrington's voice continued in the background, underscoring the gravity of the situation. "The energy disturbances seem to amplify existing vulnerabilities, leading to heightened anxiety and confusion. This is especially concerning in communities already grappling with systemic issues."

As the light pulsed, the shadows danced with increasing intensity, their movements erratic and chaotic. Clara's heart raced as she sensed a shift in the crowd's energy. Fear began to take hold, a ripple of panic sweeping through the onlookers.

"Everyone, we need to stay calm!" she shouted, her voice rising above the rising tide of anxiety. "We can't let fear control us. We need to focus on what's happening and look out for one another."

But Malik was already stepping closer to the portal, drawn by an inexplicable pull. "What if it's a sign?" he murmured, barely audible over the commotion. "What if it's a chance for something new?"

Clara grabbed his arm, her grip firm. "Don't! We don't know what's on the other side. We can't risk it."

The ground trembled again, a deeper vibration that shook them to their core. The shadows writhed more violently, and the flickering streetlights struggled against the encroaching darkness. Clara's heart raced, adrenaline coursing through her veins.

Suddenly, a loud crack echoed, and the portal widened, releasing a wave of energy that sent gusts of wind whipping through the street. Residents stumbled, their bodies pushed back by the force. Clara shielded her eyes from the brilliant light, her instincts kicking in.

"Get back!" she yelled, pushing Malik behind her. "We need to move!"

People began to scatter, some fleeing toward their homes while others stood frozen, torn between fear and fascination. The air was thick with tension, a potent mix of uncertainty and awe as the unknown threatened to envelop them.

As Clara urged her neighbors to retreat to safety, Dr. Orrington's voice echoed in her mind, a warning about the implications of the portal. This was no mere scientific anomaly; it was a disturbance that had the potential to wreak havoc on the very fabric of their community.

The air crackled with energy, and the swirling light from the portal intensified, casting long shadows that danced across the pavement. Clara turned to face the portal once more, resolute.

"We have to do something," she said, her voice steady amidst the chaos. "We can't let this take over our lives. We need to understand what's happening and protect our community."

Malik nodded, determination replacing his earlier fear. "You're right. We can't just stand by and let this happen."

Together, they rallied their neighbors, gathering those willing to confront the portal instead of retreating from it. The atmosphere shifted as people began to band together, a united front against the uncertainty that loomed before them.

Clara felt a surge of hope as they formed a circle, hand in hand. "We may not know what lies beyond this portal, but we know one thing: we are stronger together. Whatever this is, we will face it as a community."

With that declaration, they stood resolute, ready to confront the unknown that pulsed before them, determined to protect their neighborhood from the mysterious forces at play. In that moment, amidst flickering streetlights and dancing shadows, they forged a bond that transcended fear, anchoring them in the face of uncertainty.

Chapter 42

Dr. Orrington's voice carried a weight that resonated deeply within the hearts of those gathered. "These forced portals create significant disturbances and raise serious concerns." His words echoed in Clara's mind, grounding her resolve. The portal continued to pulse ominously, a beacon of chaos against the darkening sky, and she could sense the anxiety rippling through her community.

As she stood with Malik and their neighbors, the reality of Dr. Orrington's statement hung in the air like an uninvited specter. Clara knew that whatever was happening could have profound consequences, not just for them but for the environment and beyond. The energy radiating from the portal felt alive, and it was a reminder that they were not merely spectators in this unfolding drama; they were participants.

"Clara, do you think it's safe to approach?" Malik asked, glancing nervously at the swirling light. He hesitated, taking a step back as the portal flickered violently.

Clara took a deep breath, her heart racing. "We need to understand it," she replied, her voice steady. "We can't just let it control us. If we know what we're dealing with, we might find a way to protect ourselves and our community."

In that moment, Clara's mind raced back to Dr. Orrington's warnings about energy disturbances and their impact on mental clarity, especially within black communities. It was clear to her that the implications of this portal were not limited to physical disruptions; they threatened to unearth deeper, more systemic issues that could fracture their community even further.

The crowd began to murmur, uncertainty creeping in as people exchanged worried glances. Some were eager to explore, while others clung to fear. Clara felt the weight of their collective anxiety pressing down on her, but she knew that leadership required courage.

"Everyone, listen!" Clara called out, her voice slicing through the murmur. "We have the power to face this together. The energy here is overwhelming, but we can channel it. We need to figure out how to protect ourselves and our families."

A woman stepped forward, her eyes wide with fear. "What if it opens up something dangerous? We've heard stories about portals—what if it lets in something that can harm us?"

Clara nodded, acknowledging the woman's concerns. "I understand, but hiding from it won't make it go away. We need to confront it, not just for ourselves but for future generations. If we allow fear to control us, we risk losing everything we've built here."

The crowd quieted, Clara's words resonating with the shared history and struggles of their community. They had faced adversity before, and this was no different. The portal may have been a manifestation of something greater, but together, they could navigate its challenges.

Malik stepped forward, emboldened by Clara's resolve. "We can form a team. We need to gather information—see if anyone else has encountered something like this. If we document our experiences, we can have a clearer picture of what we're dealing with."

Clara's heart swelled with gratitude as she looked around at the determined faces of her neighbors. They were scared, yes, but they were also brave, ready to rise to the occasion. "That's a great idea, Malik," she said, her voice strong. "Let's set up a group to monitor the portal. We can record what we see and feel, and together, we'll figure out how to deal with it."

As they formed a plan, the portal flickered again, casting a kaleidoscope of colors over the crowd. Clara took a step closer, feeling the energy envelop her, its warmth contrasting the cool night air. It was both mesmerizing and frightening, a vivid reminder of the unknown that lay ahead.

"Let's set up a watch schedule," Clara suggested, her voice steady amidst the chaos. "We'll take turns observing. If anything unusual happens, we'll document it and share it with the group."

The residents nodded, a sense of unity forming as they exchanged ideas and strategies. Clara could feel the resolve building in the air, an invisible thread connecting them all. This was not just about confronting a portal; it was about reclaiming their power and ensuring their community remained strong in the face of uncertainty.

Dr. Orrington's voice echoed again in Clara's mind, a reminder of the potential repercussions they faced. "These forced portals create significant disturbances and raise serious concerns." She would not let those concerns become a reality for her community.

The portal surged with energy, casting an ethereal glow over the neighborhood. Clara took a deep breath, feeling the weight of responsibility settle on her shoulders. They were on the precipice of something monumental, and the path ahead would require bravery, resilience, and unity.

As the night deepened, the community rallied around Clara's vision. They began to share their own stories of encounters with strange phenomena, blending folklore with personal experiences. Each tale added depth to their understanding of the unknown, weaving a tapestry of shared history and collective memory.

"Let's not forget the lessons from our elders," an older man named Henry spoke up, his voice firm. "They've always warned us about the balance of nature and the energies we interact with. We must tread carefully."

Clara nodded, feeling the truth of his words resonate within her. "Yes, we must honor that wisdom. It's part of who we are as a community. We can't ignore our roots or the power of our shared experiences."

With the group energized, they began to strategize, each member contributing ideas and resources. Clara felt a sense of hope blossom within her. They were turning fear into action, uncertainty into purpose.

As the portal continued to pulse, Clara glanced at Malik, who stood beside her, his eyes filled with determination. Together, they would lead their community through this challenge, finding strength in their unity and resilience in their shared commitment to protect their home.

"Let's do this," Clara said, her voice resolute. "We're stronger together, and we will face whatever comes our way."

With newfound determination, they stood shoulder to shoulder, ready to confront the unknown and protect their community from the disturbances that threatened to upend their lives. The portal may have been a harbinger of chaos, but they would transform it into an opportunity for unity, strength, and understanding, forging a path forward into the darkness with courage and hope.

Chapter 43

In the dimly lit observation room, the tension was palpable as researchers leaned over their monitors, eyes darting between the screens displaying the infrared footage. The steady hum of equipment filled the air, punctuated by the soft clicking of keyboards as data streamed in. Each researcher wore an expression of focused intensity, the gravity of their task weighing heavily upon them. The glow from the screens illuminated their faces, casting eerie shadows that danced with the flickering light.

Dr. Orrington's voice resonated through the room, a calm yet urgent presence amidst the chaos. "Our visual spectrum limits our ability to perceive the full range of reality. Infrared cameras have captured light beams from rock formations that reveal phenomena beyond our usual perception." His words hung in the air, an invitation to delve deeper into the mysteries unfolding before them.

As the camera zoomed in on the screens, the researchers watched in awe. The infrared footage revealed ethereal light phenomena emerging from the rocks, pulsating with a life of their own. Patterns shifted and morphed, creating a visual symphony that was both mesmerizing and unsettling. Each flicker and flash seemed to pulse with energy, hinting at secrets hidden within the geological formations that surrounded them.

The room filled with murmurs of excitement and disbelief. "Look at that!" one researcher exclaimed, pointing to a particularly vivid display of light cascading from a mesa. "It's as if the rocks are communicating with us." The others leaned in closer, their curiosity piqued as they studied the screen intently.

Dr. Orrington stepped closer to the monitor, his brow furrowed in concentration. "This is significant. These light phenomena could indicate energy exchanges occurring at a molecular level. We must analyze the data thoroughly to understand the implications."

Another researcher, a young woman named Dr. Sinclair, turned to him, her eyes wide with enthusiasm. "If we can document these occurrences, it might lead us to new understandings of how energy interacts with geological structures. This could change everything we know about the environment."

Dr. Orrington nodded, his mind racing with possibilities. "Exactly. If we can establish a connection between these light phenomena and the energy dynamics at play, we may unlock insights into the very fabric of our reality." He gestured toward the screen, where the vibrant colors shifted in response to unseen forces. "This is just the beginning."

As the researchers continued to observe the captivating display, Clara, one of the community members who had come to learn more about the experiments, stood quietly in the corner of the room, her heart pounding with excitement and apprehension. She felt a strong pull toward the screens, her instincts telling her that this research held answers to questions that had long lingered in her mind.

Clara remembered the stories passed down through her family about the land and its mysteries. The elders often spoke of the spirits residing within the earth, guardians of nature who interacted with the world in ways that were often imperceptible to the human eye. The glowing lights on the screen felt like a bridge to those ancient tales, an invitation to explore the unseen connections that existed between humanity and the environment.

Dr. Orrington continued to guide the team, emphasizing the importance of careful documentation. "We need to capture as much data as possible," he instructed, his tone a blend of urgency and inspiration. "Every beam of light, every fluctuation in energy—these could hold the key to understanding the interplay between our surroundings and the phenomena we've been studying."

The researchers busily took notes, eager to ensure that no detail slipped through their fingers. Clara felt a sense of camaraderie with the scientists, their shared curiosity uniting them in a quest for knowledge. She stepped forward, her voice steady as she addressed the group. "Is there any way we can assist? We want to understand what's happening in our community."

Dr. Orrington turned to her, a glimmer of appreciation in his eyes. "Absolutely. Your insights and experiences can enrich our research. We welcome your perspective. Together, we can piece together the puzzle that lies before us."

As the researchers continued to monitor the lights dancing on the screens, Clara felt a growing determination within her. She understood that this was not just about science; it was about forging a connection between knowledge and the community's lived experiences. The lights flickering in the infrared footage were not merely phenomena; they were symbols of hope, a reminder that understanding the unknown could lead to empowerment and resilience.

In that moment, Clara resolved to be an active participant in the unfolding narrative. The energy emanating from the rocks and the vibrant displays of light felt like a call to action. She would not just observe from the sidelines; she would contribute to the dialogue, bridging the gap between the research being conducted and the voices of her community.

As the night wore on, the researchers remained engrossed in their observations, driven by a shared sense of purpose. The glowing lights continued to illuminate the darkened room, casting a magical aura that hinted at the mysteries yet to be uncovered. The blend of science and community spirit pulsed through the air, a testament to the potential that lay ahead.

In the depths of the observation room, amidst the swirling colors and the whispers of discovery, a new chapter was beginning to unfold. Clara felt the weight of history behind her and the promise of the future ahead, ready to embrace the unknown together with those around her.

Chapter 44

Researchers crowded around the monitors, their gazes fixated on the screens that flickered with an array of unusual light phenomena. Tension and excitement filled the air as they processed the idata, their hearts racing with the thrill of discovery. Each pulse of light, each shimmering arc, spoke of possibilities that lay just beyond the veil of the ordinary.

Dr. Orrington stood at the center of the room, his voice resonating with an urgency that captured their attention. He was a figure of authority and intellect, his years of research culminating in this moment of revelation. "Even the most sophisticated instruments reveal only a fraction of reality. What lies beyond our visual spectrum is a realm of possibilities we are just beginning to explore."

His words hung in the air, heavy with implication. The researchers leaned closer, their expressions shifting from curiosity to astonishment as they watched the screen. Ethereal lights danced and shimmered, flickering like ghostly apparitions among the rugged rock formations. Each beam seemed to defy the laws of physics, casting shadows that moved independently, as if they were sentient beings communicating in a language of light.

The patterns were mesmerizing, twisting and swirling as if they possessed a life of their own. Researchers exchanged glances, a mixture of disbelief and fascination painted across their faces. This was no ordinary data; it was evidence of something extraordinary, an unseen world that defied conventional explanation.

"Look at the way those beams interact with the rocks," one researcher murmured, pointing to the screen. "It's as if they're communicating with each other."

Dr. Orrington nodded, captivated by the unfolding spectacle. "These entities challenge everything we think we know about energy and matter. They're manifestations of a reality that operates under different principles, one that lies just outside our reach." His voice, usually measured and composed, now carried a tremor of excitement, as if he were finally grasping the threads of a long-elusive truth.

The atmosphere in the observation room grew charged, almost electric. The researchers felt a strange pull, as if the energy radiating from the screens was inviting them into a deeper understanding. They were not mere observers; they were part of a groundbreaking investigation that blurred the lines between science and the supernatural. They felt a connection to the phenomena unfolding before them, as if they were part of a larger narrative, a story woven into the very fabric of existence.

As the light patterns continued to shift, Dr. Orrington's voice remained steady, guiding the team through the significance of their findings. "We must proceed with caution. The knowledge we uncover here carries immense weight. It's not just about understanding these energy forms; it's about recognizing our place within this intricate web of existence."

His words ignited a spark of inspiration among the researchers. They shared a collective determination to understand what lay before them, aware that their quest could illuminate mysteries not just of Skinwalker Ranch but of the universe itself.

A junior researcher, Sara, leaned forward, her brow furrowed in thought. "But how do we even begin to interpret these phenomena? Are there frameworks in our existing scientific models that can accommodate what we're seeing?"

Dr. Orrington considered her question, his mind racing with possibilities. "We will need to approach this from multiple angles. Our existing models of physics may provide a foundation, but we may also need to create new paradigms that embrace the unconventional nature of these energies. Collaboration across disciplines will be crucial."

Another researcher, Marcus, chimed in, "What about the implications for our understanding of consciousness? Could these lights be a reflection of some higher state of awareness, something beyond our current understanding?"

Dr. Orrington's eyes sparkled with the idea. "It's a compelling thought, Marcus. Perhaps these energy forms are more than mere light; perhaps they represent a conscious intelligence, or a collective awareness that exists within the very structures of the Earth." He paused, letting the idea linger in the air, its possibilities echoing in the minds of his team.

The room buzzed with conversation as researchers exchanged ideas, theorizing about the implications of their findings. Each voice added to the tapestry of exploration, weaving threads of thought that connected the known with the unknown. They discussed the historical significance of Skinwalker Ranch, the legends that surrounded it, and the potential for their work to bridge ancient knowledge with modern science.

As the discussions deepened, Dr. Orrington stood back, observing the vibrant exchange. He felt a surge of pride for his team, their intellect and curiosity igniting a fire of ambition that would propel them forward. This was not just research; it was a collective awakening to the mysteries of existence.

Dr. Orrington stepped forward again, commanding the room's attention. "Let us not forget the responsibility that comes with this knowledge. The potential for discovery is vast, but we must remain grounded in our ethics. Our work has the power to influence lives, communities, and the very fabric of our understanding of reality."

His words resonated deeply with the team, and a sense of purpose infused their discussions. They knew that their journey was not merely about observation; it was about interpretation, application, and the potential consequences of their findings.

The flickering screens continued to display the otherworldly lights, each pulse seeming to respond to their heightened awareness. As the researchers' minds whirred with questions, possibilities, and theories, Dr. Orrington felt the weight of their collective mission pressing down on him.

"We stand at the edge of a precipice," he continued, his voice imbued with conviction. "What we discover here may challenge the very foundation of scientific understanding. We are not just observers; we are explorers of the unknown, stewards of knowledge that can reshape our world."

With every flicker of light, they glimpsed a hidden world rich with potential, a world that could reshape their understanding of life itself. The researchers felt a kinship with the phenomena, as if the energy was weaving its way into their very beings, urging them to pursue the unknown.

"Let's make a plan," Sara suggested, her enthusiasm palpable. "We can divide into teams to explore different aspects of the data. Some of us can focus on mapping the light patterns, while others investigate the geological formations nearby to see if there's a connection."

Dr. Orrington nodded, impressed by her initiative. "That's an excellent idea. We should also consider reaching out to experts in energy studies and consciousness research. Their insights could provide valuable context for what we're observing."

The room buzzed with energy as they discussed their next steps, the initial shock of discovery giving way to a fervor for exploration. They jotted down ideas, created diagrams, and plotted a course for their investigation. The flickering screens were no longer mere displays; they were windows into a universe teeming with possibilities.

Outside the observation room, the night air hung thick with anticipation, the vast expanse of Skinwalker Ranch harboring secrets waiting to be uncovered. The researchers knew they stood at the precipice of a monumental breakthrough, one that could redefine humanity's relationship with the natural world and its mysterious energies.

As they delved deeper into their investigation, the feeling of exhilaration intertwined with trepidation. They could not shake the sensation that they were on the brink of discovering something that would change everything. Each discussion ignited a new fire, each theory a beacon guiding them toward the unknown.

Dr. Orrington looked around the room, his heart swelling with pride and anticipation. "Remember," he said, his voice steady and resolute, "we are not just chasing data; we are uncovering the very threads of reality itself. This is our opportunity to challenge existing paradigms, to seek answers to questions that have long eluded humanity."

With renewed purpose, the researchers returned to their workstations, their fingers flying over keyboards, notes scrawled hastily on pages. The atmosphere transformed from one of uncertainty to one of determination, each member of the team fueled by a sense of camaraderie and a shared vision.

As the monitors flickered with the mesmerizing lights, they dove into their tasks, their minds racing with possibilities. They could feel the weight of history pressing upon them, the knowledge that they were part of something greater than themselves—a quest for understanding that transcended the ordinary boundaries of science.

With each passing moment, they drew closer to uncovering the secrets hidden within the luminous energy of Skinwalker Ranch, a journey that promised to challenge everything they thought they knew about reality, consciousness, and the universe itself. The stakes were high, but the potential for discovery was even greater, and as the night wore on, they knew they were embarking on a journey that would forever alter their understanding of the world.

Chapter 45

The atmosphere in the observation room was thick with tension as Dr. Orrington's words hung in the air. The researchers, gathered around the monitors, nodded in agreement. Among them, Dr. Lisa Moreno, a specialist in environmental science, spoke up, her voice laced with concern.

"Are we really prepared for the implications of this?" she asked, glancing around the room. "If these experiments are being conducted without oversight, the ramifications could be catastrophic."

Dr. Orrington met her gaze, his brow furrowing. "Exactly. We're dealing with forces beyond our comprehension. The former military and intelligence agencies have their own agendas, and I fear we might be pawns in their game."

"Pawns?" another researcher, Jason, chimed in, his voice rising. "We could be more like guinea pigs. The way they've manipulated communities already is appalling. We need to expose this."

Dr. Orrington raised a hand to quell the rising tension. "I understand your frustration, but we must approach this methodically. Panic won't serve us. We need concrete evidence before we make accusations."

Lisa leaned back in her chair, crossing her arms. "And how do you propose we gather that evidence? They control the narrative. They control the funding. We're operating in their shadow."

Dr. Orrington took a moment, his mind racing. "We'll need to investigate the origins of these experiments. Who authorized them? What data do we have on their impacts? We need to connect the dots and create a clear picture."

Jason nodded, his expression softening. "Alright, but we have to act quickly. The longer we wait, the more communities suffer. The disturbances have already begun to affect people's mental clarity and health."

Dr. Orrington glanced at the monitor, where colorful graphs displayed the rising anomalies. "I agree. But we have to be careful. If we attract too much attention, we could become targets ourselves. This isn't just about water and energy; it's about power dynamics."

The room fell silent for a moment as the weight of his words settled in. Then Lisa spoke again, her voice steady. "What about Dr. Finch? He's been vocal about these issues before. Perhaps he can provide insights or connections that we lack."

"Dr. Finch," Dr. Orrington repeated, stroking his chin. "He's a seasoned researcher with experience in community health. If anyone could help us navigate this maze, it would be him. But we'll need to approach him carefully."

"Why carefully?" Jason asked. "He's one of the good ones, right?"

"Maybe," Dr. Orrington replied, "but his previous ties to the military could complicate things. We need to ensure he's on our side before involving him."

The researchers nodded in agreement, the urgency of the situation settling over them like a thick fog. Dr. Orrington pushed back from the table, determination fueling his movements.

"Let's split into pairs and gather intel. Jason, you and Lisa investigate the community impacts and document any changes in health reports. I'll reach out to Dr. Finch and gauge his willingness to help."

As the team dispersed, the atmosphere buzzed with anxiety and purpose. Dr. Orrington took a deep breath, steeling himself for the conversations ahead.

***

The following day, Dr. Orrington found himself standing outside Dr. Finch's office. He felt a knot in his stomach as he knocked gently on the door. Moments later, it swung open, revealing Dr. Finch, a tall man in his late fifties with graying hair and kind eyes.

"Ah, Dr. Orrington! What brings you here?" Dr. Finch asked, his tone welcoming yet cautious.

"Thank you for meeting with me, Dr. Finch," Dr. Orrington replied, stepping into the office. "I wanted to discuss some recent developments that have raised serious concerns."

Dr. Finch gestured for him to sit, settling into his own chair across the desk. "I'm all ears. What's troubling you?"

"Have you been following the recent experiments involving water manipulation and energy disruptions?" Dr. Orrington asked, his voice steady.

Dr. Finch nodded, a frown crossing his features. "I've heard whispers. Some communities are experiencing strange phenomena—changes in health, energy levels. It's alarming."

"Exactly," Dr. Orrington leaned forward, urgency in his voice. "We believe these experiments may be linked to former military and intelligence agencies. There's a potential misuse of these tools to disrupt specific communities."

Dr. Finch's eyes widened slightly. "That's a serious allegation. Do you have proof?"

"Not yet," Dr. Orrington admitted. "But we're gathering data and seeking connections. I thought you could help us understand the community impacts better. Your expertise in health can shed light on the situation."

Dr. Finch rubbed his chin thoughtfully. "I appreciate your trust in me. I've been hesitant to dive into this for fear of backlash. The military's influence looms large."

"We need to act," Dr. Orrington urged. "The longer we wait, the more harm they can inflict. If we collaborate, we can create a comprehensive analysis that may compel others to take action."

Dr. Finch sighed, leaning back in his chair. "You make a compelling case. I'll need to review my records and see what I can find. But you must promise to protect my identity in this investigation."

"Of course," Dr. Orrington assured him. "We'll tread carefully."

Dr. Finch nodded, determination growing in his eyes. "Let's get to work, then. The communities affected deserve answers."

***

Meanwhile, Jason and Lisa were busy gathering information from local health clinics. They interviewed residents about their experiences and documented changes in energy levels and health conditions since the experiments began.

"Do you think the people will be willing to speak with us?" Lisa asked, eyeing the neighborhood with concern and determination.

"I think they will," Jason replied, glancing at the clipboard filled with questions. "They want their voices heard. It's about time someone listened."

As they approached a small group of residents gathered outside a community center, Lisa took a deep breath. "Alright, let's introduce ourselves and explain our purpose."

"Excuse me, everyone," Jason called, stepping forward. "We're researchers looking into recent changes in health and energy in the community. We'd love to hear your experiences."

One woman, visibly distressed, stepped forward. "My sister's been feeling anxious for weeks. She can't concentrate, and it's affecting her job."

Lisa nodded empathetically. "Thank you for sharing that. Have you noticed any other changes in the community?"

A man chimed in, his voice shaky. "It's not just her. Everyone's on edge. We're having nightmares, and the kids can't sleep. Something isn't right."

"Those are significant concerns," Jason noted, taking notes furiously. "Have you heard of any experiments or disruptions that might be related?"

"I heard a rumor about some government activity near the water supply," another resident added. "They said they're testing something, but no one really knows what's going on."

Lisa exchanged glances with Jason, excitement tingling in her veins. "That's valuable information. We'll dig deeper into these rumors."

As they continued to gather testimonials, it became clear that the community was reeling from more than just energy disruptions. There was a palpable fear in the air—a fear of the unknown, of unseen forces at play.

***

Back in the observation room, Dr. Orrington awaited updates from Jason and Lisa. His mind buzzed with thoughts of the implications of their findings. The potential for harm weighed heavily on him.

When Jason and Lisa returned, their expressions were a mixture of excitement and concern.

"We've got a lot to discuss," Jason said, his voice urgent.

"Tell me everything," Dr. Orrington replied, leaning forward in his chair.

"The residents are experiencing significant changes in their health and energy levels," Lisa began. "Anxiety, sleeplessness, and nightmares were recurring themes."

"That aligns with our suspicions," Dr. Orrington murmured, furrowing his brow. "What about the rumors regarding the water supply?"

"They're real," Jason said, nodding. "People are scared, and it seems connected to the experiments we suspect are being conducted."

Dr. Orrington felt a surge of determination. "We need to compile this information into a report. It's time to confront those responsible and demand accountability for the communities affected."

The researchers shared a look, knowing that the path ahead was fraught with challenges. But in that moment, they were united by a common goal: to uncover the truth and protect those who had been silenced for too long.

Chapter 46

Dr. Orrington leaned back in his chair, his fingers tapping softly on the edge of the desk as the soft glow from the lamp cast long shadows across the room. The stillness of the night only seemed to amplify the intensity in his gaze as he stared down at the papers scattered before him. His thoughts were heavy with the recent developments, and the silence was soon broken by his voice, calm but carrying an unmistakable urgency.

"Have you ever thought about just how fragile our technology is?" His eyes flicked up, locking onto the person sitting across from him. "All it takes is one breach, one moment of vulnerability, and everything—everything—is exposed."

The person shifted uncomfortably in their seat, clearly unnerved by the direction of the conversation. "You mean, like what happened to the researcher's phone?"

"Exactly." Dr. Orrington straightened, his fingers now tapping more insistently. "In Season One, Episode Five of 'The Secrets of Skinwalker Ranch,' we saw firsthand what can happen. A researcher's phone, taken over remotely. No warning, no sign. Just gone. Controlled by... who knows what."

There was a pause, the weight of the situation hanging in the air.

"But how can that happen?" the other person asked, their voice filled with disbelief. "I mean, aren't there security measures? Firewalls? Anti-virus software? Surely, phones and computers are supposed to be secure from things like this."

"Supposed to be," Dr. Orrington echoed, his voice now laced with a cynical edge. "But 'secure' is a word we use far too loosely when it comes to technology. These devices, the ones we trust with our most sensitive information, our conversations, our lives— they're anything but secure."

He stood, pacing slowly behind his desk, the shadows shifting with his movements. "You see, technology can be manipulated, twisted. And in this case, something, or someone, had full control. Remote access, complete takeover. No phone, no computer, nothing is completely secure."

The other person sat in stunned silence, processing the magnitude of what Dr. Orrington was saying.

They leaned forward slightly, their curiosity getting the better of them. "So, what do we do? How do we protect ourselves?"

Dr. Orrington stopped pacing, his back now turned as he stared out of the window into the dark night. "That's the question, isn't it? How do you defend yourself against an invisible enemy, one you can't see, can't touch?" He turned slowly, his expression grave. "The truth is, the moment you think you're safe, that's when you're most vulnerable."

The other person's brow furrowed. "But there must be something. Some way to keep these things out."

A soft, almost bitter laugh escaped Dr. Orrington. "The best security in the world can be bypassed if the attacker knows what they're doing. And trust me— whoever took control of that phone knew exactly what they were doing."

Silence settled between them once more, heavy and thick, until the other person broke it again. "But this wasn't just any cyberattack, was it? There was something... more to it."

Dr. Orrington's gaze sharpened. "Yes. It wasn't just about data theft or simple sabotage. There was an intelligence behind it, a purpose. Whoever—or whatever—was behind it wasn't just trying to steal information. They were probing, testing, seeing how far they could go. And that should terrify us all."

The other person swallowed hard, their voice a little quieter now. "You mean... there's something out there? Something beyond just human hackers?"

Dr. Orrington's lips pressed into a thin line. "Let's just say, there are forces at play that we barely understand. What happened on Skinwalker Ranch— what's been happening there—goes far beyond the reach of conventional explanations. And if technology can be compromised like that, it makes you wonder what else can be controlled."

The air in the room seemed to grow colder, the weight of Dr. Orrington's words pressing down on both of them. The other person could barely find their voice. "So... what do we do now?"

Dr. Orrington returned to his desk, sitting down heavily, his fingers intertwining as he stared at the documents in front of him. "We watch. We learn. And most importantly, we stay cautious. The truth is, we're living in an age where nothing is as secure as it seems. The moment we let our guard down is the moment we lose."

There was a long pause before the other person spoke again, their voice filled with uncertainty. "But how do we fight something we can't even see?"

Dr. Orrington's eyes darkened, his voice low and steady. "By understanding it. By knowing the enemy better than they know us. It's the only way to survive."

The clock on the wall ticked away the seconds as the gravity of the situation settled in. The other person leaned back, digesting everything that had been said. The silence lingered, thick with the unspoken tension that came with knowing just how fragile their security truly was.

Finally, Dr. Orrington broke the silence, his voice softer this time, almost reflective. "We've been too comfortable for too long. We've allowed ourselves to believe that our technology, our systems, are invincible. But the reality is... they're not. And it's only a matter of time before something, or someone, takes full advantage of that."

The other person's gaze dropped to the floor, the weight of Dr. Orrington's words hitting hard. "So what now? Do we just wait for the next attack?"

Dr. Orrington sighed, leaning back in his chair once more. "We prepare. We do everything we can to understand the threats we're facing, even if we don't fully comprehend them. And we hope that when the time comes, we're ready."

The other person nodded slowly, still unsure but knowing there was little else they could do. "I guess that's all we can do, isn't it?"

"Yes," Dr. Orrington replied quietly. "For now, it is."

The conversation ended on that note, both individuals lost in thought, each grappling with the same chilling realization: in a world where technology was supposed to be their greatest asset, it could also become their greatest weakness.

Chapter 47

The researcher stared at the phone in disbelief, the screen flickering and flashing symbols he couldn't make sense of. His fingers hovered over the device as though touching it might cause something worse to happen. The unnatural glow of the symbols reflected in his wide eyes.

"How is this even possible?" he muttered under his breath, swiping at the screen, but the symbols wouldn't disappear. Panic started to bubble in his chest as the device became completely unresponsive. "This is insane."

Dr. Orrington's voice pierced through the researcher's growing panic. "Don't touch it."

The researcher nearly dropped the phone at the sudden command. He glanced up and saw Dr. Orrington standing at the doorway, his face lit only by the faint light from the researcher's desk lamp. His expression was serious, calculated.

"Just put it down slowly," Dr. Orrington instructed, his voice calm but firm.

The researcher nodded, gingerly placing the phone on the desk as if it might explode at any moment. "What's happening to it?" His voice trembled.

Dr. Orrington stepped forward, his gaze never leaving the phone. "It's been compromised. Someone—or something—has taken control of it remotely. We're seeing the exact same signs as before."

"Before?" The researcher's brow furrowed. "You mean this has happened before?"

Dr. Orrington gave a slow nod. "Yes. The symbols, the takeover—this isn't the first instance. But it's escalating."

The researcher swallowed hard, his pulse quickening. "Escalating how?"

"Whoever's doing this isn't just looking for information anymore." Dr. Orrington's eyes flicked toward the researcher. "They're testing limits. Seeing how far they can push the control."

A cold shiver ran down the researcher's spine. He glanced at the phone, still flashing its eerie symbols.

"But why my phone? I don't have anything on here that—"

"It's not about what's on the phone," Dr. Orrington interrupted. "It's about what they can do with it. How they can access it, manipulate it, use it as a gateway."

The researcher blinked, confused. "A gateway? To what?"

"To more than just your personal data," Dr. Orrington said cryptically, his gaze hardening. "To you."

The researcher frowned. "To me?"

Dr. Orrington nodded again, this time more gravely. "Your habits, your routines, everything you've ever done on that phone. They can use all of that to manipulate you. Influence your decisions. And then, eventually... control you."

The researcher took a step back, his mind racing. "Control me? Through my phone? That's impossible."

"Is it?" Dr. Orrington raised an eyebrow. "You'd be surprised at what's possible when the right technology is in the wrong hands."

The researcher felt his breath quicken, his heart thudding in his chest. "What can I do? How do I stop this?"

Dr. Orrington's expression softened, but only slightly. "You can't. Not directly. This level of intrusion goes beyond traditional security measures. It's... sophisticated. But we can try to trace the source."

"How?" the researcher asked, desperation creeping into his voice.

"We'll need to analyze the data your phone's transmitting," Dr. Orrington explained. "Look for patterns, hidden codes, signals that might lead us back to the origin."

The researcher nodded frantically. "Okay, okay. Do whatever you need to. Just... make it stop."

Dr. Orrington moved swiftly to the desk, pulling out a small device from his pocket and connecting it to the researcher's phone. "It's not that simple. Whoever's doing this isn't just interested in data theft—they're playing a longer game."

The researcher furrowed his brow, watching as Dr. Orrington's fingers moved over the screen. "A longer game? What are you talking about?"

Dr. Orrington kept his eyes on the device. "It's a form of psychological manipulation. First, they make you aware of the breach. Make you feel unsafe. Then, as the days go by, they tighten their grip."

"Tighten their grip?" The researcher shook his head. "I don't understand. What's the endgame here?"

"Control." Dr. Orrington glanced up from the phone. "They're trying to control you. Slowly. It starts with your phone, then your communications, then your surroundings. Soon, every decision you make is influenced by them."

The researcher's face drained of color. "That... that can't be real. It sounds like some kind of conspiracy theory."

Dr. Orrington's expression didn't waver. "Does it? And yet, here you are. Your phone, compromised. Symbols you can't explain. You tell me—how much of this feels normal?"

The researcher opened his mouth to respond, but no words came. He felt trapped, cornered by the reality that was quickly setting in. "So... what do we do now?" His voice was barely above a whisper.

Dr. Orrington finished connecting the device to the phone and turned his attention fully to the researcher. "We track it. We figure out who's behind this and what they want. But you need to be prepared for the possibility that this... goes deeper than you think."

The researcher's mind was spinning. "Deeper? How deep?"

Dr. Orrington's gaze was steady, unflinching. "Let's just say the people behind this have resources. And they've done this before."

A thick silence settled over the room, the faint hum of the electronic devices the only sound. The researcher swallowed, his hands trembling slightly. "Are they... watching us right now? Can they hear this conversation?"

Dr. Orrington paused for a moment, then shook his head slowly. "Not yet. But they could be soon. That's why we need to move fast. We only have a small window before they realize we're on to them."

The researcher took a deep breath, trying to calm himself. "Okay. So... what do you need from me?"

"Cooperation," Dr. Orrington said simply. "I need full access to your phone, your emails, your communication logs—everything."

The researcher blinked. "Everything?"

"Yes," Dr. Orrington confirmed, his tone serious. "The only way to trace this is by going through every possible entry point they've exploited. If we miss even one, it could lead to further breaches."

The researcher hesitated, the thought of handing over all his personal information making him uncomfortable. "But... isn't there another way?"

Dr. Orrington shook his head. "Not if you want to stop this. The more we hesitate, the more time they have to strengthen their hold on your life."

The researcher stared at the flashing symbols on his phone again, weighing his options. Finally, he let out a slow breath and nodded. "Alright. Do what you need to do."

Dr. Orrington nodded in return, immediately getting to work. His fingers flew across the keyboard of his small device as he began extracting data from the compromised phone. The researcher watched in silence, anxiety gnawing at him.

After what felt like an eternity, Dr. Orrington paused, staring at the screen with narrowed eyes.

"What is it?" the researcher asked, leaning forward.

Dr. Orrington hesitated, his face tight with concentration. "This... doesn't look like a typical hack. The signals, the patterns—they're not just random."

The researcher's pulse quickened. "What do you mean?"

Dr. Orrington turned the screen toward him. "Look closely. Do you see this? These symbols—it's not just noise. It's a message."

The researcher's eyes widened. "A message? From who?"

Dr. Orrington's face darkened. "That's what we're about to find out."

Chapter 48

Dr. Orrington's voice continued, firm and authoritative. "Phones are made from elements found on Earth, meaning these elements can potentially be controlled and manipulated. What we're seeing with the phone takeovers might be just the beginning."

In a brightly lit scientific lab, scientists were busy, focused on their work. The quiet hum of advanced equipment filled the room. The team, consisting of geologists and engineers, was huddled around ground radar equipment, monitoring the readings displayed on their screens. Images of metallic formations, deep beneath the surface, flickered in real-time. The glow of the screens illuminated their faces, each of them absorbed in their task.

One of the scientists, a tall man with graying hair and a look of deep concentration, tapped the screen with his pen. "There. That's what we're looking for," he said, pointing at the readings on the display.

The others leaned in closer, eyes narrowing. They could see it now—distinct metallic formations beneath the Earth's surface. They exchanged glances, excitement flickering between them.

"This is right around Mesa," another scientist remarked, tracing a line on the map of Skinwalker Ranch spread out on the table in front of them. "We've detected similar formations around here before, but this one is... denser."

The lead scientist, Dr. Harper, nodded in agreement. "It's almost like something's concentrated there, pooling under the ground." He paused, thinking aloud. "If these formations are metallic in nature, and they've been subjected to external forces—"

"—then it's possible that whoever or whatever is responsible for the phone hack is using these same metals, manipulating them remotely," one of the junior scientists finished, her voice filled with awe and apprehension.

Dr. Harper's expression was unreadable, but his mind was racing. "There's something strange going on beneath the surface," he said slowly, leaning over the table to get a closer look at the map. "It's not just random metallic deposits. There's a pattern to it. And it's concentrated around key areas of the ranch."

"Skinwalker Ranch," one of the engineers muttered under his breath. "Of course, it had to be this place."

Another scientist, a woman with sharp eyes and a calm demeanor, pointed to a section of the map near the mesa. "We've always suspected that there's more going on underground than we've been able to detect. But now, with these readings..."

Dr. Harper nodded grimly. "Now we have proof. But what we don't know is whether these formations are naturally occurring or... something else."

The group fell silent, the weight of the situation sinking in. They all knew the history of Skinwalker Ranch—the strange occurrences, the unexplained phenomena. And now, this new layer of mystery was unfolding before them, right beneath their feet.

One of the younger scientists, barely out of his twenties, broke the silence. "If these metals are being controlled somehow, what does that mean for the rest of the ranch? Or for us?" His voice quivered slightly, betraying the fear behind his curiosity.

Dr. Harper exhaled, running a hand through his hair. "That's what we're here to figure out. But we need more data before we jump to conclusions." He gestured to the team. "Let's focus on getting more detailed scans of this area. We need to understand the composition and extent of these formations."

The group nodded, immediately going back to their screens and equipment. The air buzzed with tension as the scientists worked, their focus entirely on uncovering the secrets beneath the surface. The metallic readings, flashing across their screens, felt like breadcrumbs leading them to a truth they weren't entirely sure they wanted to find.

Dr. Harper glanced at the map again, his gaze lingering on the mesa. He couldn't shake the feeling that this was only the beginning. Whatever forces were at play here, they were growing stronger—and they were about to find out just how far that power extended.

Chapter 49

Dr. Orrington's voice, calm and analytical, cut through the air once more. "Ground radar has provided evidence of metallic planetary orbits beneath the ground in Mesa, Skinwalker Ranch. This suggests that extraterrestrial life forms or unidentified aerial phenomena, or UAP, could reside in these subterranean metallic orbits, not in outer space."

As the researchers stared at their screens, each seemed lost in thought, pondering the implications of what they had just heard. Dr. Harper leaned back in his chair, rubbing his chin. "If what Dr. Orrington is suggesting is true," he began, "then we've been looking in the wrong place all along. We've been scanning the skies, when the answers might be right beneath our feet."

Another scientist, Karen, tilted her head slightly, a look of skepticism crossing her face. "So, you're saying these metals underground are acting like planetary orbits? That they're holding something, or someone?"

Dr. Harper nodded slowly. "That's exactly what I'm saying. These formations are too uniform to be a coincidence. Something—whether natural or artificial—is at work here."

Karen raised an eyebrow. "But...extraterrestrial lifeforms? Are we really jumping to that conclusion?"

"Not jumping," Dr. Harper clarified, his voice measured. "But we can't ignore the possibility. Skinwalker Ranch has a history of strange occurrences, and now we've got physical evidence suggesting there's more going on underground than we've ever realized."

One of the junior researchers, David, who had been silently listening, finally spoke up. "But how would these metals be connected to UAPs or extraterrestrials? I mean, we've always thought of them as being...out there, in the sky, or in space. Why would they be underground?"

Dr. Harper sighed, clearly having wrestled with that same question. "We don't know for sure. But what if we've been wrong about the nature of extraterrestrial life this whole time? What if they're not just in the skies but have found a way to exist within the Earth's elements?"

Karen crossed her arms, frowning. "That's a pretty big leap, Harper."

Dr. Harper shrugged. "Maybe. But think about it. If we were an advanced civilization, able to manipulate elements at a molecular or even atomic level, why wouldn't we use the Earth's natural metals to create a safe haven, or even a base? It's perfect. Hidden. Undetectable by normal means."

David looked from Karen to Harper, absorbing their words. "You think these metals are being manipulated by something...intelligent?"

Harper nodded. "It's possible. And if they are, that means we're dealing with something far beyond what we understand."

A tense silence filled the lab as each person mulled over the enormity of the possibility.

Karen broke the silence, her tone softer now, as if trying to grasp the full weight of their findings. "So...what's next? What do we do with this information?"

"We need more data," Dr. Harper said firmly, his mind already racing with plans. "We can't just make assumptions. We need to conduct deeper scans, run tests on the metals we've found. If there's a way to determine if these orbits are being controlled or manipulated, we need to find it."

David nodded in agreement, his earlier doubt replaced with determination. "If there's something down there, we have to figure out what it is. But if this is extraterrestrial in nature...we need to be prepared for what that means."

Karen exhaled slowly. "This could change everything we know."

"Exactly," Harper said, leaning forward. "Which is why we need to approach this carefully. We're not just dealing with science anymore—we could be crossing into territory that's been untouched for centuries, maybe millennia."

"Or something that was never meant to be touched," Karen murmured, her eyes narrowing as she stared at the radar screen.

David glanced at the map of the Mesa, unease settling in his stomach. "Do you think it's dangerous? I mean, if there's something controlling these metals, something living down there..."

Dr. Harper's expression grew serious. "We have to assume it's a possibility. But we won't know until we dig deeper—both literally and figuratively."

Karen pushed back her chair, standing up as if the conversation had sparked a fire within her. "Alright, then. Let's get to work. The sooner we get more data, the sooner we can understand what we're dealing with."

The rest of the team followed her lead, the tension in the room morphing into a collective determination. Each of them knew that what they were about to uncover could either revolutionize their understanding of the universe or plunge them into the unknown.

As the team dispersed to continue their research, David lingered, staring at the map of Skinwalker Ranch. The idea that something—or someone—was potentially controlling the metals beneath the earth sent a chill down his spine. "You really think we're ready for whatever's down there?"

Dr. Harper, who had been gathering his notes, paused and looked at David. "I don't know if anyone's ever truly ready for something like this, David. But that's what makes discovery so important. It's not about being ready—it's about being willing to learn."

David nodded, but the worry didn't leave his face. "I just hope we're not opening Pandora's box."

Dr. Harper offered a reassuring smile. "Curiosity is what drives us. But caution is what keeps us alive. We'll proceed carefully."

David gave a small nod, still unsettled but trusting his mentor's judgment. "Alright. I guess we'll find out soon enough."

As Dr. Harper turned back to his work, his expression shifted from calm to contemplative. Deep down, he knew they were standing on the edge of something monumental. The metals beneath the Mesa were only the beginning, and he wasn't sure if even his team was prepared for what lay ahead. But they would press on, searching for answers to questions that had remained buried for too long.

"Let's hope we're asking the right questions," Harper muttered to himself as the lab buzzed with renewed activity.

Chapter 50

Scientists moved purposefully, placing sensors around the area with a sense of urgency. The cool night air buzzed with anticipation as they monitored every inch of the ground beneath their feet. Various pieces of equipment—ground scanners, electromagnetic field detectors, and even motion sensors—were scattered around the site. Each scientist checked and rechecked their tools, knowing that this moment could redefine everything they understood about extraterrestrial life.

Dr. Orrington's voice, clear and concise, echoed in their minds. "In simpler terms, extraterrestrial beings might be living inside our planet, rather than in the vastness of space."

David, still uneasy from their previous conversation, knelt down next to one of the scanners, carefully adjusting its position. "Living inside our planet?" He muttered to himself, shaking his head. "I always thought we'd find them in the skies, not under our feet."

Karen, standing nearby, glanced over her shoulder at David. "I know it sounds insane, but it's starting to make sense, isn't it?" She squinted at her tablet, where the data from the sensors was being streamed. "I mean, think about it. If we were looking for intelligent life, why wouldn't they hide where we're least likely to look? Right beneath us."

David shrugged, unsure. "I just can't wrap my head around it. If there's life down there, why now? Why haven't we detected it before?"

Karen gave him a tight-lipped smile. "Maybe we weren't looking hard enough. Or maybe they didn't want to be found. Either way, we're the ones stepping into their world now."

Dr. Harper walked over, his presence commanding the attention of everyone around. "How are the readings looking?" he asked, his voice betraying a mixture of excitement and concern.

Karen handed him the tablet. "So far, we're picking up minor fluctuations, but nothing too out of the ordinary. However..." She trailed off, looking at the monitor.

"However?" Harper pressed, his eyes narrowing.

She pointed at the screen. "There's something happening just beneath the surface. Small pulses, almost like a signal."

David peered over her shoulder. "A signal? Are you saying it's...communicating with us?"

"It's possible," Karen responded, her voice barely above a whisper. "The pattern isn't random. It could be some form of coded communication. Or...it could be something else entirely."

Dr. Harper's brow furrowed as he studied the data. "If these readings are what I think they are, we could be looking at the first contact—whether that's intentional or not."

David glanced at him, concerned. "What do you mean by 'not intentional'?"

Harper didn't respond immediately. He was focused on the tablet, analyzing the signals flashing across the screen. "It's just a theory, but what if they don't know we're here? What if these pulses are something like an automated response or a defense mechanism triggered by our equipment?"

Karen nodded slowly, her mind turning over the possibilities. "So, you're saying we might be disturbing something? Something that's been lying dormant for who knows how long?"

Harper met her gaze, his expression grave. "Exactly. We could be waking up something that's been hidden for centuries. And we have no idea what that might be."

David swallowed hard, suddenly feeling the weight of their mission pressing down on him. "And what if whatever's down there doesn't want to be disturbed? What if it's hostile?"

"That's a possibility we have to consider," Harper admitted, crossing his arms. "But we won't know until we investigate further."

Karen exhaled sharply, glancing around at the other scientists, who were all focused on their tasks, oblivious to the conversation. "So, what's the plan? We can't just stop now. We're too far in."

Harper nodded, his jaw set. "We continue with the scans. We gather as much data as we can. But we proceed cautiously. We need to be ready for anything."

Just then, one of the other scientists, a tall man named Jacob, jogged over, looking concerned. "Dr. Harper, you need to see this," he said, handing over a small handheld device displaying a live feed from one of the underground sensors. The readings were spiking dramatically, a series of rapid pulses flashing across the screen.

Harper's eyes widened. "What the hell..."

Karen leaned in closer, her mouth dropping open. "Those pulses—they're increasing in frequency."

Jacob nodded, his face pale. "It's like something down there is reacting to us. The closer we get, the more active it becomes."

David took a step back, the uneasy feeling in his stomach growing stronger. "This...this can't be good, right? We're pushing too hard."

Karen shot him a look. "David, we're scientists. We knew the risks going into this. We're here to uncover the truth, no matter how unsettling it might be."

"But what if the truth gets us killed?" David blurted out, his voice shaky. "I mean, come on—signals from underground, metal formations moving or being controlled? What if whatever's down there is a threat?"

Dr. Harper raised a hand, silencing him. "Enough, David. We're all aware of the risks, but panic isn't going to help anyone. We need to stay calm and focused. Let's not make any assumptions until we know more."

David clenched his jaw, biting back his anxiety. He knew Harper was right, but it didn't make the situation any less terrifying.

Karen turned her attention back to the feed. "These pulses… they're too rhythmic to be natural. It's like a heartbeat. Steady, controlled." She paused, her face grim. "It's alive."

The group exchanged nervous glances. The idea that they might be detecting something living beneath the ground, something far beyond human understanding, sent a chill through them.

Harper was the first to speak. "We need to triangulate the source of these pulses. Narrow down the exact location."

Karen nodded, already moving toward one of the nearby computers. "On it."

As she began typing in commands, the rest of the team gathered around, tension thick in the air. David crossed his arms, staring at the ground beneath his feet. "I really hope we're not about to open a can of worms we can't close."

Karen's fingers flew across the keyboard, bringing up multiple layers of data. "I'm getting close to a pinpoint location." Her voice was calm, but her eyes flickered with concern. The pulses were growing faster, almost as if they were responding to her actions.

"There!" she exclaimed. A single point on the map lit up, marking the source of the strange signals.

Dr. Harper leaned in, his face inches from the screen. "It's directly beneath the mesa."

David paled. "That's where we detected the highest concentrations of those metals earlier. The same place where we think something's been manipulating them."

Karen nodded. "Exactly. Whatever is down there, it's in the middle of that metallic orbit. It's like... it's using the metals as a shield, or even a habitat."

Harper rubbed the back of his neck, his mind racing. "We need to go deeper. Conduct a more thorough investigation, but..." His voice trailed off, and he turned to Karen. "Is there a way we can continue monitoring without triggering a reaction from below? We don't want to provoke anything."

Karen frowned, considering the question. "We can try using less invasive methods. Maybe rely more on passive monitoring rather than sending out strong signals. But there's no guarantee it won't still respond."

Dr. Harper sighed. "We're walking a fine line here. We need to be careful."

Jacob, who had been listening quietly, spoke up. "Dr. Harper, are we even sure we want to go further with this? I mean, what if we're dealing with something that's beyond us, something we can't handle?"

Harper looked at him, his face serious. "We don't back down from discovery, Jacob. We're here to understand the unknown, no matter how dangerous it might be."

David shook his head, muttering under his breath. "I just hope we're not biting off more than we can chew."

Karen turned back to her screens, eyes fixed on the pulsing signals. "Whatever's down there," she said softly, "it knows we're here."

The team fell silent, the weight of that realization hanging in the air. They had come searching for answers, but now it seemed that the answers were reaching up to meet them. The question was: would they be ready for whatever lay hidden beneath the earth?

Chapter 51

The researchers crowded around the large tank, their faces illuminated by the soft, bluish glow of the water flowing within. Karen, her hands on her hips, leaned closer to the surface, watching the water swirl as if it held secrets beneath its calm exterior. "It's fascinating, isn't it?" she said, her voice barely above a whisper. "The way water interacts with everything here—like it's alive, or part of some bigger system."

David, standing beside her, looked skeptical. "Alive? Come on, Karen. It's just water. I mean, I get the whole underground planetary orbits thing, but water being a part of their system? That's a stretch, even for you."

Karen shot him a glance. "You've seen the readings, David. It's not just water. There's something in it— some element or energy we haven't identified yet. And it's reacting to the metallic formations underground."

David scratched the back of his head. "Still feels like science fiction."

Dr. Harper walked over, clipboard in hand, his expression serious as always. "Water is a conductor, David. If these orbits really do host some kind of advanced technology, water could be the key to their power source. It's not far-fetched to assume that life—interterrestrial or otherwise—would use what's already abundant on Earth to fuel their systems."

David crossed his arms, unwilling to let go of his doubt. "And what about air? Gravity? All the other stuff that we depend on? Why aren't we talking about that?"

Karen's fingers drummed against the edge of the tank. "We are. But water is where we're seeing the most consistent activity. There's something here, David, and we need to understand it before we can move on to the bigger picture."

Dr. Harper nodded. "Karen's right. We start with what we know, then build from there." He handed her the clipboard, pointing at a specific set of readings. "The fluctuation levels in the water—they're off the charts compared to other natural sources around the ranch."

Karen scanned the data, her brow furrowing. "It's as if something is drawing energy from it, feeding off the water itself."

David rolled his eyes. "You're making it sound like there's a giant alien power plant underneath us."

Harper ignored his sarcasm. "We can't rule out the possibility of advanced technology using water as a power source, especially when we're talking about civilizations that may have been here long before us."

David sighed, clearly unconvinced, but he didn't push the point. Instead, he peered over Karen's shoulder at the clipboard. "So, what's next? Are we just going to sit around watching water swirl?"

Karen chuckled. "No, David. We're going to collect more data, run some tests, and see if we can isolate whatever it is that's causing these fluctuations."

Harper nodded in agreement. "Exactly. We need to better understand what's happening beneath the surface. If there's something down there—whether it's a technological system or an entirely new form of life—it's interacting with the water. That's our best lead right now."

Just then, Jacob entered the room, looking frazzled. He clutched a tablet to his chest, his eyes darting between the others. "We've got a situation."

Harper turned to face him, his expression unreadable. "What is it?"

Jacob swallowed hard, stepping closer. "The sensors we placed near the Mesa—they're picking up movement."

Karen's head snapped up. "Movement? As in, something's moving underground?"

Jacob nodded, thrusting the tablet into Dr. Harper's hands. "Look for yourself. The readings show a steady increase in activity—something's shifting down there. It's subtle, but it's definitely happening."

David, leaning over to get a look at the data, furrowed his brow. "What the hell is that? It looks like...like waves. But under the ground?"

Karen's eyes widened as she studied the screen. "It's not waves. It's...pressure. Something is building up down there, and it's moving toward the water source."

Harper cursed under his breath. "This isn't good. If there's pressure building beneath the surface, it could be a natural occurrence—like an earthquake. But with everything we've seen, I'm not convinced that's the case."

Jacob shifted uncomfortably. "So, what are we looking at, then? Some kind of...release of energy? Or something more...intentional?"

Harper didn't answer immediately. He set the tablet down and rubbed his temples, deep in thought. "I don't know. But whatever it is, we need to be prepared for the worst-case scenario. If there's any chance this is tied to the orbits or their energy systems, it could have massive implications for what's happening here."

David glanced nervously at Karen. "You're not saying this could be an attack, right? I mean, there's no way that's what this is...right?"

Karen's expression remained neutral. "We can't rule anything out, David. We don't know enough about what's down there. But if there's an advanced species living underground, it's possible they're reacting to our presence."

Jacob looked between them, his voice uncertain. "So, what do we do? Keep monitoring? Pack up and leave? I'm not exactly eager to stick around if something dangerous is about to happen."

Harper shook his head firmly. "We can't leave. Not yet. We've come too far to turn back now. If this is the breakthrough we think it is, we need to understand what's happening, no matter the risk."

David exhaled sharply, his anxiety clear. "You're saying we're going to just sit here and wait for something to come up and—what? Make contact?"

Harper met his gaze with unwavering resolve. "We're scientists, David. Our job is to observe, document, and understand. If something's down there, we need to know what it is, why it's reacting, and what it means for us. If that means taking a risk, so be it."

Karen nodded in agreement. "He's right. We can't let fear dictate our actions. This could change everything we know about life, about the universe. We have to see it through."

David groaned, running a hand through his hair. "Fine. But if something comes up and tries to eat us, I'm out."

Karen smirked. "Noted."

Harper turned his attention back to the tablet, tapping a few commands into the interface. "Jacob, I want you to increase the monitoring frequency around the water source. Keep a close eye on those pressure readings. If anything changes, I want to know immediately."

Jacob nodded quickly, already moving toward the equipment. "Got it, Dr. Harper."

As Jacob rushed to comply, the tension in the room seemed to thicken. Karen crossed her arms, staring at the water tank with a contemplative expression. "Do you think we're dealing with something sentient down there?" she asked softly, not looking at anyone in particular.

Harper paused, his eyes still on the tablet. "I don't know. But it's possible. If these fluctuations are tied to a system—technological or biological—it's reacting in real time to what we're doing. That suggests a level of awareness."

David, still pacing, muttered under his breath. "Awareness...great. Just what we need—conscious water and a pissed-off underground civilization."

Karen laughed softly. "David, you've got to admit—
it's exciting. Terrifying, but exciting."

He stopped pacing long enough to give her a deadpan
look. "I'd feel more excited if we weren't standing on
top of it."

Harper chuckled lightly, despite the gravity of the
situation. "David, you're going to look back on this
and realize it was the defining moment of your career.
You'll thank us later."

David rolled his eyes but couldn't help a small smile.
"Yeah, sure. If we make it out of here alive."

Just then, Jacob's voice cut through the room, tense
and urgent. "Dr. Harper, the pressure—it's spiking.
Something's happening."

Harper, Karen, and David all rushed to the
equipment, eyes wide as they stared at the screen. The
readings were going off the charts, and the ground
beneath their feet seemed to vibrate ever so slightly.

Karen's voice was barely audible. "Oh my God. It's
waking up."

Harper's gaze hardened, his mind racing. "Everyone, stay calm. We're not leaving until we know exactly what we're dealing with."

David swallowed, staring at the ground. "I just hope we're not too late."

Chapter 52

Dr. Orrington leaned closer to the camera, urgency etched on his face. "Water is immensely valuable to these underground beings. Their technology relies heavily on it. Thus, we must act swiftly to address the global water crisis." He paused, allowing the gravity of his statement to sink in.

Rebecca shifted uneasily in her chair, glancing at her notes. "Dr. Orrington, what exactly do you mean by their technology relying on water? How does that connect to what we've been seeing at Skinwalker Ranch?"

He straightened up, steepling his fingers as he thought. "Consider this: water is not just a resource; it's a key element in sustaining life and technology. In the case of these interterrestrial beings, their systems might be designed to harness the unique properties of water—its conductivity, its molecular structure. It's essential for their survival and operational efficiency."

Rebecca frowned, her brow furrowing. "So, if we're facing a global water crisis, does that mean we could be endangering them too?"

Dr. Orrington nodded. "Precisely. If they depend on the water we often take for granted, we might inadvertently be pushing them to act in ways we can't predict. We must explore how we can mitigate this crisis—not just for ourselves, but for them as well."

"How do we even begin to do that?" Rebecca asked, her voice tinged with concern. "It feels like we're fighting a losing battle with our own planet."

He sighed, running a hand through his hair. "We need to gather more data. This isn't just about technology and extraterrestrial life; it's about understanding our ecosystem as a whole. We must collaborate with environmental scientists, hydrologists, and policymakers."

INT. RESEARCH FACILITY - DAY

The next day, Dr. Orrington and Rebecca gathered with a group of researchers in the facility's conference room, the walls adorned with maps of Skinwalker Ranch and the surrounding areas. They sat around a large table, laptops open, as Dr. Orrington began the meeting.

"Thank you all for coming," he said, his tone shifting to one of determination. "As we discussed, our research indicates a pressing need to address the global water crisis, especially considering the implications for the beings beneath our feet. We need a plan."

One of the senior researchers, Dr. Harris, leaned forward, adjusting his glasses. "What kind of data are we looking at? Do we have evidence that connects the water levels to the activity we're seeing at the ranch?"

Dr. Orrington nodded. "Yes, the readings from the underground sensors show fluctuations in water levels correlating with increased electromagnetic activity. We believe this is not a coincidence. The water is a conduit for their technology, allowing them to operate their systems more effectively."

Rebecca interjected, "So, if we can stabilize the water supply, we might be able to create a buffer. This could help both the environment and whatever is down there."

Dr. Harris raised an eyebrow. "That's ambitious. But how do we achieve that? It sounds like we need a comprehensive approach to water conservation and possibly even restoration techniques."

Another researcher, Dr. Lee, chimed in, "We could start with community engagement. If we raise awareness about the water crisis, we might inspire local action. It could be as simple as promoting water-saving practices."

Dr. Orrington agreed. "Absolutely. We also need to push for policy changes at the state and national levels. It's crucial to incentivize water conservation measures. This has to be a collective effort."

INT. MESA - DAY

As part of their initiative, Dr. Orrington and his team ventured to Mesa, armed with portable equipment and an enthusiasm to engage with the local community. They set up a booth in the town square, where residents gathered, curious about the research being conducted at Skinwalker Ranch.

"Welcome, everyone!" Dr. Orrington called out, smiling as he addressed the crowd. "We're here to discuss an urgent issue: the global water crisis and its implications for both our community and the extraordinary phenomena we're investigating at Skinwalker Ranch."

A local farmer stepped forward, skepticism in his eyes. "You think we're in a crisis? We've got water right here! Our wells are full."

Rebecca jumped in, "That's a great point, but what we're seeing is a larger trend. Water levels are dropping across the region due to climate change and overuse. We want to ensure that what we have stays sustainable for the future."

Dr. Orrington added, "And it's not just about us. If these underground beings depend on this water too, we might be compromising their technology and our potential for understanding them."

A young woman in the crowd raised her hand, intrigued. "How do we know they even exist? What proof do you have?"

Dr. Orrington smiled, "Great question! We've gathered extensive readings and data that suggest unusual activity beneath the surface. The combination of water and the metallic formations we're detecting points to something extraordinary."

INT. COMMUNITY CENTER - LATER

After the outdoor presentation, the team moved to a nearby community center for a more in-depth discussion. The room buzzed with energy as locals engaged with the scientists.

Rebecca stood by the refreshment table, pouring coffee for attendees. A middle-aged man approached her, his expression serious. "I've lived here my whole life. Are you really saying there's something down there?"

"Potentially, yes," Rebecca replied, trying to gauge his reaction. "Our readings show signs of metallic formations and unusual energy fluctuations. We believe there's a connection between these and the water beneath the ranch."

He shook his head, still unconvinced. "Sounds like science fiction to me. I'm not sure I buy into it."

"That's understandable," Rebecca said, maintaining a friendly demeanor. "But we have to keep an open mind. If there's any truth to this, it could change everything we know about our world."

Just then, Dr. Orrington joined them, overhearing the conversation. "What we're proposing is a partnership between science and community. Whether you believe in the phenomena or not, we all share the same water supply. It's in our best interest to ensure it's protected."

The man crossed his arms, still skeptical but visibly intrigued. "I guess that makes sense. What can we do to help?"

Rebecca brightened, sensing a shift in his perspective. "We're gathering stories from the community, sharing knowledge about sustainable practices, and we'd love your input on how to improve water conservation locally. Every voice

Chapter 53

Dr. Orrington leaned over the table, his urgency palpable. "Water is immensely valuable to these underground beings. Their technology relies heavily on it. Thus, we must act swiftly to address the global water crisis."

Rebecca glanced at her notes, her brow furrowing. "Dr. Orrington, how exactly does their technology rely on water? What's the connection to what we're seeing at Skinwalker Ranch?"

He straightened, considering her question carefully. "Water is not merely a resource; it's a key element that sustains life and technology. For these interterrestrial beings, their systems may be designed to harness the unique properties of water—its conductivity, its molecular structure. It's essential for their survival and operational efficiency."

Rebecca frowned. "So, if we're facing a global water crisis, does that mean we could be endangering them too?"

"Exactly," he replied. "If they depend on the water we often take for granted, we might be pushing them to act in ways we can't anticipate. We need to explore how we can mitigate this crisis—not just for ourselves, but for them as well."

She shifted in her seat. "But how do we even begin?"

"We must gather more data. This isn't just about technology and extraterrestrial life; it's about understanding our ecosystem as a whole. We need collaboration—environmental scientists, hydrologists, policymakers."

***

The following day, Dr. Orrington and Rebecca gathered with a group of researchers in the facility's conference room. The walls were adorned with maps of Skinwalker Ranch and surrounding areas. They sat around a large table, laptops open, as Dr. Orrington began the meeting.

"Thank you all for coming," he said, his tone firm. "As discussed, our research indicates a pressing need to address the global water crisis, especially considering the implications for the beings beneath us. We need a plan."

Dr. Harris leaned forward, adjusting his glasses. "What kind of data do we have? Do we see evidence connecting the water levels to the activity at the ranch?"

"Yes," Dr. Orrington replied. "The readings from our underground sensors show fluctuations in water levels that correlate with increased electromagnetic activity. We believe this is significant. The water acts as a conduit for their technology."

Rebecca added, "If we stabilize the water supply, we might create a buffer, helping both the environment and whatever is down there."

Dr. Harris raised an eyebrow. "That's ambitious. But how do we achieve that? It sounds like we need a comprehensive approach to conservation and possibly restoration techniques."

Dr. Lee chimed in, "Community engagement could be a starting point. If we raise awareness about the water crisis, we might inspire local action. Promoting water-saving practices could make a difference."

Dr. Orrington nodded in agreement. "Absolutely. We also need to advocate for policy changes at both state and national levels. Incentivizing water conservation measures is crucial. This has to be a collective effort."

***

To implement their initiative, Dr. Orrington and his team ventured to Mesa, equipped with portable equipment and eager to engage the local community. They set up a booth in the town square, where residents gathered, curious about the research being conducted at Skinwalker Ranch.

"Welcome, everyone!" Dr. Orrington called out, smiling as he addressed the crowd. "We're here to discuss an urgent issue: the global water crisis and its implications for our community and the extraordinary phenomena we're investigating at Skinwalker Ranch."

A local farmer stepped forward, skepticism evident in his eyes. "You think we're in a crisis? We've got water right here! Our wells are full."

Rebecca jumped in, "That's true, but we need to consider the bigger picture. Water isn't just about what's in our wells; it's about the sustainability of our resources. If we don't manage it wisely, we could face severe shortages in the future."

Another resident, an elderly woman, crossed her arms. "You scientists always say there's a crisis. Why should we believe you?"

Dr. Orrington stepped forward, sincerity in his voice. "Because we've seen the data. Fluctuations in water levels can lead to unpredictable environmental changes. This affects not only us but potentially other life forms as well."

"Life forms?" the farmer scoffed. "You mean those supposed aliens?"

"Not just aliens," Dr. Orrington clarified. "These beings might hold knowledge or technology that could help us address our water issues. We need to understand our connection to them."

Rebecca added, "What if they depend on the same water we do? What if our actions endanger them? It's not just about saving ourselves; it's about finding a balance."

The crowd murmured, some exchanging glances of curiosity. The elderly woman leaned in. "So, what do you propose we do?"

Dr. Orrington smiled, sensing the shift in the room. "We need to work together. We want to educate you on sustainable practices and gather your input on water conservation efforts. We believe that by coming together, we can create a plan that benefits both our community and the beings we're studying."

A young man in the crowd raised his hand. "How do we start?"

"Great question!" Rebecca replied enthusiastically. "We'll be holding workshops to share best practices for water conservation. We want to hear your ideas too. Let's brainstorm solutions together."

Dr. Orrington gestured toward the equipment they had set up. "We'll also be conducting water tests and monitoring levels in the area. The more we understand our local environment, the better we can protect it."

***

As the weeks passed, the initiative began to take shape. The community responded positively, with residents attending workshops and sharing their own ideas for conserving water. Dr. Orrington and his team worked diligently, conducting tests and gathering data.

One afternoon, Rebecca was busy organizing workshop materials when Dr. Orrington walked in, a stack of folders in his arms.

"Hey, Rebecca! Look at this data," he said, dropping the folders onto her desk. "We've seen a noticeable drop in water levels in the last few months, particularly in areas where we previously detected electromagnetic activity."

She glanced up, her interest piqued. "That's concerning. Do you think it's connected to the underground activity?"

"Possibly," he replied. "We need to analyze the data further. If the water is being affected, it might indicate that something below is shifting, possibly impacting their technology or even their habitats."

Rebecca's eyes widened. "So, if they're being affected, they might respond in ways we can't predict."

"Exactly," he said, his expression serious. "We need to keep our focus on both water conservation and understanding what's happening beneath us. It's a delicate balance."

As the day turned into night, the two continued to work side by side, driven by the urgency of their mission.

Weeks later, the research facility was buzzing with activity. Dr. Orrington stood at the front of a crowded room, preparing for a community update. He glanced at the audience, locals and team members eager to hear what they had accomplished.

"Thank you all for being here tonight," he began. "We've made significant strides in our efforts to address the water crisis while simultaneously investigating the phenomena at Skinwalker Ranch. I want to share some of our findings with you."

Rebecca stood beside him, ready to present their research. "We've collected water samples from various locations, analyzing their quality and levels. What we've found is alarming."

The room quieted, all eyes on her.

"We've noticed significant contamination in areas adjacent to electromagnetic activity," she continued.

"This supports our theory that the underground entities are somehow linked to the water quality in this region."

A murmur swept through the crowd, and Dr. Orrington took the opportunity to engage them further. "We're not just studying these beings; we're also understanding how our actions impact the environment they inhabit. This is a call to action for all of us."

A young woman in the front row raised her hand. "What can we do to help? It sounds like we need to take immediate steps."

Dr. Orrington smiled, grateful for the enthusiasm. "Absolutely. We need your help in raising awareness and advocating for policies that protect our water sources. Organize community cleanups, promote water-saving measures in your homes, and share what you learn with your neighbors."

The young woman nodded, a spark of determination in her eyes. "I can help organize a community event! We could involve schools and local businesses."

"Great idea!" Rebecca encouraged. "The more people we involve, the greater impact we'll have."

As discussions continued, it became clear that the community was ready to take action. A sense of unity filled the room, igniting hope for the future.

As the meeting drew to a close, Dr. Orrington felt a surge of optimism. "Together, we can make a difference. Let's not just act for ourselves but for the beings that share this land with us. Our future depends on it."

With that, the community's commitment to preserving their water resources and understanding the mysteries of Skinwalker Ranch began to take shape, setting the stage for a collaborative effort that could change everything.

Chapter 54

Dr. Orrington's voice resonated through the airwaves as the scene transitioned from the vibrant cityscape to a local community center where he was set to lead a discussion on water conservation efforts.

The room buzzed with anticipation as locals gathered, chairs arranged in a semicircle. Dr. Orrington stood at the front, flanked by Rebecca, who was setting up a projector. The screen flickered to life, displaying images of thriving ecosystems and clean water sources.

"Thank you all for coming today," Dr. Orrington began, his enthusiasm infectious. "We've seen incredible progress in our conservation efforts since the initiative started. Today, I want to talk about how we can take these efforts further, particularly considering our past experiences during the lockdown."

Rebecca chimed in, "During that time, we noticed a significant reduction in pollution and a marked improvement in water quality. Nature responded beautifully to our absence, and it made us realize how impactful our daily activities can be."

An elderly man in the front row, Mr. Thompson, raised his hand. "So, what you're saying is that if we just stop using water for a while, it'll fix everything?"

Dr. Orrington chuckled. "Well, it's not quite that simple, but taking a period of inactivity can help. By reducing water consumption significantly over a set period, we give our resources a chance to replenish. It's about creating a balance."

A young woman, Lisa, leaned forward. "But isn't it difficult to get everyone on board with something like that? People have routines and habits they don't easily change."

Rebecca nodded. "That's absolutely true. The key is to create awareness and motivation. We can introduce a community-wide 'Water Reboot Week' where everyone commits to reducing their usage and participates in activities that promote water conservation."

Mr. Thompson scratched his chin thoughtfully. "I like that idea, but how do we encourage people to join in? Not everyone is going to care about water conservation."

Dr. Orrington smiled. "This is where you all come in. We need champions in the community. People who can influence others to participate—friends, family, social media advocates. If you show the benefits, people will want to join."

Lisa raised her hand again, excitement gleaming in her eyes. "What if we held events during Water Reboot Week? Like workshops, clean-up days, and competitions for the best water-saving practices?"

"That's brilliant!" Dr. Orrington responded, his enthusiasm evident. "We could also invite local schools to get involved. Educating children about water conservation can instill lifelong habits."

As the group brainstormed, a sense of camaraderie filled the room. Ideas flowed freely, and conversations buzzed with creativity.

***

Later that week, the community mobilized to prepare for the Water Reboot Week. Dr. Orrington, Rebecca, and the local volunteers met at the community center, surrounded by flyers and promotional materials.

"Alright, team," Rebecca said, looking over the gathered crowd. "We need to finalize our events and spread the word. Let's make this week memorable!"

A volunteer named Greg spoke up, "I can handle social media! I'll create a campaign to raise awareness and encourage people to share their water-saving tips."

"Excellent!" Dr. Orrington replied. "We should use hashtags to create a sense of community online. Something like #WaterRebootChallenge."

"Let's make a video!" Lisa suggested. "We could interview residents about why water conservation is important to them. It'll personalize the campaign."

"I love it!" Rebecca exclaimed. "Personal stories resonate with people. It makes the issue feel real and urgent."

As they continued to brainstorm, an older woman named Mrs. Johnson spoke up. "What about a community potluck? We could invite everyone to bring a dish that showcases local produce while emphasizing how conserving water benefits our farms."

Dr. Orrington beamed at the idea. "That's a fantastic way to connect everyone and celebrate our local resources. We can use that event to share information on water-saving techniques while enjoying good food."

The room buzzed with excitement, ideas building on one another as they crafted a plan for Water Reboot Week. As the meeting wrapped up, they felt invigorated, united by a shared purpose.

***

The atmosphere in the community center was vibrant as the week commenced. Banners hung from the walls, displaying the Water Reboot Week logo. Residents filled the room, chatting and laughing, ready to engage in the activities.

Dr. Orrington took to the front of the room, raising his hands to capture everyone's attention. "Welcome, everyone, to the kickoff of our Water Reboot Week! I'm thrilled to see so many of you here, ready to make a difference."

Cheers erupted from the crowd, and he continued, "This week, we'll explore various ways to conserve water and understand its importance to our community and the beings we've been studying. We have workshops, challenges, and a potluck planned, so let's get started!"

Rebecca stepped up next, holding a clipboard. "First, we're going to break into groups for our water-saving challenge. Each group will be tasked with coming up with creative ideas for reducing water usage at home and in public spaces. You'll have an hour to brainstorm, and then we'll share our ideas with the whole group."

A buzz of energy filled the room as participants quickly divided into groups, eager to tackle the challenge.

***

After an hour, the groups reconvened, and excitement filled the air as they shared their ideas. Lisa stood up first, beaming.

"Our group came up with a shower timer challenge. We can create a fun app that tracks how long you spend in the shower and rewards you for reducing your time. The more you save, the more points you earn for local businesses!"

"That's a fantastic idea, Lisa!" Rebecca exclaimed. "Incentives work wonders!"

Next, Greg shared, "We thought about implementing rain barrels in our backyards. It's a simple yet effective way to collect rainwater for gardening and washing cars. Plus, we could have a workshop on how to set them up!"

Dr. Orrington nodded. "Absolutely! Collecting rainwater not only saves water but also reduces runoff. It's a win-win!"

Mrs. Johnson stood up next, her voice filled with enthusiasm. "We discussed planting drought-resistant plants in community gardens. Not only does it save water, but it also beautifies our neighborhood!"

"Great thinking!" Dr. Orrington responded. "It's important to choose plants that are suited for our climate. That way, we'll encourage biodiversity and minimize water usage."

Finally, an enthusiastic teenager named Alex spoke up. "What if we create a water usage pledge? Everyone can sign it and commit to reducing their water consumption. We can display it prominently in the community center!"

Rebecca clapped her hands, "I love that idea! It'll show our commitment to the cause and inspire others to join in."

As the group continued sharing ideas, the room buzzed with creativity and collaboration. The energy was infectious, and the residents felt empowered to take action.

***

The first day of Water Reboot Week concluded with the potluck. The smell of home-cooked dishes wafted through the community center, drawing residents into the dining area, where tables were adorned with colorful tablecloths and decorations.

Dr. Orrington stood at the entrance, greeting everyone as they arrived. "Welcome! I hope you're all ready to share some delicious food and learn more about water conservation."

Rebecca helped direct traffic as residents filled plates with dishes made from local produce. "This is fantastic! Look at all the creativity on display," she said, her eyes shining with pride.

The potluck began with introductions as each dish was shared. Residents explained the ingredients and how they sourced them sustainably.

Mr. Thompson stood up with a hearty dish. "This is a vegetable stew made from my own garden! I don't use any chemicals, and I collect rainwater to water my plants."

Cheers erupted as others applauded his efforts, and Lisa followed suit. "I made a salad with veggies from the local farmer's market. It's important to support our farmers, and they use sustainable practices!"

As the evening progressed, residents mingled, discussing their newfound knowledge of water conservation. Dr. Orrington and Rebecca moved through the crowd, answering questions and engaging in conversations about the impact of their collective efforts.

"Rebecca, I can't believe how much excitement there is in the room," Dr. Orrington remarked, his heart swelling with pride. "The community is truly embracing this."

"I know! It's incredible to see everyone come together," she replied, her eyes gleaming. "It feels like we're creating a movement, one that could genuinely make a difference."

As the night wore on, the conversations turned to the future. Residents shared their commitment to continue the water-saving practices beyond the week, pledging to keep the momentum alive.

***

By the end of the week, the community had successfully implemented various water-saving measures. Dr. Orrington and Rebecca stood at the front of the community center for the final wrap-up meeting, a sense of accomplishment filling the air.

"Thank you all for being part of Water Reboot Week," Dr. Orrington began, his voice steady. "Your efforts have made a remarkable impact, not just on our water resources but also on the spirit of this community."

Applause echoed through the room as Rebecca chimed in. "We've gathered data on water usage during this week, and I'm excited to report that we've seen a reduction in consumption across the board. That's a testament to your dedication!"

Mr. Thompson raised his hand. "What's next? How do we keep this going?"

"That's an excellent question," Dr. Orrington

Chapter 55

Dr. Orrington stood at the podium in the town hall, his presence commanding attention. The room was filled with residents, each eager to hear about the water conservation initiative that had captured their community's imagination. A projector flickered to life behind him, displaying images of lush landscapes, clean rivers, and thriving ecosystems.

"Thank you all for coming today," he began, his voice steady and passionate. "We're gathered here to discuss a crucial issue that affects us all: water conservation. As we've seen, our actions have a direct impact on our environment, and it's time we acknowledge the urgency of this situation."

A murmur of agreement rippled through the audience. Dr. Orrington continued, "By committing to a period of inactivity in our water usage, we can create a remarkable change. This isn't just a local effort; it's a global one. If we can demonstrate our commitment to preserving this vital resource, who knows what could happen?"

From the back of the room, a young woman named Mia raised her hand. "Are you saying that if we reduce our water usage, we might get something in return? Like advancements in technology?"

"Yes!" Dr. Orrington replied, a glint of excitement in his eyes. "If we show our dedication to conservation, it's possible that the interterrestrial species we've been studying might recognize our efforts. They could choose to share their knowledge with us, leading to advancements that could help solve many of our problems."

Mr. Thompson, an older gentleman with a skeptical look, stood up. "That sounds a bit far-fetched, don't you think? How can we be sure any of that will happen?"

"Fair question," Dr. Orrington responded, his tone respectful. "While we can't guarantee results, the principle of reciprocity is deeply rooted in many cultures. If we show the universe that we're willing to care for our planet, it stands to reason that others might respond positively."

A man in the front row, James, leaned forward, intrigued. "So, what can we do specifically? How can we take action?"

"Great question, James," Dr. Orrington said. "I propose we initiate a 'Water Reboot Challenge' over the next month. During this time, we'll reduce our water consumption collectively, share our strategies, and track our progress."

Mia raised her hand again, her curiosity piqued. "What kind of strategies are we talking about?"

Rebecca, who had been observing the discussion, jumped in. "There are several ways we can approach this. For instance, we can install rain barrels to collect rainwater for gardening, set timers for showers, and limit our use of appliances that consume excessive water."

"And we can organize workshops to teach everyone about water-saving techniques," Dr. Orrington added. "Engaging our community in practical solutions is key."

The room began to buzz with conversation as residents discussed their ideas.

"Why don't we hold a community clean-up day?" suggested Sarah, a local teacher. "We can clean our rivers and parks while educating people about how litter impacts water quality."

"Excellent idea, Sarah!" Dr. Orrington exclaimed. "We can promote this as part of our challenge. It's about making our community more aware of the issues we face."

A man named Carl chimed in, "What about involving local businesses? They could sponsor events or offer discounts for those who participate in water conservation efforts."

"That's a fantastic suggestion!" Rebecca said. "We could create partnerships that encourage businesses to promote sustainability while supporting the community."

As ideas flowed freely, a sense of unity formed among the residents. The shared goal of conserving water sparked passion and determination in their hearts.

Later, as the meeting continued, Dr. Orrington encouraged attendees to break into small groups to discuss their water-saving strategies and plan community events.

"Let's take about twenty minutes to brainstorm. Focus on what you can implement in your households and how you can engage others in this challenge," he instructed.

The audience members split into groups, their energy palpable as they exchanged ideas.

In one group, Mia sat with Sarah and James.

"I think we should create a social media campaign," Mia suggested. "We can share tips and success stories, encouraging others to join in."

Sarah nodded enthusiastically. "And we can use visuals to show how much water we're saving. Pictures of rain barrels or before-and-after images of gardens could really draw attention."

James added, "We could even have a friendly competition—whoever saves the most water in a month could win a prize. It would motivate people to get involved."

Meanwhile, another group, led by Mr. Thompson, focused on practical changes they could implement in their homes.

"We need to be realistic," Mr. Thompson said. "Not everyone is going to want to change overnight. But if we focus on small steps, like fixing leaks and using water-efficient appliances, we can make a real difference."

"Yes, and let's not forget about education," suggested another member of his group. "We can create flyers to distribute at the community center and local stores, making it easy for everyone to learn about water conservation."

Back at the main meeting area, Dr. Orrington surveyed the room, a smile on his face as he observed the collaborative spirit of the community.

***

The atmosphere was electric as the community gathered for a follow-up meeting to kick off the Water Reboot Challenge. Colorful posters decorated the walls, and tables were set up with information about water-saving techniques.

"Welcome back, everyone!" Dr. Orrington exclaimed as he stepped to the front. "I'm thrilled to see so many of you here, ready to take action. Let's hear about the progress you've made since our last meeting."

Mia stood up, excitement bubbling in her voice. "Our social media campaign is live! We've started using the hashtag #WaterRebootChallenge, and people are already sharing their tips and successes!"

"Fantastic!" Dr. Orrington replied. "Engaging the community through social media is a great way to spread awareness."

James added, "We've also organized a community clean-up day for this Saturday. We're inviting everyone to join us in cleaning up the local river and parks. It'll be a great opportunity to educate participants about the importance of keeping our water sources clean."

"Wonderful initiative!" Dr. Orrington said, his voice filled with pride. "Let's make sure to promote that heavily. Education is a vital part of our mission."

Mr. Thompson then spoke up, "Our group has been working on a list of water-saving tips that we want to distribute. We're also planning to host a workshop on fixing leaks and using water-efficient appliances."

"That's crucial!" Rebecca interjected. "We should also consider doing a demonstration of installing rain barrels during the workshop. Seeing it in action will inspire people to take the plunge."

As the meeting continued, attendees shared their plans and ideas, each person fueled by a sense of purpose.

***

On the day of the community clean-up, the sun shone brightly, and residents of all ages gathered with gloves, trash bags, and plenty of enthusiasm.

Dr. Orrington and Rebecca arrived early to set up a table filled with flyers and information about water conservation. The air was filled with laughter and chatter as neighbors greeted one another.

"Thanks for organizing this, Dr. Orrington," Sarah said as she approached. "It's so great to see everyone come together like this."

"I couldn't agree more, Sarah," he replied, smiling at the collective effort. "This is what community looks like—united for a common cause."

As the clean-up began, participants spread out along the riverbank, picking up litter and debris. Mia and

James worked together, chatting as they collected trash.

"This feels good, doesn't it?" Mia said, lifting a plastic bottle out of the water. "Knowing we're making a difference."

James nodded. "Absolutely. And it's amazing how many people showed up today. I didn't think it would attract this many!"

Nearby, Mr. Thompson instructed a small group on how to properly dispose of recyclables. "Remember, folks, every little bit counts. Keeping our water clean is crucial for conservation efforts."

A child named Lucy ran up to Dr. Orrington, her face lit up with excitement. "Look! I found a cool rock!" she exclaimed, holding it up proudly.

"That's a beautiful find, Lucy!" Dr. Orrington encouraged. "Nature has so many treasures. Let's make sure we keep our environment clean so others can enjoy them too."

As the clean-up progressed, participants shared stories and tips about their own efforts to save water, creating a warm sense of camaraderie. Laughter and chatter filled the air, reinforcing the bonds of community.

***

After a long day of hard work, the community center buzzed with energy as residents gathered for a celebration to wrap up the clean-up event. The smell of food wafted through the air, and tables were filled with dishes donated by local businesses.

"Welcome, everyone! Thank you for coming together today to make a difference," Dr. Orrington said, standing at the front of the center. "Your efforts have not gone unnoticed. We've collected an incredible amount of trash today, and I can already see the positive impact we're making."

As applause filled the room, Rebecca added, "And we've got some exciting news! We've partnered with a local farm for this evening's dinner. They've prepared a delicious meal using sustainable, locally sourced ingredients."

Residents began to fill their plates, excited to share a meal together. Conversations flowed, filled with laughter and excitement about their shared accomplishments.

"I never thought I'd enjoy cleaning up so much," James said to Mia as they settled.

Chapter 56

The laboratory hummed with the sound of computers and equipment, casting a soft glow over the researchers gathered around the large screen. On the monitor, Professor Luc Montagnier's image flickered, presenting his theories on water memory. The atmosphere was thick with curiosity and anticipation as they absorbed every word he said.

"Isn't it fascinating?" Dr. Lara Simmons remarked, leaning closer to the screen. "Water can hold information, like a living record of its environment. This could revolutionize our understanding of how we approach water conservation."

"Right?" Dr. Malik Chen replied, tapping his pen on the table. "If water has memory, then that means our actions could have long-lasting impacts—far beyond what we initially thought. It makes our conservation efforts even more critical."

A graduate student named Zoe leaned back in her chair, arms crossed. "But how does that actually work? Can water really remember things? It sounds almost too good to be true."

Dr. Simmons turned to her, eager to clarify. "Think of it this way: water interacts with its surroundings, absorbing frequencies and vibrations. Montagnier suggests these interactions create a kind of imprint. If we can understand that process, we might learn to enhance our water sources."

Zoe frowned, still skeptical. "It sounds like pseudoscience to me. How can we measure something like that? What's the evidence?"

Dr. Chen chimed in, his tone encouraging. "There have been experiments that show how water can retain the influence of substances it's been in contact with. If we can harness that, we could create better purification methods or even improve crop irrigation."

"Imagine the implications for agriculture," Lara said, her excitement palpable. "If we can tap into water memory, we might be able to enhance crop yields while using less water."

"But it's not just agriculture," Zoe countered. "What about health? If water can remember beneficial frequencies, could we potentially create water that improves health?"

"Absolutely!" Dr. Chen agreed. "Think about how much cleaner our water supply could be. If we develop a method to program water with healing frequencies, it could change lives."

Dr. Simmons glanced at the clock on the wall. "Let's not get too ahead of ourselves. We need to focus on the research we can conduct right now. What experiments can we design to explore water memory further?"

Zoe sat up, her expression shifting from skepticism to curiosity. "We could set up control groups with water samples, exposing them to different frequencies. Then we could test if the water retains any memory of those frequencies."

"That's a solid idea," Dr. Chen said, nodding. "We could measure changes in the water's chemical properties before and after exposure. If we observe any significant differences, it could lend credibility to the theory."

As they discussed their plans, the excitement in the room grew. Each researcher began to bounce ideas off one another, sketching outlines for experiments on notepads and typing notes on their laptops.

Lara stood, energized by the brainstorming session. "I'll start drafting a proposal for the necessary materials. If we can demonstrate even one aspect of water memory, it could attract funding for larger projects."

Zoe added, "And I can compile existing research and studies related to Montagnier's theories. It's important we build on what's already out there."

Dr. Chen looked around the room, sensing the collaborative spirit. "Let's meet again tomorrow to discuss our findings. We need to keep this momentum going."

"Agreed," Lara said. "We have to be thorough. This could be groundbreaking."

As the meeting wrapped up, the researchers gathered their things, excitement bubbling over as they exchanged thoughts on the next steps. Zoe lingered for a moment, catching Dr. Simmons before she left.

"Do you really believe in this water memory concept?" she asked, her voice low.

Lara paused, contemplating her answer. "I think there's potential. Science is about exploring the unknown. Whether we prove or disprove it, we'll learn something valuable in the process."

Zoe nodded slowly, absorbing the response. "I guess it's worth exploring. Let's see where this leads."

The researchers filed out of the lab, energized by the discussions. The prospect of investigating something so profound ignited a spark in their minds, and they were eager to dive deeper into the mysteries of water.

***

The following week, the lab was buzzing with activity as the team prepared for their experiments. Tables were covered with glassware, pipettes, and other scientific equipment. Dr. Chen organized materials while Zoe entered data into a spreadsheet.

"Hey, Zoe," he called, "can you check if we have enough distilled water for our samples? We don't want any impurities affecting our results."

"Sure thing," she replied, pulling out a jug from a shelf. "We should have just enough, but I'll grab another bottle just in case."

As she walked over to the storage area, Lara entered the lab, a stack of papers in hand. "Good news, everyone! I've secured funding for our project! The board is intrigued by the water memory concept and wants to support our research."

"Wow, that's incredible!" Zoe exclaimed, returning to the table with the additional water bottle. "This gives us a real opportunity to dive deeper into our experiments."

Dr. Chen smiled widely. "Now we just need to finalize our experimental design. I think we should include a variety of frequencies to see if there's a significant response from the water."

"Absolutely," Lara said, laying out her proposal on the table. "I've outlined the different frequencies we can test, along with potential measurement techniques for tracking changes in the water."

As they reviewed the proposal, Zoe raised her hand. "What if we also include a group that's exposed to no frequencies at all? It'd be important to see if any changes are happening due to natural factors or if they're solely a result of the frequencies."

"Good thinking, Zoe," Dr. Chen acknowledged. "A control group is essential for validating our results."

They continued refining their proposal, throwing ideas back and forth, their synergy palpable. The clock ticked away, but they hardly noticed as they immersed themselves in their work.

Later that day, Dr. Chen led a discussion on the logistics of their upcoming experiments. "Let's plan to start testing next week. We'll need everyone on board for the initial setup. It'll be a long process, but I believe we'll see something remarkable."

"Should we prepare a presentation for the board?" Lara suggested. "They might want updates on our progress as we go along."

"Definitely," Dr. Chen agreed. "Let's keep them in the loop. They'll appreciate being part of our journey."

Zoe, inspired by the collaborative energy, asked, "What if we document everything we do? Video our experiments, take photos, keep a detailed journal of our observations?"

"That's a brilliant idea!" Lara responded, her eyes shining with enthusiasm. "It'll not only help us with reporting but could also be valuable for future research."

Excitement filled the lab as the researchers began to visualize the journey ahead of them. They knew they were stepping into uncharted territory, but the thrill of discovery drove them onward.

***

The following week, the lab was abuzz with anticipation. The team gathered around the setup, where several water samples were placed under different frequency emitters. Zoe checked the equipment while Dr. Chen prepared to start the first test.

"Everything looks good," she said, adjusting the dials. "I'm ready when you are."

Dr. Chen nodded, a focused expression on his face. "Let's do this. Starting with the low-frequency sound waves."

As he activated the equipment, a soft hum filled the room. The researchers watched intently, excitement and nerves mixing in the air.

"Can you feel the energy in the room?" Zoe whispered to Lara, who stood beside her, eyes fixed on the water samples.

"Absolutely," Lara replied, her voice barely above a whisper. "It's like we're on the brink of something huge."

After the initial test, they carefully documented their observations. Dr. Chen glanced at the clock. "Let's give it a few minutes before we move on to the next frequency. Everyone, make sure to note any changes you see in the samples."

Zoe wrote quickly in her notebook, her mind racing with possibilities. "Do you think we'll see anything noticeable after just one exposure?"

"It's hard to say," Dr. Chen answered, a hint of uncertainty in his voice. "Water memory is a complex phenomenon, and we may need to conduct multiple tests to draw any significant conclusions."

Lara looked at the samples with hope and skepticism. "Whatever happens, we're breaking new ground here. Even if we don't see immediate results, we're contributing to a body of knowledge that could change the way we understand water."

Zoe nodded, encouraged by her words. "I just hope we're able to capture something worthwhile."

As the hours passed, the researchers moved through their planned frequency tests, documenting results and engaging in spirited discussions. After each round, they paused to reflect on their observations, analyzing every detail.

"Look at this," Zoe exclaimed, pointing to her notes. "When we exposed the water to the medium frequency, there was a noticeable change in the pH levels compared to the control group."

"Interesting!" Dr. Chen leaned closer, examining the data. "We need to run additional tests to confirm this. But if it holds true, it could suggest that the water is reacting to the frequency."

Lara interjected, "Let's make sure to repeat the experiment to eliminate any variables. We can't afford to overlook anything."

As they prepared for the next round of tests, the excitement in the room was palpable. Every researcher was fully engaged, their minds buzzing with ideas and possibilities.

"Okay, team," Dr. Chen announced, drawing everyone's attention.

Chapter 57

"Did you hear what Dr. Orrington said?" Zoe asked, her eyes wide with fascination. "Water functioning like a supercomputer? That's mind-blowing."

Lara nodded, leaning in closer to the screen where Professor Montagnier's video was playing. "It changes everything we thought we knew about water. If it can actually store signals, think about the implications for health and environmental science!"

"Right? Imagine if we could develop ways to program water with specific frequencies," Dr. Chen replied, jotting down notes. "We could revolutionize how we approach water purification and distribution. It could help with everything from agriculture to medicine."

Zoe bit her lip, thinking. "But how do we even begin to test these ideas? There's so much we don't know about water's memory."

Dr. Orrington stepped into the lab, interrupting their conversation. "I couldn't help but overhear you all discussing water memory. It's a fascinating topic with endless possibilities."

"Dr. Orrington, do you really believe water can remember?" Zoe asked, curiosity etched on her face.

"I do," he said, his eyes brightening. "Montagnier's research shows that water can absorb and transmit signals. We're just scratching the surface of what that means."

Lara crossed her arms, contemplating. "So if we can tap into that potential, we could potentially create water that's enhanced for various purposes?"

"Exactly," Dr. Orrington said, pacing the room. "Imagine water that retains healing properties or water programmed to promote plant growth. We could make a substantial impact on agriculture and health care."

Dr. Chen raised an eyebrow. "But how do we ensure the reliability of these results? We'd need a controlled environment and precise measurements."

"Of course," Dr. Orrington replied. "We'll need to design a rigorous experimental protocol. First, we should define the types of signals we want to test. Then, we can establish control groups to measure any changes."

Zoe chimed in, "What kind of signals should we focus on? Are there specific frequencies known to have effects on living organisms?"

"Great question," Dr. Orrington said, nodding in approval. "There's a body of research suggesting that certain frequencies can influence cellular processes. We should start there."

As the conversation progressed, the team began brainstorming ideas for their experiments.

"Let's categorize the frequencies we'll use," Dr. Chen suggested. "We could have low, medium, and high frequencies, each exposed to the water samples for a set duration. This way, we can compare the results effectively."

"That makes sense," Lara said, jotting down notes. "And we can take measurements of the water's pH, conductivity, and even biological activity if we introduce plant seeds into the samples."

Zoe's excitement grew. "What if we also document any physical changes in the water? Like how it looks or smells before and after exposure to different frequencies?"

"Good idea," Dr. Orrington replied, enthusiasm bubbling over. "Visual observations could provide additional insights into the effects we're investigating."

Dr. Chen looked at the team, a sense of purpose settling over him. "Let's divide up the tasks. We need to gather the materials, design our experiments, and develop a timeline for the project."

Zoe raised her hand, eager to contribute. "I can handle the literature review. I'll compile studies on water memory and related frequencies. That way, we'll have a solid foundation for our experiments."

"Excellent," Dr. Orrington said. "And I can oversee the experimental design. We'll need to make sure everything is methodical and replicable."

"I can help with setting up the lab and the actual experiments," Lara added, her enthusiasm evident. "Let's make sure we have everything in place before we begin testing."

"Perfect," Dr. Chen concluded. "Let's aim to have our initial setup ready by the end of the week. We need to hit the ground running."

The team dispersed, each person energized by their roles in the upcoming project. Zoe grabbed her laptop and began typing furiously, eager to dive into her research.

***

The following days were a whirlwind of activity as the team prepared for their experiments.

"Zoe, how's the literature review going?" Lara asked one afternoon, glancing up from her own work.

"I'm making progress," Zoe replied, glancing at her screen. "There are some fascinating studies on how specific frequencies affect plant growth and cellular regeneration. I'll compile the key points and share them with everyone."

"That'll be super helpful," Lara said, organizing the lab equipment. "We want to make sure we have all the relevant data at our fingertips."

Meanwhile, Dr. Orrington was meticulously setting up the experimental apparatus. "We'll need to ensure that our equipment is calibrated properly. I want to eliminate any variables that could skew our results."

Dr. Chen approached, examining the setup. "It looks great. Have we decided on the control group parameters yet?"

"Yes," Dr. Orrington replied. "We'll have samples that are not exposed to any frequencies, as well as samples exposed to a variety of conditions. It's critical to compare these results against our experimental groups."

Zoe returned to the conversation, her laptop in hand. "I found a study that discussed how sound frequencies influenced the growth of tomato plants. It might be beneficial for us to include some biological elements in our tests."

"That's a brilliant idea," Dr. Chen said, clearly impressed. "We can use seeds to assess any changes in growth after exposure to our water samples. It would add another layer to our research."

"I'll get started on that," Zoe said, enthusiasm radiating from her. "What kind of plants should we use? I think something that grows quickly would be ideal."

"How about radishes?" Lara suggested. "They germinate quickly, and we can measure their growth over a short period."

"Great choice," Dr. Orrington agreed. "Let's add that to our experimental plan."

After finalizing their tasks, the team worked diligently throughout the week, setting up their experiments and gathering materials. They shared ideas, debated methodologies, and supported each other, creating a dynamic and collaborative atmosphere.

On the day of their first experiment, the lab buzzed with anticipation.

"Alright, team," Dr. Chen announced, clapping his hands together. "Today's the day. Let's make sure everything is in place before we begin."

Zoe checked her notes, glancing around the room. "I'm ready with the frequency emitters. I'll start with the low-frequency sound waves."

"I'll handle the control group samples," Lara said, positioning the water samples on the table. "Everything is organized."

"Perfect. Let's begin!" Dr. Chen said, his excitement infectious.

As Zoe activated the low-frequency emitter, a soft humming filled the room. The researchers watched intently as the water samples reacted to the sound waves.

"Do you think we'll see any changes right away?" Lara asked, her voice laced with anticipation.

"Probably not immediately," Dr. Chen replied, maintaining focus on the samples. "We'll need to let them sit for a while to observe any effects. Let's set a timer for fifteen minutes."

"What should we do in the meantime?" Zoe asked, glancing around.

"Let's prepare for the next frequency," Dr. Orrington suggested. "We can set up the medium-frequency emitter while we wait."

The team got to work, bustling around the lab as they set up the next phase of their experiment.

Zoe positioned the medium-frequency emitter while Lara took notes on the progress of the low-frequency exposure.

"Okay, we're almost ready," Zoe said, adjusting the settings. "I think we'll be able to see some interesting results with this one."

As the timer for the low-frequency samples went off, Dr. Chen gathered everyone's attention. "Alright, let's document our observations. What do we see?"

Zoe peered into the first water sample, frowning slightly. "It looks clear, but I don't notice any significant changes."

"Let's test the pH levels," Lara suggested, grabbing the pH strips. "That might give us more information."

As they conducted the tests, a sense of nervous excitement filled the air.

"Well?" Dr. Chen prompted, watching closely.

"The pH seems stable," Lara reported. "No noticeable changes yet."

"Okay, let's move on to the medium frequency," Dr. Chen said, encouraging everyone to keep their spirits up. "We have a lot of samples to get through, and I believe we'll start seeing results soon."

Zoe activated the medium-frequency emitter, and the lab filled with a different hum, slightly higher than the previous one.

"I can feel the vibrations through the table," Zoe noted, her enthusiasm building. "It's amazing how sound can affect something as simple as water."

"We'll let this run for fifteen minutes too," Dr. Orrington said, setting a timer. "In the meantime, let's discuss what we'll measure after this round."

"I think we should focus on both physical properties and any biological changes," Lara suggested. "We can track the growth of the radish seeds and see how they respond to the treated water."

"Agreed," Dr. Chen nodded. "And we'll want to take careful notes of our observations for each round of tests."

The team continued to brainstorm, discussing various measurements and methods for the remainder of their first day of experimentation.

As the time ticked down, anticipation hung in the air.

"Five seconds!" Zoe exclaimed, excitement bubbling over. "Get ready!"

When the timer went off, Dr. Chen encouraged everyone to gather around as they prepared to analyze the medium-frequency water samples.

"Well, what do we see?" he asked, eyes shining with curiosity.

Zoe peered into the sample. "It looks slightly different."

Chapter 58

"Dr. Orrington, what exactly do you mean by external interdimensional entities?" Zoe asked, her brow furrowing in confusion.

Dr. Orrington leaned forward, a grave look on his face. "There are theories suggesting that there are forces beyond our understanding that might intervene if we neglect our responsibilities. If we don't take action to conserve water and replenish our resources, they may impose their own solutions, which could be detrimental to humanity."

Lara, sitting across from him, exchanged glances with Zoe. "That sounds a bit far-fetched, don't you think? I mean, we should focus on our immediate challenges with water scarcity before worrying about... other dimensions."

Dr. Orrington shook his head slowly. "It's not far-fetched if you consider the patterns we've observed. History shows that when societies ignore their ecological responsibilities, they face consequences beyond their control. I'm not suggesting we panic, but we need to be proactive."

"Proactive how?" Zoe pressed. "What steps can we take that we're not already doing?"

"We need to inspire community action," Dr. Orrington said. "Hold workshops, educate people about water conservation, and encourage grassroots initiatives. We also need to leverage technology—monitoring systems, apps for tracking water usage, and ways to incentivize conservation at every level."

Lara leaned back, contemplating. "So you're saying we should start with our local communities and build from there?"

"Exactly," Dr. Orrington replied. "Change often begins at the grassroots level. If we can mobilize our communities, we'll have a better chance of influencing larger systems."

Zoe nodded, enthusiasm growing. "We could organize a community meeting. Bring people in to discuss the importance of water conservation and brainstorm ideas."

"That's a great idea," Dr. Orrington said, a hint of a smile breaking through his serious demeanor. "We should invite local leaders, educators, and even students. Engaging the younger generation is crucial—they'll be the ones living with the consequences of our actions."

Lara chimed in, "And we could showcase our recent findings on water memory. If we can show how water can be influenced positively, people might be more inclined to participate."

"I can design a presentation," Zoe suggested, pulling out her laptop. "I can highlight our research and the practical steps we can all take to make a difference."

Dr. Orrington leaned back, a glimmer of hope in his eyes. "Now you're thinking like true scientists. When we combine knowledge with action, we can create change."

"Do you think we could also get some media coverage?" Lara asked. "If we can generate enough buzz, it could really motivate people to get involved."

"Absolutely," Dr. Orrington agreed. "We need to leverage every avenue available to us. Local news outlets, social media—anything that can amplify our message."

Zoe grinned, typing furiously on her laptop. "I can reach out to some of my contacts in the local news. They might be interested in covering the meeting."

Dr. Orrington nodded. "Good. Let's make sure we have a clear agenda for the meeting. We need to outline what we want to achieve and how we'll engage the community."

"I can handle the logistics," Lara said, standing up. "I'll book a venue, create flyers, and handle the refreshments."

"Perfect," Dr. Orrington replied, his expression softening. "Your organizational skills will be invaluable."

The energy in the room shifted as the team began to feel a renewed sense of purpose. They started brainstorming ideas for the community meeting, throwing out suggestions and building on each other's thoughts.

"What if we had interactive stations?" Zoe suggested. "People could learn about different conservation techniques and even sign up for challenges to reduce their water usage."

"I love that idea," Lara exclaimed. "We could even have a water conservation pledge wall where attendees can commit to specific actions they'll take."

Dr. Orrington nodded appreciatively. "These are the kinds of initiatives that engage people. Making it personal and actionable is key."

"Should we invite some local experts or activists?" Zoe asked. "They could provide additional insights and perhaps share their own experiences with water conservation."

"Yes, that would be beneficial," Dr. Orrington agreed. "They can help validate our message and inspire the audience with real-life examples."

As they continued to brainstorm, the room filled with laughter and excitement. Ideas flowed freely, and everyone felt invigorated by the prospect of making a difference in their community.

"We should set a date for the meeting," Dr. Orrington suggested. "The sooner we act, the better."

"Next Saturday?" Zoe proposed, glancing at her calendar. "That gives us a week to prepare."

"Works for me," Lara said, jotting down the date. "I'll make sure everything is organized by then."

"Let's touch base regularly to ensure we're all on the same page," Dr. Orrington added. "Communication will be crucial."

The team nodded, and as they began to wrap up their meeting, Zoe felt a sense of purpose wash over her. "I can't believe how quickly this is coming together. It feels like we're actually going to make a difference."

Dr. Orrington smiled. "We're starting to build a movement. Remember, every small action counts. Together, we can create ripples that will lead to significant change."

The team dispersed, each member energized and ready to tackle their tasks.

As the days passed, they worked tirelessly to prepare for the community meeting. Zoe reached out to local media outlets, while Lara handled logistics and coordinated with community leaders. Dr. Orrington reviewed their research findings and finalized the presentation.

When Saturday arrived, the atmosphere in Dr. Orrington's study was electric. The team gathered early to finalize their plans and set up the space for the meeting.

"I've printed out all the flyers," Lara said, handing them out to the group. "We should have enough to distribute around the community center."

"Great job," Zoe replied, sticking a flyer to the wall. "And I've got my laptop ready for the presentation. I can't wait to share our findings."

Dr. Orrington glanced at his watch. "Okay, we have about thirty minutes until the meeting starts. Let's go over the agenda one more time."

Zoe nodded, her excitement bubbling over. "We'll start with introductions, then I'll present our research on water memory, and finally, we can open the floor for discussions and brainstorming."

"I'll lead the discussion part," Lara said, looking at Dr. Orrington. "I think we should encourage people to share their own ideas and experiences."

"Excellent approach," Dr. Orrington replied, a hint of pride in his voice. "Engaging the community in dialogue will be key to building momentum."

As the clock ticked closer to the meeting time, more attendees began to trickle into the room.

Zoe glanced around, her heart racing with anticipation. "I hope we have a good turnout. This is so important."

"Don't worry, it'll be great," Lara assured her, adjusting the seating arrangements. "We've done all the groundwork. Now we just need to execute."

When the room was full, Dr. Orrington stepped forward to address the gathering crowd. "Thank you all for being here today. Water conservation is a critical issue that affects us all, and I'm thrilled to see so many engaged community members."

As he spoke, Zoe felt a swell of pride. They were all here for a common purpose, and that sense of unity was palpable.

Zoe took a deep breath, stepping up to present. "Today, I want to share some exciting findings about water memory. Research suggests that water can store and transmit signals, functioning much like a supercomputer. This has significant implications for our approach to water conservation."

She clicked through her slides, showcasing key points and research findings. The audience listened intently, some taking notes and others nodding in agreement.

Lara chimed in, "We need to think about the role we each play in conserving our water resources. Simple changes at home can lead to significant impacts in our community."

"I'd love to hear what others have experienced," Dr. Orrington said, inviting participation. "What actions have you taken to conserve water?"

A woman raised her hand. "We installed low-flow fixtures in our house. It's made a noticeable difference in our water bill."

"Excellent!" Zoe encouraged. "That's a perfect example of how small changes can add up."

Another attendee spoke up, "I've been part of a community garden, and we've started a rainwater collection system. It's been great for reducing our reliance on city water."

"Fantastic idea," Lara said, smiling. "That's the kind of innovation we need to spread."

As the discussion continued, ideas flowed freely, and the energy in the room surged. Attendees shared their own experiences and brainstormed new solutions together.

"We should create a community challenge," one person suggested. "Encourage everyone to reduce their water usage for a month and track their progress."

"Yes!" Zoe exclaimed. "We could offer prizes for the most creative solutions or the biggest reductions. That could really get people involved."

Dr. Orrington watched the conversation unfold, a sense of hope swelling in his chest. "It's this kind of collaboration that will drive real change. We need to keep this momentum going."

As the meeting drew to a close, the atmosphere buzzed with excitement. They had not only educated the community but also inspired them to take action.

Zoe glanced at Lara, grinning. "I can't believe how well this went. People are so passionate about this issue."

"It's only the beginning," Lara replied, her eyes sparkling with enthusiasm. "We've sparked something important here."

Dr. Orrington stepped forward, addressing the group one last time. "Thank you all for being here today."

Chapter 59

Dr. Orrington paused, allowing the weight of his words to settle in. He leaned back in his chair, contemplating the implications of what he had just said. "It made me realize how much we still don't understand about the universe we live in."

From the corner of the room, Zoe raised her hand, curiosity dancing in her eyes. "Are you saying that the show suggests there are things in nature that defy our scientific understanding? Like the laws of physics?"

"Exactly," Dr. Orrington replied, nodding. "When you see a mountain behaving like water, it forces you to question everything. If such phenomena exist, what else are we missing?"

Lara, sitting across the desk, furrowed her brow. "But isn't it just entertainment? A dramatization of events? How can we take that seriously in scientific discourse?"

Dr. Orrington smiled slightly, appreciating her skepticism. "That's a valid point, Lara. However, sometimes it takes dramatization to engage the public and spark interest in scientific inquiry. Just because something is presented in a show doesn't mean the underlying concepts can't lead us to explore deeper truths."

Zoe leaned forward, intrigued. "So, you think there's merit in exploring the connection between the show's claims and actual scientific phenomena?"

"Definitely," Dr. Orrington said, his voice firm. "We should always question what we think we know. The laws of physics we hold as absolutes might not be as rigid as we believe. Investigating these phenomena can lead us to discoveries that can transform our understanding of the natural world."

Lara crossed her arms, contemplating. "But how do we approach this scientifically? We can't just take everything at face value. We need evidence, data, repeatability."

Dr. Orrington nodded in agreement. "Absolutely. We need a methodical approach. But first, we should explore these ideas and gather observations. The more we investigate, the more we can discern what holds water—no pun intended."

Zoe chuckled. "You're right. We could start a project around this. We can analyze reports and eyewitness accounts of similar phenomena and see if any patterns emerge."

"Good idea," Dr. Orrington encouraged. "Documenting these observations could lead to a compelling research proposal. If we can find a connection between popular media and unexplained natural phenomena, we might just have something noteworthy."

Lara uncrossed her arms, her interest piqued. "And what if we found credible sources or similar cases? That could lend more weight to the conversation."

"Exactly," Dr. Orrington replied, his eyes sparkling with enthusiasm. "We could create a database of unusual phenomena reported around the world. It's time we take the conversation beyond the confines of traditional science."

Zoe nodded eagerly. "I can start gathering materials and compiling them into a comprehensive report. We could even categorize them based on geography and nature of the phenomena."

"And I can research the scientific principles that could explain these occurrences," Lara added, her mind racing with ideas. "I'll dig into quantum physics and theories of space-time."

Dr. Orrington's expression shifted to one of pride. "This is how science evolves. By questioning, researching, and collaborating. I'm excited to see where this leads us."

Zoe glanced at the clock on the wall. "Should we set up a timeline for our research? I think it'll keep us on track."

"Great idea," Lara replied. "How about we meet weekly to discuss our findings and share ideas? That way, we can keep the momentum going."

"I can handle setting up a shared document for our notes and resources," Zoe suggested. "It'll be easier to track our progress that way."

"Perfect," Dr. Orrington said. "Collaboration is key, and a structured approach will help us make significant strides."

Zoe grinned, her excitement palpable. "I can't wait to see what we discover. This feels like a real adventure."

As the three of them continued to brainstorm, the conversation flowed naturally, full of energy and enthusiasm. They dove into potential topics they could explore, such as unexplained geological formations and historical accounts of peculiar natural occurrences.

"Have you ever heard about the phenomenon of ball lightning?" Dr. Orrington asked, sparking another wave of discussion.

Lara leaned forward, her eyes bright. "I've read about that! It's so strange—people have witnessed these glowing orbs appearing during thunderstorms. There's no consensus on what causes it."

"That could definitely fit into our research," Zoe added. "It's a well-documented phenomenon, but the explanations are all over the place. Some scientists think it's an electromagnetic event, while others have more speculative theories."

Dr. Orrington nodded thoughtfully. "Exactly. That kind of inconsistency is what we need to investigate further. It highlights the gaps in our understanding and shows how much more we can learn."

"Should we also consider folklore and cultural interpretations of these phenomena?" Lara suggested. "Many cultures have legends that describe similar events."

"That's a fantastic angle," Dr. Orrington said, clearly impressed. "Cultural narratives can often hold kernels of truth, reflecting humanity's relationship with the natural world. It could also provide insight into how societies interpret the unexplained."

Zoe's fingers danced across her laptop keyboard as she took notes. "I'll research different cultural stories related to unexplained phenomena. That could add depth to our findings."

"Great. We'll need to present a well-rounded approach," Dr. Orrington replied. "And don't forget to document any scientific literature on these subjects, too. It's crucial we ground our research in credible sources."

"Got it," Lara said, determination clear in her voice. "I'll compile the scientific studies and literature I find, along with the folklore. We'll weave it all together."

As they wrapped up their discussion, a sense of purpose enveloped the room. They were embarking on a journey of discovery, fueled by their curiosity and commitment to exploring the unknown.

"Let's aim to meet next week with our preliminary findings," Dr. Orrington suggested, his excitement palpable. "I believe we're on the verge of something significant."

Zoe beamed. "I can't wait to share what I find. This is going to be amazing!"

With plans set and spirits high, the three of them exited the study, energized by their mission. As they moved forward, each step felt like a stride into uncharted territory.

The following week, the trio reconvened in Dr. Orrington's study, eager to share their findings.

"I've gathered a bunch of reports on ball lightning," Lara announced, setting down a stack of papers. "There are some fascinating case studies from around the world, but no definitive answers yet."

"That's great!" Zoe said, eyes gleaming with excitement. "I found several cultural stories that reference mysterious lights in the sky. It seems to be a common theme across different societies."

"Perfect," Dr. Orrington replied, looking over the papers. "Let's integrate these narratives into our research. They'll provide a broader context for our findings."

As they discussed their discoveries, Zoe couldn't help but feel a sense of camaraderie growing between them. "This feels more like a collaborative effort rather than just research. I love it."

Dr. Orrington smiled. "Science thrives on collaboration. When we pool our knowledge, we can uncover deeper insights."

"I also found some interesting literature on water memory," Lara added, glancing at Dr. Orrington. "It ties into the concept of water functioning as a supercomputer. We could incorporate that into our overall findings."

"That's an excellent connection," Dr. Orrington said. "Water is fundamental to life, and exploring its properties could lead us to significant breakthroughs."

Zoe's fingers flew over her keyboard. "I'll summarize the water memory findings and how they relate to our other topics. It'll strengthen our argument."

"Let's also prepare a presentation for when we compile our research," Lara suggested. "We'll want to communicate our findings clearly when we share them with the larger scientific community."

Dr. Orrington nodded in agreement. "Absolutely. A well-structured presentation will help convey our message effectively."

The trio continued to bounce ideas off one another, energized by the collaborative spirit. As the hours passed, their discussion evolved into a passionate exploration of the topics at hand.

"Should we also consider reaching out to experts in related fields?" Zoe proposed. "They might provide additional insights and expertise that could enhance our research."

"That's a smart move," Dr. Orrington replied. "Networking within the scientific community can open doors and lead to fruitful collaborations."

"Plus, if we find someone with experience in geology or folklore, they might help us contextualize our findings further," Lara added.

As they continued planning, a shared vision emerged. They were not just conducting research; they were becoming part of a larger conversation about the mysteries of the natural world and humanity's place within it.

By the end of the meeting, they had a clear plan of action and a growing sense of purpose. Each team member was energized, eager to contribute to this project that felt increasingly significant.

"Let's reconvene next week with our updates," Dr. Orrington suggested. "And be sure to gather any additional resources or contacts that could help us."

Zoe nodded enthusiastically. "I'll reach out to some of my contacts in the folklore community. I'm sure I can find someone willing to chat."

"And I'll dive deeper into the water memory research," Lara added. "This project is turning out to be more exciting than I initially thought!"

Dr. Orrington smiled at his team, pride swelling in his chest. "I'm grateful to work with such passionate and driven individuals. Together, we'll uncover some remarkable insights."

As they parted ways, Zoe couldn't shake the feeling of anticipation. They were embarking on a journey that could reshape their understanding of the world.

Chapter 60

As the camera zoomed in on the researchers, disbelief and excitement filled the air. They stood atop a rocky outcrop, watching the mountains shift and sway.

"Did you see that?" Jack, a young researcher, exclaimed, his eyes wide. "It looked like the whole mountain just... undulated."

Marissa, an experienced geologist, squinted into the distance. "I know what I saw, Jack. But we can't just jump to conclusions. We need to document this carefully."

"Document what, exactly?" Jack asked, pulling out his notebook. "What do we even call this? 'Mountain Rippling'?"

"Let's focus on what we can objectively observe," Marissa replied, her tone measured. "What we need is clarity. If we start calling it something outlandish, it will only detract from the seriousness of our research."

"Right," Jack muttered, jotting down notes. "But I mean, how often do you get to see a mountain do... that?"

"I've seen enough weird things in my career that I've learned to be cautious," Marissa said. "We need to gather data and formulate a hypothesis before we draw any conclusions."

Meanwhile, Dr. Orrington approached them, carrying his own set of observations. "What's the situation here? I could feel the ground vibrating as I walked over. It's extraordinary!"

Jack turned to Dr. Orrington, excitement bubbling. "It looked like the mountain was... alive. Like it was moving like water. It's incredible!"

Dr. Orrington raised an eyebrow. "Incredible, yes, but also perplexing. What did the other team members observe? Were they as astonished?"

Marissa shook her head. "Surprisingly, they didn't report it as water-like movement. They're chalking it up to natural seismic activity."

"Seismic activity?" Dr. Orrington echoed, deep in thought. "Interesting. But this doesn't feel like the aftermath of an earthquake or geological shift. There's something more to it."

"Maybe they just didn't want to seem crazy," Jack suggested, glancing at the other researchers in the distance. "I mean, who's going to take you seriously if you claim you saw a mountain ripple like water?"

"Perhaps we should have a discussion with the other researchers," Marissa said. "Get a consensus on what's happening here before we proceed."

"I'll gather everyone," Jack offered. "I want to hear their thoughts firsthand. If they're all convinced it's seismic, we might have to think creatively to convince them otherwise."

As Jack walked away, Dr. Orrington turned to Marissa. "What do you think? Is it seismic activity, or is there something else at play here?"

"I'm not sure," Marissa admitted. "I've studied geological patterns for years, and this... this is unlike anything I've encountered. It doesn't fit neatly into any established theories."

Dr. Orrington nodded, his mind racing. "We need to be careful how we present our findings. If we claim this is extraordinary without sufficient evidence, we risk losing credibility."

"Agreed," Marissa said. "But we also have to be open to the possibility that our understanding of geology is limited. Maybe there's a phenomenon we don't yet understand."

At that moment, Jack returned, flanked by several researchers. "Okay, everyone, let's hear what you all observed. We need to discuss this movement we're seeing in the mountain."

The group gathered, their expressions curiosity and skepticism. Dr. Orrington took the lead. "Thank you all for coming together. We've noticed some unusual activity in the mountains that needs addressing. I'd like to hear each of your observations."

Kira, a biologist, stepped forward first. "I've been focusing on the flora in the area, and I did notice some plants seemed to sway even when there was no wind. It felt... unsettling, like they were responding to something."

"That's interesting," Marissa said, taking notes. "Did you observe any patterns in their behavior?"

"Not really. It was sporadic," Kira replied, frowning. "But I thought it was just an anomaly until I saw the mountain moving too."

Marcus, a geophysicist, chimed in. "I didn't feel any seismic activity that would correlate with what you're describing. My instruments are showing nothing unusual in the area."

Jack leaned closer, intrigued. "So, you're saying there's no scientific explanation for the movement we're seeing?"

"Not from what I can gather," Marcus replied, shaking his head. "But it could be a minor tectonic shift. We might just be at the wrong place at the wrong time."

"Or the right place at the right time," Dr. Orrington interjected, his voice firm. "We need to investigate this further. I propose a detailed study of the geological activity in this region."

"Count me in," Kira said, her enthusiasm evident. "If there's something more going on, I want to know."

"I'm in as well," Jack added. "This could be groundbreaking."

"Let's set up a plan," Marissa suggested. "We can gather more data, possibly even bring in some additional equipment to measure fluctuations in the area."

Dr. Orrington nodded, pleased with the team's enthusiasm. "Excellent. Let's make it our mission to find answers. If we can document this phenomenon accurately, we'll not only contribute to science but perhaps redefine some of our existing theories."

As the group dispersed to gather equipment and set up for further observation, Jack found himself walking alongside Kira. "Are you as excited about this as I am? We could be on the cusp of a major discovery!"

Kira smiled, her eyes sparkling with anticipation. "Absolutely! It's not every day you see a mountain behave like that. I just hope we can figure out what's causing it."

"Me too," Jack said, glancing back at the undulating mountain. "It's almost like it's alive, isn't it?"

"Right? It makes you wonder what else is out there that we haven't seen or understood," Kira replied thoughtfully. "The natural world is full of mysteries, and this feels like just one of many."

Meanwhile, Dr. Orrington gathered the other researchers, setting a sense of urgency in the room. "This is not just an oddity. If we can uncover the truth behind this movement, it could shift our understanding of geology and perhaps even physics. Let's keep an open mind and be thorough in our investigation."

Marissa nodded in agreement. "We need to approach this scientifically, but we also have to remain open to unconventional possibilities. There's no harm in exploring the unknown, as long as we stay grounded in evidence."

As the sun began to set, casting long shadows over the mountains, the team set to work. They positioned sensors and cameras, documenting every aspect of the unusual movement.

"Look at this," Jack called, crouching by one of the sensors. "The readings are fluctuating. It's almost like the ground is breathing."

"Breathing?" Kira teased, playfully nudging him. "You're getting a little poetic there, Jack. But I have to admit, it does look odd."

Dr. Orrington approached, scrutinizing the readings on Jack's device. "Let's not overlook the importance of accurate language, but you're correct. There's something unusual here."

"Perhaps we should take a sample of the soil," Marcus suggested. "It could reveal more about the geological properties at play."

"Good idea," Marissa agreed. "We should analyze the composition to see if there are any unusual minerals or geological features that might explain the movement."

As the team collected samples and continued monitoring the situation, their conversations flowed freely, filled with excitement and speculation about the mountain's behavior.

"I wonder if we'll find evidence of something entirely new," Jack mused, placing his collected sample into a container.

"Or something that challenges everything we thought we knew," Kira added, her enthusiasm infectious. "Imagine being the team that discovered a new phenomenon!"

"Let's not get ahead of ourselves," Marissa cautioned, but she couldn't help but smile at their optimism. "The key is to remain grounded in our findings, regardless of how extraordinary they may seem."

"Right," Dr. Orrington interjected. "We need to avoid sensationalism and focus on the data we gather. Whatever we uncover must be rooted in factual evidence."

As night fell, the mountain's ripples seemed to glow under the stars, casting an eerie yet beautiful light over the landscape. The researchers worked diligently, documenting their observations and sharing ideas late into the night.

"We should take shifts monitoring the sensors," Kira suggested, stifling a yawn. "This movement might not just happen during the day."

"Good call," Jack replied. "I can take the first shift. I'm too wired to sleep anyway."

"I'll join you," Marissa volunteered. "I'd rather keep an eye on things than risk missing any sudden changes."

"Great! I'll get some coffee brewing," Jack said with a grin. "We'll need to stay sharp if we want to catch anything unusual."

As the two settled in for their shift, they talked about their backgrounds and what led them to this research.

"So, Kira, what got you into biology?" Jack asked, leaning back against the rocky surface.

"I've always been fascinated by living organisms," Kira replied, her voice thoughtful. "It's incredible how interconnected everything is. Studying ecosystems gives me a sense of purpose. And when I see something like this," she gestured toward the mountain, "it reminds me of how much we still have to learn."

Jack nodded, appreciating her passion. "I get that. For me, geology has always felt like piecing together a puzzle."

Chapter 61

Zen leaned back in his chair, a furrow forming on his brow as he replayed the voice of Dr. Orrington's latest broadcast in his mind. The man's claims were always wild, but this time, the talk of "portals" and "electrical entities" took it to a new level. He was still trying to wrap his head around the idea that this scientist—known for his controversial work—was suggesting that something so outlandish could be real.

"Portals opening and electrical entities," Zen muttered to himself. "What next, aliens showing up in my backyard?"

He chuckled dryly, shaking his head, when suddenly the door to his small apartment creaked open. Sinclair, his trusted subordinate, stepped inside, carrying a stack of documents. Without saying a word, Sinclair tossed the files onto the table in front of Zen, crossing his arms.

"You're still listening to that nonsense?" Sinclair asked, clearly unimpressed. "I told you Dr. Orrington is a crackpot. Electrical entities? Come on."

Zen waved a hand dismissively. "I'm not saying I believe him. But you have to admit, the man's been right about a few things before. We can't just ignore this."

Sinclair sighed, pulling up a chair beside him. "I don't know why you're even wasting your time on this. We've got real problems to deal with—actual enemies, not some sci-fi ghost stories."

Zen leaned forward, flipping open one of the files Sinclair had brought in. "If there's even a one percent chance that this is true, we have to be prepared. You don't think I'm taking this seriously enough?"

Sinclair raised an eyebrow. "Prepared for what exactly? For random portals to pop open and zap us with these 'electrical entities'? What does that even mean, Zen?"

"It means," Zen started, running a hand through his hair, "that if there's something out there—anything—that we don't understand, we need to get ahead of it. Dr. Orrington said he has a method to weaken or trap them. We need to find out more."

Sinclair scoffed, clearly frustrated. "And how exactly are we supposed to do that? Knock on his door and ask nicely? That man's been off the radar for years. Nobody's seen him in person for a long time."

Zen nodded, flipping through the file. "Which is why we need to figure out where he is. If this turns out to be true and these entities are dangerous, we're going to need that method."

"And if it's all a hoax?" Sinclair challenged.

Zen paused, his fingers tracing the edges of a document. "Then we move on, but I'm not willing to take that risk without checking it out."

Sinclair sighed again, leaning back in his chair. "Alright, fine. I'll put some people on it, see if we can track down Orrington. But don't get your hopes up. This whole thing sounds like a wild goose chase."

Zen smiled faintly. "I've been on wilder."

They sat in silence for a moment, the tension in the room easing as Sinclair flipped through another folder, seemingly lost in thought. Zen tapped his fingers on the table, his mind still buzzing with the possibilities Orrington had presented.

Suddenly, Sinclair broke the silence. "You know, there's one thing that's been bugging me."

"What's that?" Zen askcd, looking up from his own file.

Sinclair hesitated, glancing toward the window as if weighing his words carefully. "If Orrington's right... if there really are entities out there that can come through portals... why haven't we seen more signs? Why now?"

Zen shrugged. "Maybe the portals are opening in isolated places. Maybe it's only starting."

"Or maybe," Sinclair said, leaning forward, "this is just the beginning of something bigger, and Orrington's just scratching the surface."

Zen's expression darkened. "That's exactly what I'm worried about."

They continued discussing potential scenarios for what could happen if Orrington's theories proved true. As far-fetched as it all seemed, Zen had learned to never completely dismiss the unbelievable. His life had already been turned upside down once—he wasn't about to be caught off guard again.

As the conversation wound down, there was a knock on the door. A moment later, one of their operatives, Riley, stepped in, holding her phone in her hand, an unreadable look on her face.

"What's up, Riley?" Zen asked, curious.

She hesitated before speaking. "You guys aren't going to believe this."

Sinclair rolled his eyes. "Try us."

Riley handed Zen the phone, where a blurry video was paused on the screen. "This was recorded an hour ago, outside of town. People are saying it's… well, just watch."

Zen hit play, and the grainy footage showed a darkened sky over a forest clearing. Suddenly, the screen flickered, and what looked like a glowing rip in the air appeared. From that rip, something almost translucent and crackling with energy began to emerge—an indistinct, shapeless mass of light that writhed and pulsed.

Zen's eyes widened. "Is this…?"

Riley nodded, her voice tight. "People are calling it a portal. And that… whatever that is, came out of it."

Sinclair stared at the screen in disbelief. "You've got to be kidding me."

Zen paused the video, his mind racing. "Get me the location where this was recorded. We're going there. Now."

Sinclair frowned, his skepticism still evident. "You really think that's real? That could be anything— some trick with the camera, a glitch…"

Riley shook her head. "I don't think so. There are eyewitnesses. People are scared, Zen."

Zen stood, grabbing his jacket from the back of his chair. "We need to see this for ourselves. If it's real, then Dr. Orrington might not be as crazy as we thought."

Sinclair grumbled under his breath but followed Zen's lead. "Fine, but if this turns out to be a wild goose chase, I'm going to be very annoyed."

"You'll live," Zen replied, his voice firm. "Let's go."

The three of them left the apartment, heading for the vehicles parked outside. As they drove toward the location of the supposed portal sighting, Zen's mind raced. He couldn't shake the feeling that things were about to change—and fast.

The journey was tense, with Sinclair occasionally muttering doubts while Riley remained uncharacteristically quiet. As they approached the forest, Zen slowed the car, his eyes scanning the surroundings.

"We're close," Riley said, pointing toward a break in the trees where the clearing was located.

Zen parked, and they all stepped out, the weight of the situation settling over them. The clearing seemed peaceful at first glance, but there was an odd energy in the air, something almost electric. It made Zen's skin prickle.

"Well?" Sinclair said, hands on his hips. "I don't see any glowing portals."

Riley pointed to a spot in the grass. "There. That's where it happened."

Zen crouched down, studying the area carefully. The grass seemed charred, as if it had been scorched by something. There was no other sign of the strange entity from the video, but the air still felt heavy, charged with something unseen.

"We missed it," Zen muttered, standing back up. "But something definitely happened here."

Sinclair looked around skeptically. "Or it could be kids playing with fireworks."

Riley shot him a look. "You really think fireworks caused that video?"

Zen turned to Sinclair, his voice firm. "We can't ignore this. Whether it's real or not, we need to be prepared. If portals are opening, we need to figure out how and why."

Sinclair sighed, running a hand through his hair. "Alright, fine. What's the plan then?"

"We track down Dr. Orrington," Zen said decisively. "He's the only one who claims to have a way to stop these things. If this is real, we need him."

"And if it's all a load of crap?" Sinclair asked, still clearly doubtful.

Zen didn't hesitate. "Then we find out the truth one way or another. But I'm not willing to bet everything on the idea that this is all fake."

Riley nodded in agreement. "I'm with you, Zen. We can't afford to dismiss this."

Sinclair groaned. "Alright, fine. Let's go find the good doctor. But don't say I didn't warn you if we end up chasing shadows."

As they left the clearing, Zen's mind raced with possibilities. If Orrington's theories were true, the world was about to change in ways they couldn't yet comprehend. He just hoped they could stay ahead of whatever was coming through those portals—because the alternative was too terrifying to consider.

Chapter 62

The sun hung low in the sky, casting a warm glow over the wide-open fields that stretched for miles. The only sounds were the soft rustling of the wind through the tall grass and the occasional lowing of cattle. A quiet, rural area like this wasn't used to much commotion.

The retired sheriff, Charles Bryant, sat in his old wooden chair on the porch, watching the fields in front of him. He hadn't thought much about those days until recently, but now… they haunted him. He reached for his glass of iced tea, his hand trembling ever so slightly as he lifted it to his lips.

Across from him, Dr. Orrington leaned forward. The doctor's notebook was open, pen poised, but he wasn't writing. Instead, he waited, his eyes focused on the sheriff, waiting for the next word.

"You still think I'm crazy, Doc?" Sheriff Bryant asked, squinting as he studied the man sitting across from him.

"No," Dr. Orrington replied calmly, setting the pen down. "I wouldn't be here if I thought that."

The sheriff nodded, his gaze drifting back to the fields. He hadn't told many people the full story, and those who had heard parts of it didn't believe him. But he could still remember every detail—those long, strange nights on patrol, when things weren't as quiet as they seemed.

"Guess you want to hear the rest, then," Sheriff Bryant said, his voice rough from years of shouting commands.

Dr. Orrington said nothing, only giving a slight nod, letting the sheriff take his time.

Sheriff Bryant took a deep breath, setting the glass of tea down on the small table beside him. "It wasn't just one time, you know? This wasn't some single occurrence, Doc. It happened… over and over. I was seeing things out there, things no one else was seeing. Lights in the sky, strange sounds. But it wasn't until we started losing cattle that it really got strange."

Dr. Orrington leaned forward, intrigued now. "Losing cattle? You mean, they were disappearing?"

Bryant shook his head. "Not disappearing. We'd find them, but they'd be dead… and it was always the same thing. Females. Always females, Doc. Their reproductive organs—well, they'd been... tampered with."

Dr. Orrington furrowed his brow, his pen hovering over the page again. "Tampered with? In what way?"

The sheriff looked away, his jaw tightening. "I'm no expert, but I've seen enough of the world to know what looks natural and what doesn't. These weren't natural. It was like someone—or something—had been... studying them. Taking samples. There wasn't a drop of blood anywhere. Clean cuts."

There was a long pause, the weight of the sheriff's words settling in the air between them.

"You think it was extraterrestrial beings," Dr. Orrington finally said, his voice low but steady.

Sheriff Bryant didn't answer right away. He let out a slow breath before nodding. "I don't think, Doc. I know. I saw them. They weren't human. Too tall. Too thin. Eyes like nothing I've ever seen. They were... studying them, like it was some kind of experiment."

Dr. Orrington scratched a note on his pad, the only sound breaking the silence. "And you were the only one who saw these... beings?"

"I was the only one who had the guts to talk about it," Bryant said, his voice tinged with frustration. "There were others. Farmers, ranchers, even a few of my deputies—they saw the lights, heard the strange sounds, but they didn't want to be the crazy one. They didn't want to ruin their lives with something no one would believe. But I saw them up close, Doc. I could smell 'em. I could feel the cold air whenever they showed up."

The doctor leaned back, his pen still hovering. "How did they appear to you? You mentioned lights—was that how they arrived?"

Bryant nodded slowly. "Always started with the lights. Sometimes it was just one, other times there were a few, hovering out there over the fields. Then, there'd be this low hum. Not something you'd hear, more like you felt it in your bones. After that, the lights would drop down, and then... they'd be there. Right in the middle of the field."

Dr. Orrington scribbled down a few more notes before looking back up. "Did they ever communicate with you?"

The sheriff barked out a laugh. "Communicate? Hell, no. They weren't interested in me, Doc. I was just a bystander. They were focused on the cattle. They'd do whatever it was they were doing and then vanish. No words. No contact. Just… gone."

Dr. Orrington closed his notebook, tapping the edge of it lightly. "Have you ever considered telling this story publicly?"

Bryant gave him a hard look. "You think people would believe me? No, Doc. They'd call me a lunatic, like they already do. You think I like living like this, out here in the middle of nowhere, with nothing but the sound of cows to keep me company? I've got no family left. No job. Hell, I barely leave the property. Because people talk. And when they talk, it ain't good."

"You're not alone in this, Sheriff," Dr. Orrington said, his voice softer now. "There have been other reports, not just in this country but all over the world. Strange lights, livestock mutilations… even people have claimed to be abducted. It's not as rare as you might think."

Bryant's eyes narrowed. "You saying you believe me?"

Dr. Orrington paused, studying the sheriff for a moment. "I'm saying… there's more to this world than what we can explain. And I'm not here to call you a liar."

The sheriff leaned back in his chair, exhaling slowly. For the first time in a long while, the tension in his shoulders seemed to ease. "Well, that's something, I guess."

They sat in silence for a moment, the only sound the gentle rustling of the wind through the trees.

Finally, Dr. Orrington broke the silence. "I'd like to examine the site where this happened. The fields where you saw the lights, where the cattle were found."

Bryant glanced out at the vast, empty fields. "I can take you there," he said after a pause. "But I can't promise you'll see anything. It's been years. Might be nothing left."

"Still, I'd like to see it," Dr. Orrington insisted.

The sheriff stood up slowly, groaning as his knees cracked. "Alright then, Doc. Let's go see if we can find some ghosts."

The Life of Dr. Orrington

Chapter 63

The research facility buzzed with a quiet intensity. Rows of screens lined the walls, displaying a flurry of data: DNA sequences, genetic structures, and complex models of chromosomes. The sterile white light reflected off the shiny surfaces, giving everything an otherworldly glow.

Dr. Orrington stood at the front of the room, hands clasped behind his back as he watched the large monitor with curiosity and apprehension. On the screen, a digital model of human chromosome 2 spun slowly, illuminated by vibrant colors that marked the points of fusion.

Dr. Keller, one of the lead scientists, adjusted his glasses and turned to the team. "This fusion… it's not just unique. It's intentional. The way the two chromosomes combined is too precise to be a natural evolutionary accident."

"Are you suggesting extraterrestrial involvement?" Dr. Howard, another scientist, asked, his voice skeptical. He tapped his pen against his clipboard. "We've been over this. There's no concrete evidence of outside interference in human evolution. Not yet."

Keller shook his head. "We keep circling the same point. The fusion is unlike anything we've seen in any other species. Human chromosome 2… it's almost as if it was engineered."

Dr. Orrington interjected, stepping forward. "That's what I've been saying all along. The extraterrestrial presence we're seeing today, with cattle and livestock, is just the tip of the iceberg. If they've been observing and experimenting on us now, who's to say they weren't involved from the start? This could go back thousands, if not millions, of years."

Howard scoffed. "You're saying aliens had a hand in the creation of human beings?"

Orrington met his gaze steadily. "I'm saying it's possible. Think about it. Human evolution took a massive leap when this fusion happened. No other species shares this trait. Why us? Why then?"

Dr. Patel, who had been quietly observing the conversation, finally spoke up. "There are too many gaps in the fossil record. We know that. But this… if it's true… it changes everything we thought we knew about our origins."

Keller nodded. "Exactly. The fusion isn't random. It's too clean, too organized. Look at this." He gestured to the monitor, zooming in on the structure of the chromosome. "These telomeres… they're not where they should be. Normally, you'd expect to see the remnants of these sequences at the ends of chromosomes, but here—"

"They're fused in the middle," Patel finished, her eyes narrowing as she studied the image. "Almost as if someone…"

"Spliced them together," Keller said. "Exactly."

Howard leaned back in his chair, crossing his arms. "So you're proposing that extraterrestrial beings somehow intervened in the genetic development of early humans? That's a pretty big leap, even for you, Orrington."

Orrington shrugged. "I'm not proposing anything. I'm presenting evidence. And the evidence suggests that something—or someone—played a role in the formation of human chromosome 2. Whether that's extraterrestrial or something else entirely, we don't know. But we can't ignore the signs."

Patel sighed. "The problem is, the moment we start talking about aliens, we lose credibility. The scientific community won't take this seriously unless we have undeniable proof."

"Proof is exactly what we're working toward," Orrington replied. "But we need to keep an open mind. What if the reason we've never been able to fully explain our own evolutionary leap is because we've been looking in the wrong direction?"

There was a long pause, the room growing still as the weight of his words settled over the team.

Keller broke the silence. "So what's the next step? How do we prove this? Or at least get closer to the truth?"

Orrington stepped closer to the monitor, staring at the fusion points. "We start by analyzing the anomalies in the cattle. The genetic manipulation they've been undergoing, the reproductive experiments—it's all connected. These beings, whatever they are, have a vested interest in our biology. They're studying us, just like they studied our ancestors. We need to trace the patterns."

Patel glanced at the screens showing data from the cattle experiments. "If they're targeting specific reproductive organs, they might be mapping genetic traits, tracking how these traits pass down through generations."

"Exactly," Orrington said, nodding. "And that's why the cattle are so important. They're a window into understanding the broader picture. Cows are one of the primary food sources for humans. If they're manipulating their DNA, they could be testing how changes in livestock affect the human population."

Howard frowned. "So, what… they're farming us? Experimenting on our food supply to control us?"

"Not control," Orrington corrected him. "Study. We're part of their experiment. They want to see how we adapt, how we evolve. If they were involved in our genetic past, they're still monitoring us, watching how their 'work' progresses."

The room fell silent again as the implications hung in the air. Orrington knew the team was struggling to come to terms with the idea. It wasn't easy to accept that humanity might be part of some grand experiment conducted by beings far beyond their understanding.

Finally, Patel spoke. "If what you're saying is true, then we need to gather more data. The cattle experiments are key. But we also need to look at human genetics more closely. What if there are other anomalies? Other signs that point to this kind of intervention?"

Keller nodded. "I agree. We've been so focused on explaining the fusion through natural processes that we haven't considered all the possibilities. We need to widen our scope."

Howard rubbed his temples, clearly frustrated. "This is going to take years. And even if we do find something, convincing the rest of the scientific community..."

Orrington smiled faintly. "I'm not asking you to convince anyone yet. I'm asking you to help me find the truth. Whether that truth is extraterrestrial, natural, or something else entirely... we owe it to ourselves to explore every avenue."

Keller leaned forward, eyes locked on Orrington. "So where do we start?"

Orrington tapped the screen, where the image of the fused chromosome still rotated slowly. "We start here. With the cattle, with human chromosome 2, with every genetic anomaly we can find. If there's a pattern, we'll uncover it."

Patel stood, her face set with determination. "Then we better get to work."

Howard sighed but stood as well, albeit more reluctantly. "You realize this could ruin all of our careers if we're wrong."

"We won't be wrong," Orrington said, his voice firm. "And if we are... well, then at least we'll know we followed the evidence, wherever it led."

Chapter 64

Dr. Orrington sat at a wide wooden table, surrounded by ancient manuscripts and weathered texts, each filled with cryptic symbols and faded ink. He flipped through the brittle pages of a particularly old volume, carefully tracing the words with his finger. His brow furrowed in concentration as he examined the text before him.

On the nearby monitor, flickering infrared footage showed the faint image of a glowing, circular portal opening in the middle of a desolate field. The soft hum of the monitor filled the otherwise silent library.

Dr. Patel entered the room, her footsteps echoing softly across the stone floor. She approached Dr. Orrington, glancing at the monitor before looking at the book in his hands.

"Is that what I think it is?" Patel asked, raising an eyebrow.

Dr. Orrington didn't look up from the page. "Yes. It's the same book we saw referenced in the old footage from the temple excavation. The one the cleric used to open the portal."

Patel leaned closer, peering at the ancient script. "Are you telling me this book is real? That it's not just some myth passed down through the ages?"

Dr. Orrington nodded slowly, still fixated on the words. "It's very real. The language is archaic, but I've been able to translate a portion of it. The cleric recited this exact passage when the portal opened."

Patel crossed her arms, her gaze shifting back to the monitor. "And you're sure that what we're seeing in the footage is a portal? Not some optical illusion or atmospheric anomaly?"

"I'm certain," Orrington replied, his voice low and certain. "Everything matches—the symbols, the alignment of the stars, the incantation. This is a portal."

Patel shook her head, her skepticism apparent. "You realize what you're saying, don't you? You're suggesting that we're dealing with some kind of supernatural force. Something that science can't explain."

Orrington finally looked up, meeting her eyes. "That's exactly what I'm saying. And it's not just science that can't explain it. This goes beyond our understanding of the universe. These texts… they're describing a connection between worlds. Between dimensions."

Patel hesitated, processing his words. "So what's on the other side of that portal? Where does it lead?"

Orrington exhaled, his expression grim. "That's what we need to find out."

Patel leaned against the table, glancing down at the open book again. "And how exactly do we do that? We're talking about opening a gateway to… what, another reality?"

"Potentially," Orrington said, flipping another page. "The cleric believed that the portal led to the realm of the gods. A place beyond life and death, where ancient beings reside."

Patel frowned. "And you believe that?"

"I don't know what to believe yet," Orrington admitted. "But I do know that this is bigger than us. Bigger than anything we've ever encountered before. And we need to be prepared for what happens if we open that portal again."

Patel narrowed her eyes, her voice lowering. "You're not seriously considering activating it, are you?"

Orrington closed the book with a soft thud, his gaze steady. "If we don't, someone else will. This knowledge is already out there. It's only a matter of time before others try to exploit it."

Patel sighed, running a hand through her hair. "This is madness. We're scientists, not occultists. How can we possibly justify—"

"We justify it by finding the truth," Orrington interrupted. "If there's even the slightest chance that these portals are real, we owe it to ourselves to investigate. To understand what we're dealing with."

Patel was silent for a moment, her eyes drifting back to the monitor, where the portal footage continued to loop. "And what happens if we open it and something comes through? Something we can't control?"

Orrington stood up, moving to the monitor and pausing the footage. "That's a risk we have to take. But we'll be prepared. We'll have the tools, the knowledge, everything we need to contain whatever might come through."

Patel shook her head. "This sounds like a bad idea."

"Maybe," Orrington conceded. "But it's a necessary one. If we don't do this, we'll be left in the dark, while others use this knowledge for their own gain. We can't afford to be ignorant."

Patel stared at the monitor, then at the ancient book in front of her. "Alright," she said quietly. "But if we're going to do this, we do it carefully. Step by step. No rushing into things."

Orrington nodded in agreement. "Of course. We'll take every precaution."

Patel picked up one of the old manuscripts, scanning the strange symbols and inscriptions. "These texts... do they say anything about how the portals were used? What happened after they were opened?"

Orrington tapped the side of the book he had been reading. "There are references to battles, wars between beings from different realms. Some of these texts are vague, but the overall theme is consistent— whoever controls the portal controls the power that comes with it."

"Power," Patel muttered, shaking her head. "That's always the driving force, isn't it?"

Orrington smiled faintly. "It always is."

The two stood in silence for a moment, the weight of the discovery settling over them.

Finally, Patel spoke. "So what's the next step? Are we trying to activate this thing ourselves?"

Orrington turned back to the book, flipping to a page marked with several bookmarks. "First, we need to fully understand the ritual. The incantations are precise, and there can be no mistakes. If we do this wrong, we could open a portal to… well, anywhere. We need to be certain."

"And how do we get certain?" Patel asked.

"We translate more of the text," Orrington replied. "There are still parts I haven't deciphered. They could hold the key to controlling the portal properly."

Patel sighed. "This is going to take time."

"Time we have," Orrington said, sitting back down. "But we need to move quickly enough to stay ahead of anyone else who might be looking into this."

Patel nodded reluctantly, sitting beside him and picking up one of the translations. "Alright. Let's get to work."

***

The hours passed in silence, the two scientists pouring over the ancient texts, their concentration unbroken. Every once in a while, Orrington would jot down a note or mutter a word of translation under his breath, while Patel scanned the pages for patterns or clues.

Finally, after what felt like an eternity, Patel leaned back, rubbing her eyes. "I think I found something," she said, her voice hoarse from hours of silence.

Orrington looked up from his notes, his eyes sharp. "What is it?"

Patel pointed to a passage on the page. "This part here… it talks about the alignment of celestial bodies. It mentions a specific time and place for the portal to be opened."

Orrington squinted at the text, then nodded. "Yes, that makes sense. The stars need to be aligned properly for the ritual to work. It's all about timing."

Patel frowned. "But this alignment... it hasn't occurred in centuries. According to this, the next time it'll happen is..."

She trailed off, her eyes widening.

Orrington leaned forward. "When?"

"Next week," Patel whispered. "The alignment will happen next week."

Orrington's eyes lit up with a mixture of excitement and dread. "Then we don't have much time."

Patel stared at the text, her mind racing. "If we're going to do this, we need to be ready. We can't afford any mistakes."

Orrington nodded grimly. "Agreed. We'll prepare everything. Gather the materials, run the simulations, double-check every translation."

"And what if something goes wrong?" Patel asked, her voice barely above a whisper.

Orrington's gaze was steady. "Then we'll deal with it. But we won't let fear stop us. This is our only chance."

Patel nodded slowly, her heart pounding in her chest. "Alright. Let's do it."

Chapter 65

Dr. Orrington sat in his dimly lit office, his fingers tapping rhythmically on the polished wooden desk as the weight of recent events settled on him. The clock ticked loudly in the silence, each second stretching on, amplifying the tension that hung in the air. He glanced toward the window, the night outside offering little comfort. Shadows crept along the walls, flickering with the movement of the trees outside, but his mind was on something far more sinister.

A soft knock on the door snapped him out of his thoughts. "Come in," he called, his voice slightly hoarse from hours of silence.

The door creaked open, and Dr. Patel stepped inside. She hesitated in the doorway, her eyes quickly scanning the room before landing on Dr. Orrington. "You look like you haven't slept in days," she remarked, concern lacing her tone as she moved closer. "What's going on?"

Dr. Orrington rubbed his temples before motioning for her to sit. "It's getting worse," he said flatly. "The portals… they're not just theories anymore. They're real. And they're opening up right here, near my home, my business."

Patel's eyes widened, and she sank into the chair across from him. "Wait, what do you mean they're opening near your home? You're not serious."

"I wish I weren't," Orrington muttered, leaning forward. "Two nights ago, I saw it with my own eyes. One of the portals opened in the field across from my house. I heard the same sounds—the low hum, the distortion in the air. And the energy… you could feel it. Like the air itself was bending."

Patel's expression grew more incredulous. "You're saying a portal opened, and you didn't tell anyone? You didn't report it?"

Orrington let out a bitter laugh. "Report it to who? The government? Do you know what they'd do with this information? It's too dangerous. And besides…" He paused, glancing out the window as though expecting something to be lurking in the darkness. "They're keeping me from sharing what I know. Whoever—or whatever—is behind these portals doesn't want the truth getting out."

Patel's voice was sharp. "Wait, they're preventing you from sharing this? Who are they? What's really going on?"

Orrington clenched his fists. "I don't know who exactly. But I do know that every time I try to communicate outside about my findings—emails, phone calls—they get intercepted. It's like they're watching me. Every move I make, every conversation I have, it's like they're one step ahead."

Patel was silent for a moment, processing his words. "And you think these portals are connected to that? That someone's deliberately opening them near you to keep you from sharing what you know?"

Orrington leaned back in his chair, the exhaustion evident in his face. "Not just someone. Something. It's not just about control anymore. These portals... they're more than a scientific curiosity. They're being used as weapons."

Patel blinked, her voice barely above a whisper. "Weapons? How?"

Orrington sat up straighter, his voice steady as he explained. "Remember the infrared cameras we used during the first experiments? They captured the initial portal opening, but when we replayed the audio recordings, we realized something terrifying. The sound frequencies associated with the portal's opening had a profound effect on the surrounding area. Animals, people... anyone in proximity to the sound experienced disorientation, nausea, even hallucinations. It's like the portals are warping reality itself."

Patel frowned, leaning closer. "And you think they're using this as a weapon? Who would do that?"

"Not just who," Orrington said, his gaze intense. "But why. There are entities out there—beings, civilizations, I don't know what exactly—who have figured out how to weaponize this technology. It's no longer just about exploration or discovery. It's about control. And if we don't figure out how to stop it..."

His voice trailed off, but Patel finished his thought for him. "They'll use it against us."

Orrington nodded grimly. "They already are. The portal near my house wasn't an accident. It was a warning. A way of telling me to stay silent, to stop digging into this. But I can't. Not now."

Patel sat back in her chair, shaking her head slowly. "This is too much, Orrington. If they're watching you, if they're threatening you… we need to be careful. This isn't just about science anymore. This is about survival."

"I know," Orrington said, his voice soft but resolute. "But that's exactly why we need to keep going. The more we learn about these portals, the better equipped we'll be to defend ourselves."

Patel stared at him, her brow furrowing in concern. "But how can we fight against something we don't fully understand? We barely have control over the data we've gathered, and now you're telling me there's a coordinated effort to suppress it?"

Orrington stood up, pacing the length of his office. "We can't just sit back and let them dictate what we do. If we don't act now, we'll be caught off guard. These portals—they're not natural phenomena. They're being controlled, and whoever controls them holds immense power."

Patel watched him pace, her own anxiety growing. "But what can we do? We don't even know who's behind this. And if they've already targeted you…"

"We keep researching," Orrington interrupted, stopping in his tracks. "We keep digging. The answers are in these texts, in the data we've gathered. We're close, Patel. Closer than anyone has ever been to understanding how these portals work."

Patel leaned forward, resting her elbows on her knees. "And then what? Let's say we figure out how the portals function. How do we stop them? Or worse, how do we protect ourselves if they use them against us?"

Orrington turned to face her, his eyes filled with a determination that bordered on desperation. "We use their own technology against them. We turn the portals into our weapon."

Patel's eyes widened, her voice trembling slightly. "You're suggesting we open our own portals? Deliberately?"

"Yes," Orrington replied without hesitation. "If we can figure out the exact frequencies, the exact conditions needed to open and control a portal, we could defend ourselves. Maybe even take the fight to them."

Patel stood up, shaking her head. "That's insane. You're talking about playing with forces we don't understand. We could unleash something far worse than what we're already facing."

Orrington took a step closer, his voice low but intense. "And if we do nothing, we're just sitting ducks, waiting for them to strike again. We can't afford to be passive, Patel. Not anymore."

Patel swallowed, her gaze falling to the floor. "I don't like this, Orrington. None of it. But… you're right. If what you're saying is true, then we don't have a choice."

Orrington placed a hand on her shoulder, his expression softening slightly. "I know this isn't easy. But we're the only ones who can stop this. No one else knows what we do."

Patel sighed, nodding slowly. "Alright. I'm with you. But we need to be careful. We can't rush into this."

Orrington gave her a small smile. "Careful is my middle name."

Patel smirked, though her concern was still evident in her eyes. "I'll hold you to that."

As they stood in silence, the weight of their decision hanging heavy in the room, a soft beep echoed from Orrington's desk. He glanced over at his computer screen, where a message flashed ominously.

"They know," Orrington said, his voice tight with fear.

Patel moved quickly to his side. "What is it?"

Orrington stared at the screen, the message clear and chilling: **"STOP NOW, OR YOU WON'T LIKE WHAT HAPPENS NEXT."**

He swallowed hard, his heart pounding in his chest. "They're watching us."

Patel's face drained of color. "What do we do?"

Orrington's jaw clenched as he turned off the monitor. "We keep going. No matter what."

Patel nodded, though the fear in her eyes mirrored his own.

Chapter 66

Dr. Orrington stood at the center of the lab, surrounded by a dizzying array of monitors and advanced equipment. The hum of machinery created a constant background noise, but his focus was on the team gathered around the main table, their expressions skepticism and curiosity.

"Are you telling us that someone is deliberately opening these portals?" Dr. Patel asked, leaning forward. "And that they're doing it to stop you?"

Orrington nodded, his face tight with determination. "Exactly. These organized individuals want to keep me quiet about my findings on nanorobots inhibiting hydrogen. If we don't act quickly, we could lose our chance to counter their plans."

"Nanorobots?" asked a young intern, Sam. "What do they have to do with portals?"

"They're the key to understanding how these portals work," Orrington explained, gesturing to a large monitor displaying complex diagrams. "By manipulating hydrogen, they can create unstable energy fields. These fields can destabilize matter and open portals at will."

"Why would anyone want to inhibit hydrogen?" Patel questioned, her brow furrowing. "Hydrogen is essential for life."

"Precisely," Orrington replied, his voice steady. "Controlling hydrogen means controlling water. Water is vital for survival. If they gain the upper hand in this technology, they could dictate who has access to these essential resources."

"What's your plan?" Patel asked, her tone shifting from doubt to concern.

Orrington took a deep breath, scanning the room. "I've developed a method to weaken and trap these electrical entities. We can use physics to our advantage. By creating a field that disrupts their energy signatures, we can force the portals to close."

"Disrupt their signatures?" Sam echoed. "How do we do that?"

Orrington pointed to a series of equations projected on the screen. "Using these calculations, we can manipulate electromagnetic frequencies. When the portals open, they emit a specific range of frequencies. If we can generate a counter-frequency, we might close them or at least contain whatever is coming through."

"Are you sure this will work?" Patel asked, skepticism creeping back into her voice.

"We won't know until we try," Orrington said, his eyes gleaming with urgency. "But we have to move fast. If they realize we're onto them, we'll be in even deeper trouble."

A silence fell over the group, the weight of Orrington's words sinking in.

"Alright," Patel finally said, breaking the tension. "What do we need to do?"

"First, we need to gather all the data we have on the portals. We can't rely on the government or any official channels for this. They're likely compromised," Orrington instructed, his voice gaining momentum. "We need to work independently and discreetly."

Sam raised his hand hesitantly. "What about security? If they're watching you, what's to stop them from monitoring us?"

"Good point," Patel said, her gaze shifting to Orrington. "We need to ensure that our communications are secure."

"I've got that covered," Orrington replied, his confidence returning. "I've set up a secure channel that only the three of us can access. We can use it to share information without being intercepted."

Patel crossed her arms. "What about the equipment we need? We'll require some specialized tools to generate those frequencies."

"We can use what we have here in the lab," Orrington said, his mind racing. "I've been stockpiling equipment for just this kind of situation. It's not ideal, but it'll have to do for now."

"Let's get to work, then," Patel said, determination lacing her voice. "We need to move quickly before they close in on us."

As they gathered around the table, Sam flipped through a stack of papers. "I found this report on recent portal sightings. There's a pattern. It seems they're focusing on rural areas. This one—" he pointed to a highlighted section— "mentions an uptick in unexplained phenomena right near Dr. Orrington's home."

Orrington leaned in closer. "That's just a few miles from here. If they're opening portals that close, we need to be on high alert."

"What's the next step?" Patel asked, ready to dive into action.

"We'll split up," Orrington said decisively. "I'll stay here and run simulations to find the exact frequencies we need to disrupt the portals. Patel, you work with Sam to gather as much intel as you can. Look for any signs of their activity."

"What about you?" Patel asked, concern creeping back into her voice.

"I'll be fine," Orrington assured her. "I know how to keep a low profile. Just focus on your tasks. We need to cover as much ground as possible."

"Be careful," Patel said, her eyes narrowing. "We can't afford to lose you too."

"I will," he promised, though the weight of his own fears pressed on him. "And if anything feels off, you contact me immediately."

As they split off to their respective tasks, the air was thick with anxiety and urgency. Orrington began typing furiously on his computer, his mind racing through calculations and possibilities.

Orrington's fingers danced across the keyboard as he ran simulations, his heart pounding in his chest. The monitors flickered with data, each line of code bringing him closer to understanding the phenomenon. A notification pinged, pulling him from his concentration.

"What now?" he muttered to himself, glancing at the screen. An alert from his secure channel flashed. It was Patel.

PATEL: *We found something. Meet us at the usual spot.*

Orrington's pulse quickened. He grabbed his notes and headed out of the lab, navigating the familiar corridors as he made his way to the designated meeting point. The air was thick with tension, and he felt the weight of the moment bearing down on him.

He arrived at the warehouse, its silhouette looming against the night sky. Patel and Sam were already waiting outside, their faces pale under the moonlight.

"What's going on?" Orrington asked, concern creeping into his voice.

Patel took a deep breath, her eyes wide with urgency. "We found evidence of their operation. There's a warehouse not far from here, and it looks like they're stockpiling something. We need to investigate."

Orrington frowned. "What kind of evidence?"

"Here," Sam said, handing over a flash drive. "We hacked into their security system. There are video feeds of the portals opening and closing. They're using some kind of technology that we've never seen before."

"Technology?" Orrington repeated, a mixture of fear and intrigue flooding his senses. "What do you mean?"

"Just watch," Patel urged, plugging the flash drive into a portable monitor they had brought along.

As the video began to play, Orrington leaned closer. The footage showed a group of masked individuals standing around a swirling portal, their faces obscured. They were chanting in unison, their hands raised as energy crackled around them.

"This is them," Patel whispered, her eyes fixed on the screen. "They're invoking something."

"What are they invoking?" Orrington asked, his heart racing. "And why here?"

The footage continued, revealing the portal pulsating with energy, the air shimmering around it. Then, without warning, the screen went black.

"Was that intentional?" Sam asked, confused.

"Possibly," Orrington replied, frustration evident in his voice. "But that wasn't all. We need to dig deeper. If they're summoning these portals, we need to find out how they're doing it and stop them."

"Let's head back to the lab and analyze this," Patel suggested. "We need to know everything we can about their operation."

Orrington nodded, determination igniting within him. "Agreed. And we need to move quickly. If they're aware we're onto them…"

"They'll come for us," Sam finished, his voice low.

The trio made their way back to the lab, urgency propelling them forward. As they entered, the familiar hum of machinery greeted them, but the atmosphere was charged with tension.

Orrington immediately went to his workstation, ready to analyze the footage. "We need to extract any data from that video. Every frame could hold crucial information."

"I'll get right on it," Patel said, her fingers flying across the keyboard. "Let's see if we can find any identifiable technology."

Orrington's heart raced as he watched her work. "We can't let them gain any more ground. We have to be the first to figure this out."

As they worked in tandem, Sam hovered nearby, looking increasingly anxious. "What if they come here while we're in the middle of this?"

"They won't," Orrington assured him, though he felt the weight of uncertainty. "We're safe for now. But we need to be ready for anything."

Patel glanced up from the monitor, her expression grave. "Orrington, I found something. There's a pattern in their chanting. It's not random; it's a language."

"Language?" Orrington echoed, intrigued.

"An ancient one, I think," Patel continued, her eyes scanning the screen. "It's a form of invocation, possibly summoning energy to fuel the portals."

"Can we decipher it?" Sam asked, leaning in closer.

"I'm working on it," Patel replied, her brow furrowed in concentration. "But it might take some time."

Orrington felt a sense of urgency rise within him. "We can't afford to waste time. If they're using this language to control."

Chapter 67

The lab buzzed with energy as the researchers gathered around a series of monitors, each displaying complex waveforms and frequencies. Dr. Orrington stood at the front, his brow furrowed in concentration as he addressed the group.

"Listen up, everyone," he said, raising his voice to be heard over the low hum of equipment. "We're at a critical juncture here. Our experiments with sound frequencies, particularly those around 192 GHz, could be the key to opening and closing portals effectively."

Dr. Patel, who had been reviewing the data, looked up, intrigued. "You're saying that sound at that frequency can actually open portals?"

Orrington nodded, his enthusiasm palpable. "Exactly. It's not just about the frequency; it's about how we can manipulate it. In Season Four, Episode Ten, we saw firsthand the power of sound. With the right tools and methods, we can replicate that."

Sam, the young intern, furrowed his brow. "What kind of tools do we need? Do we have them here?"

Orrington pointed toward the equipment lined up against the wall. "We've got some devices that can generate those frequencies, but we'll need to fine-tune them. We also need to ensure our safety measures are in place. If these entities respond to the sound, we don't know what could come through."

"Right," Patel said, jotting down notes. "But what if we attract more than we can handle? We've already seen the footage of the portals opening. We don't know what's on the other side."

"That's why we have to be careful," Orrington replied, pacing the floor. "We can't just go blasting frequencies without a plan. We need to observe and understand what we're dealing with first."

Sam's eyes widened. "So, are we going to use infrared cameras to monitor the portals? You mentioned that infrared could help us see these entities."

"Exactly," Orrington confirmed. "We'll set up the cameras around the lab and any potential portal sites. It's crucial we document everything that happens, especially if we're opening new ones."

Patel looked up from her notes, her expression serious. "And if we see something? What's our protocol?"

"First, we observe," Orrington instructed. "If we encounter anything dangerous, we retreat to the safe zone. Our priority is data collection without putting anyone at risk."

Sam nodded slowly. "So, we need to establish a command center where we can monitor everything from a safe distance?"

"Exactly," Orrington said, impressed. "Let's set it up in the back room. We can have multiple screens running the infrared feeds and the frequency outputs. Patel, you'll lead that effort."

"Got it," Patel replied, already gathering her materials. "What about you, Dr. Orrington?"

"I'll focus on calibrating the frequency generators," he said, moving toward the equipment. "We need to be precise. A single miscalculation could have catastrophic consequences."

As Orrington began adjusting the dials on the frequency generators, Patel and Sam set up the command center in the back room. Patel linked the monitors together, checking each feed from the infrared cameras.

"Do you think we'll really see anything?" Sam asked, his voice tinged with excitement and anxiety.

Patel shrugged, a determined smile on her face. "With our luck? Probably. But the real question is: what happens if we do?"

Orrington chimed in from the other room, "If we see anything, remember to keep calm. Our goal is to collect data, not to engage. We're not equipped for a confrontation."

Sam took a deep breath. "Okay, I get it. I just hope we're ready for whatever might come through."

Patel turned to him, her expression softening. "We'll be fine. We've prepared for this. We have each other's backs."

As Orrington continued to calibrate the equipment, he felt a growing sense of urgency. He checked the time on his watch and turned back to the two. "Are we ready?"

"Almost," Patel replied. "Just a few more adjustments on the camera feeds. How's the frequency calibration going?"

"I'm almost done," Orrington said, twisting a knob. "Just a few more tweaks, and we'll be ready to test."

"Testing sounds exciting," Sam said, a grin breaking out on his face. "What if we really can open a portal?"

"We need to be prepared for anything," Orrington reminded him, though he couldn't help but share in Sam's enthusiasm. "This could be a groundbreaking moment in our understanding of these phenomena."

"Okay, I'm ready to see what we can do," Patel said, checking the final connections on the monitors. "Let's make history."

Orrington straightened up, a determined glint in his eyes. "Alright, everyone. Let's start with the frequency test. We'll begin at a lower range and gradually increase to 192 GHz."

As Orrington adjusted the settings, the air in the lab seemed to crackle with anticipation. "Here we go," he announced, pressing a button to initiate the test.

The sound filled the room, a low hum that gradually increased in intensity. The monitors flickered as the cameras began to pick up unusual readings.

"Infrared cameras are active," Patel reported, her eyes glued to the screens. "I'm not seeing anything yet."

"Stay focused," Orrington urged. "We'll keep ramping up the frequency."

As the sound escalated, the atmosphere shifted. The air thickened, and an electric charge filled the room. The monitors began to show strange distortions.

"Look!" Sam shouted, pointing at one of the screens. "There's something—"

Suddenly, the monitor flickered wildly, and a shadowy figure appeared in the infrared feed. The room fell silent, tension tightening around them.

"What is that?" Patel whispered, her eyes widening.

"I don't know," Orrington admitted, his heart racing. "But we need to stay calm and keep observing."

The figure on the screen shifted, its outline unclear but undeniably present. It seemed to pulse with energy, flickering in and out of visibility.

"Are we sure this isn't just a glitch?" Sam asked, trying to convince himself.

Orrington shook his head. "It's too consistent to be a glitch. Keep recording, Patel. We need this data."

The figure began to expand and contract, almost as if it were reacting to the sound waves. Orrington felt a chill run down his spine.

"What if it's trying to communicate?" Sam suggested, his voice barely above a whisper.

"Let's not jump to conclusions," Patel cautioned. "We need to analyze this scientifically, not emotionally."

"Agreed," Orrington said, focusing on the readings. "Let's keep increasing the frequency and see how it reacts."

As they continued to adjust the equipment, the figure on the screen became more defined. It was no longer just a shadow; it seemed to take on shape and form.

"Is it—? It looks like it's… dancing?" Sam exclaimed, his eyes wide with disbelief.

"Dancing? That's a stretch," Patel replied skeptically, though she couldn't deny the strange movements on the screen. "It's definitely reacting to the sound, but we can't assign human traits to it."

Orrington was captivated. "It's almost as if it's a response to the frequency modulation. Let's experiment with different sound patterns and see if we can get a clearer reaction."

As Orrington worked to modify the sound waves, Patel leaned closer to the monitor. "I can't believe we're actually witnessing this. It's incredible."

Just then, the figure surged forward, pulsing with energy, and the monitor emitted a loud crackle.

"Shut it down! Shut it down!" Orrington shouted, panic rising in his chest. "We can't risk an overload!"

Patel quickly pressed buttons, frantically cutting the sound. The figure flickered violently before disappearing completely.

"Did we lose it?" Sam asked, breathless.

"I think so," Orrington replied, his heart still racing. "But we got the data. Let's analyze what we just witnessed."

As they calmed down, Patel glanced over the readings. "That was surreal. I've never seen anything like it."

"Neither have I," Orrington said, shaking his head in disbelief. "But we need to make sure we can replicate this phenomenon without causing harm."

"What's next?" Sam asked, his excitement barely contained.

"We analyze the data, refine our frequencies, and prepare for another test," Orrington said, a determined glint in his eyes. "But we have to be cautious. The last thing we need is to attract unwanted attention."

Patel nodded, her expression serious. "We need to consider what we're dealing with. If there are entities coming through portals, we must protect ourselves."

"I agree," Sam said. "We should set up some defenses in case things get out of hand."

"Good thinking," Orrington said, his mind already racing with possibilities. "Let's formulate a plan for security while we analyze the data. This could change everything we know about interdimensional travel."

As they settled into the analysis phase, the atmosphere in the lab shifted from apprehension to excitement. They were on the brink of something extraordinary, and each of them felt the weight of their mission. With careful planning and teamwork, they would unlock the secrets of the portals—and perhaps even find a way to control them.

Chapter 68

The conference room buzzed with tension as scientists huddled around a large table strewn with charts, graphs, and reports. Dr. Orrington stood at the front, pointing to a series of data on a projection screen.

"Everyone, thank you for coming on such short notice," he began, his voice steady but urgent. "We're facing unprecedented challenges with these interterrestrial phenomena, and we need to address them now."

Dr. Patel, seated at the table, frowned as she scrutinized the data. "The signals we've been detecting are becoming increasingly potent. They're not just random noises; they seem to have a pattern."

"Exactly," Orrington replied, tapping the screen to highlight a chart that showed escalating signal strength. "These signals appear to correspond with significant fluctuations in our environment, particularly in areas where we've recorded portal activity."

Dr. Thomas, an astrophysicist, interjected, "What concerns me is their potential impact on organic life. If these signals can interfere with biological systems, we could be looking at serious consequences."

"Are we sure these signals are even meant for us?" Sam, a junior scientist, asked, leaning forward in his seat. "They could be a form of communication between their own entities."

Orrington nodded thoughtfully. "That's a valid point, Sam. But whether they're intended for us or not, the effects are real. We've already noted anomalies in local wildlife, not to mention the disturbances in our agricultural areas."

"Let's not forget the reports from farmers," Dr. Patel added. "Cattle are exhibiting unusual behavior. They've been restless, and some have even died under strange circumstances."

A heavy silence fell over the room as everyone absorbed the weight of her words. Dr. Thomas rubbed his temples. "We need a comprehensive study. If these signals are affecting life on Earth, we must act before it escalates."

"What kind of study?" Sam asked, his curiosity piqued. "Are we talking about a field investigation or lab experiments?"

Dr. Patel leaned back in her chair, arms crossed. "Both. We need to analyze the signals in controlled environments while also monitoring their effects in the field. Perhaps we can set up observation points in the most affected areas."

Orrington's eyes sparkled with determination. "That's the right approach. We can gather data on both fronts. But we must also consider safety protocols. If the signals are causing these disturbances, we need to ensure our team is protected."

"What do you propose?" Dr. Thomas asked, shifting his focus back to Orrington.

"First, we enhance our monitoring systems with real-time data analysis. We can deploy drones equipped with sensors to track these signals from multiple angles," Orrington explained, pacing as he spoke. "Next, we establish teams to work with local farmers. We need to gather firsthand accounts of any strange occurrences."

"Are we prepared for potential confrontations?" Sam asked hesitantly. "If these signals are indeed from interterrestrial entities, we might encounter more than just electromagnctic interference."

Dr. Patel nodded in agreement. "It's crucial we stay vigilant. We have no idea what we might be dealing with if we come face-to-face with these phenomena."

Orrington leaned forward, his expression serious. "I understand the risks, but we have to approach this scientifically. We cannot let fear dictate our actions. Knowledge is our best defense."

Dr. Thomas glanced at the charts again. "So, what's our timeline for this investigation? We can't afford to waste time."

"We need to start immediately," Orrington said decisively. "We'll break into teams: one focusing on fieldwork, the other on data analysis. Sam, you'll lead the data analysis team alongside Dr. Patel. Gather every piece of information we have on the signals."

"Understood," Sam replied, energized by the responsibility.

"And Dr. Thomas," Orrington continued, "you'll coordinate the field teams. Make sure they're equipped with the necessary safety gear and communication devices. We need to maintain contact at all times."

Dr. Thomas nodded, scribbling down notes. "I'll get a list of what we need ready. We should also consider setting up emergency protocols in case of unexpected encounters."

"Good thinking," Orrington praised. "Let's make sure we're prepared for anything."

As the discussion continued, the atmosphere in the room shifted from concern to determination. Each scientist began to feel the weight of their responsibility and the urgency of the situation.

"Before we break, let's discuss our communication strategy," Patel suggested. "We need to ensure all teams are aligned on our findings and strategies as we gather data."

"Absolutely," Orrington agreed. "Regular updates will be crucial. I want each team to report their findings daily, whether it's in the field or in the lab."

As the meeting concluded, the scientists felt a renewed sense of purpose. They were no longer just researchers; they were pioneers on the frontlines of an extraordinary phenomenon that could reshape their understanding of life on Earth.

"Let's move quickly and stay safe," Orrington reminded them as they began to disperse. "We're about to uncover truths that could change everything."

"Dr. Orrington," Sam called out as he was packing up his materials. "Do you really think these signals are connected to the portals? I mean, can we make that leap yet?"

Orrington paused, considering the question. "The data suggests a correlation, but we need more evidence. That's why our investigations are crucial. Until we understand what's truly happening, we can't draw definitive conclusions."

"Right," Sam said thoughtfully. "It just feels like we're on the brink of something huge."

Dr. Patel overheard their conversation and chimed in. "We are. But let's not lose sight of the potential dangers involved. This isn't just science; it's our responsibility to ensure the safety of our world."

"Agreed," Orrington said, his gaze sweeping across the room. "We're stepping into uncharted territory. Let's tread carefully but boldly."

As the scientists began to organize themselves for the work ahead, Orrington felt excitement and trepidation. They were embarking on a journey that would test their skills, their courage, and their understanding of the very fabric of reality.

In the days that followed, teams split off into their designated roles, each scientist focused on their task. Sam and Dr. Patel delved into the data, analyzing the intricate patterns of the signals and searching for connections to the environmental anomalies they had witnessed.

"Look at this," Sam said, pointing at the screen. "There's a spike in signal frequency that coincides with an increase in strange animal behavior."

Dr. Patel leaned closer, her eyes narrowing as she examined the data. "It's almost like there's a trigger point. We need to correlate these signals with the reports from the farmers. It might give us a clearer picture of what's happening."

As they worked late into the night, the atmosphere in the lab grew more intense. They were piecing together a puzzle that held implications beyond their current understanding.

Meanwhile, Dr. Thomas led the field teams, driving to various agricultural sites to interview farmers and document any unusual occurrences. The tension was palpable as they approached their first stop.

"Remember, we're here to listen and observe," he reminded his team. "We need to gather as much information as possible without raising alarm."

The team arrived at the farm, where the owner, Mr. Jensen, awaited them. He looked worn and anxious, glancing nervously at the fields.

"Thanks for coming," he said, his voice low. "I've been worried sick about my cattle."

"What exactly have you been experiencing?" Dr. Thomas asked, pulling out his notebook.

Mr. Jensen sighed heavily. "They've been restless for weeks. Some even started acting... strange. It's like they sense something is wrong."

"Have you noticed any unusual sounds or changes in the environment?" Dr. Thomas inquired, scribbling down notes.

"Yeah, that's just it," Mr. Jensen replied. "I've heard these weird noises at night—like a low hum. It's been keeping me awake."

The team exchanged glances, their minds racing with possibilities. "And has anything happened to your livestock?" Dr. Thomas pressed.

"Three of my cows just... collapsed," Mr. Jensen said, shaking his head in disbelief. "One of them had to be euthanized. The vet couldn't figure out what was wrong."

"That's alarming," Dr. Thomas said, taking a deep breath. "We're conducting a study on these phenomena, and your reports are crucial. If you notice anything else, please contact us immediately."

"I will," Mr. Jensen assured him, his eyes wide with concern. "I just want to protect my animals. I don't want to lose any more."

As they finished the interview, Dr. Thomas felt the weight of their mission. They were racing against time to understand these signals before it was too late.

Back in the lab, Sam and Dr. Patel continued their analysis, sorting through the data they had collected. Sam's eyes lit up as he pointed to a significant trend on the screen.

"Dr. Patel, look at this! The frequency patterns are almost identical to the fluctuations we recorded during the last significant portal opening."

Dr. Patel leaned in closer, excitement sparking in her eyes. "You're right! This could mean the signals are a precursor to portal activity. We need to present this data to Dr. Orrington immediately."

"Let's go," Sam said, rushing to gather their findings.

As they headed toward Dr. Orrington's office, the weight of their discovery hung in the air. They had unearthed something that could change the course of their investigation—and perhaps their understanding of the entire phenomenon.

When they arrived, they found Dr. Orrington deep in conversation with Dr. Thomas, who was sharing.

Chapter 69

"Understanding and defending against these signals is a daunting challenge," Dr. Orrington stated, his voice steady and commanding as he faced the assembled group of scientists in his study.

The room was dimly lit, lined with bookshelves filled with texts that spanned centuries. The atmosphere was thick with anticipation, the air charged as the team awaited the next steps.

Dr. Patel leaned forward, her brow furrowed with concern. "What are our options, Dr. Orrington? With these signals increasing in potency, we need a solid plan of action."

Dr. Orrington rubbed his chin thoughtfully. "I agree. First, we need to gather as much data as possible. This requires us to work both in the field and in the lab simultaneously. I want each team to report daily on their findings."

Dr. Thomas, always eager for action, chimed in. "I can head up the field team. We should check the most affected areas first and gather information on any environmental changes."

"Good idea, Thomas," Dr. Orrington replied, nodding approvingly. "Make sure to keep in contact with the farmers. Their observations are invaluable. We can't overlook the human element in this situation."

Sam, who had been silently processing the information, raised his hand. "What about the equipment we'll need? If these signals can disrupt our technology, we should invest in protective gear for our instruments."

"That's essential," Dr. Patel added. "We need to ensure our monitoring systems can withstand any interference we encounter in the field. Perhaps we should look into shielding technologies."

"Let's consult with the engineering team," Dr. Orrington suggested. "They might have insights into creating protective measures for our equipment."

As the conversation continued, a sense of urgency enveloped the group. Dr. Orrington felt the weight of their mission pressing down on him, and he knew they had to act swiftly. "Our perception of reality is constantly evolving. The discoveries we've made challenge our understanding and require us to rethink our approach. We must act with urgency to address these phenomena and protect our world."

"Do you think the public needs to be informed?" Sam asked, his voice laced with concern. "I mean, if these signals are affecting organic life, shouldn't we be transparent?"

"Transparency is vital," Dr. Orrington replied, "but we must be cautious. We don't want to incite panic without solid evidence. Let's focus on our research first. Once we have concrete data, we can present our findings responsibly."

Dr. Patel nodded. "We should draft a preliminary report that outlines our initial findings and our action plan. It will help keep everyone on the same page."

"Let's do it," Dr. Thomas said, enthusiasm in his voice. "We can start compiling data from both the field and the lab right away. I'll assemble the field team and meet with the farmers again. I want to ensure we don't miss any crucial information."

As the team began to break up, Dr. Orrington called out, "Before we go, I want to stress the importance of safety. Whatever we encounter, we must remain vigilant and follow our protocols. We're stepping into uncharted territory."

"Understood, Dr. Orrington," Sam replied, his eyes bright with determination. "We'll be careful."

Once everyone had left, Dr. Orrington sat alone in his study, the weight of the world on his shoulders. He stared at the flickering monitor displaying the data they had collected, contemplating the challenges ahead. The stakes were higher than ever, and he was determined to guide his team through the storm.

The following day, Dr. Thomas gathered his field team in the lab, the air buzzing with anticipation. "Alright, everyone, listen up! We've got reports of unusual activity at two farms. I want each of you to be prepared for anything. We're going to start by interviewing the farmers, taking notes on any changes they've observed, and collecting samples if necessary."

"Are we expecting any kind of interference?" one of the team members, Lisa, asked, her voice tinged with worry.

"That's a possibility," Dr. Thomas replied. "We need to keep our equipment in working order. Ensure everything is calibrated correctly before we head out. I'll lead the first visit; the rest of you can split up into smaller teams to cover more ground."

"Sounds like a plan," Lisa said, her resolve strengthening. "Let's do this."

As they loaded the vchicles with equipment, the team couldn't shake the feeling that they were on the brink of something monumental. Dr. Thomas felt excitement and dread; they were venturing into the unknown, and the stakes were high.

Meanwhile, in the lab, Sam and Dr. Patel were working tirelessly to analyze the signals. "I'm convinced there's a connection between the signals and the portal activity," Sam said, his eyes glued to the screen. "Look at this pattern. Every time we detect a spike, there's a corresponding report of strange occurrences."

Dr. Patel leaned closer, examining the data closely. "You're right. It's almost as if these signals are influencing the environment. We should cross-reference these findings with the historical data on portal openings."

Sam nodded vigorously. "Let's compile everything we have. We need to present this to Dr. Orrington as soon as possible."

The two worked in tandem, their fingers flying over the keyboards as they sorted through mountains of data, correlating the signals with environmental changes. The excitement in the lab was palpable, and the energy fueled their determination.

"Got it!" Sam exclaimed after several minutes. "Look at this correlation! Each major spike in signal strength aligns with documented portal openings in this region. We have solid evidence here!"

"Let's prepare a report and get it to Dr. Orrington before he returns from the field," Dr. Patel suggested. "This is crucial information that could change our approach."

Meanwhile, Dr. Thomas's field team arrived at the first farm, a sprawling expanse of farmland. The sun beat down as they approached the farmer, Mrs. Carter, who stood nervously at the edge of her field.

"Thank you for meeting with us, Mrs. Carter," Dr. Thomas said, introducing his team. "We're here to discuss the unusual activities you've reported."

"Thank you for coming," she replied, wringing her hands. "I've been worried about my crops. They're not growing like they used to, and some of the plants have died suddenly."

Dr. Thomas took out his notebook. "Can you describe what you've noticed? Any strange sounds or changes in the weather?"

Mrs. Carter nodded, glancing around as if the ground might betray her. "There's been this low hum at night. It's unlike anything I've ever heard. And then, just last week, I found three of my plants completely wilted, as if they'd been scorched."

"Did you notice any changes before that?" Dr. Thomas probed.

"Only the hum," she answered. "But it's not just the plants. My chickens have been acting strangely, too. They're skittish, and some won't leave their coop."

"Thank you for sharing this information," Dr. Thomas said. "It's crucial for our research. We'll be collecting samples and monitoring the area for any further signs."

As they set up their equipment to gather data, Lisa stepped forward. "Mrs. Carter, have you heard anything about other farms experiencing similar issues?"

"I have," she said, her voice dropping. "I heard from Mr. Jensen down the road. He's been having problems with his cattle, and I believe he lost one recently."

"Did he mention anything specific about the sounds or strange occurrences?" Lisa asked, her curiosity piqued.

"Yes, he said he heard a humming sound too," Mrs. Carter replied. "I thought it was just my imagination."

Dr. Thomas exchanged a glance with Lisa. "We need to connect with Mr. Jensen next. If there's a pattern, we might be able to determine the cause of these disturbances."

As they finished collecting samples, Dr. Thomas felt a sense of urgency build within him. "Alright, team, let's pack up and head to Mr. Jensen's. We need to gather as much information as we can."

The team quickly packed their equipment, their minds racing with the possibilities of what they might discover.

As they arrived at Mr. Jensen's farm, the atmosphere shifted. The sun hung low in the sky, casting eerie shadows across the fields. Dr. Thomas could feel the weight of the moment as he approached the farmer, who looked visibly shaken.

"Thank you for meeting with us again, Mr. Jensen," Dr. Thomas said, trying to gauge the man's state of mind. "We're here to gather more information about the issues you've been experiencing."

Mr. Jensen's eyes darted around, anxiety evident on his face. "I'm glad you came. It's getting worse. Just last night, I heard the hum again, and I thought I saw something moving out in the fields—something… unnatural."

"What did you see?" Lisa asked, her tone serious.

"I don't know how to explain it," he replied, rubbing his hands together. "It was like a shadow moving against the light. I thought I was imagining it until my cows started acting up again. It was as if they sensed something was wrong."

Dr. Thomas nodded, taking notes. "This is important information. We need to monitor the area closely.

Have you noticed any other changes—maybe in the soil or water?"

"Yeah, the soil feels… different," Mr. Jensen said, kneeling to scoop up a handful. "It's drier than usual, and I've had to water my crops more often. It's not normal for this time of year."

"Let's collect soil samples as well," Dr. Thomas said.

Chapter 70

Dr. Orrington sat at his desk, the soft glow of the lamp casting shadows across the walls of his study. The tension in the room was palpable as he addressed the camera, his gaze unwavering.

"In Season Two, Episode Seven, researchers observed a highly charged river of water flowing near the planetary orb underground. This revelation aligns with my confidence that interdimensional species, or E.T.s, harness water in ways akin to a supercomputer." He leaned in closer, emphasizing his words. "Understanding this phenomenon is crucial."

A group of scientists surrounded a large monitor displaying footage of the charged river. The flickering images captured their collective attention, and excitement buzzed in the air. Dr. Patel, a physicist, pointed at the swirling mass of energy on the screen, her eyes bright with curiosity.

"Look at how the water interacts with the energy fields! It's almost as if it's alive," Dr. Patel exclaimed, her voice laced with excitement.

Sam, a junior researcher with a skeptical streak, leaned closer, his brow furrowing. "Alive? That's a strong word. Are we sure this isn't just a natural phenomenon?"

Dr. Thomas, the head of the research team, shook his head, his expression serious. "Natural or not, we need to consider the implications. If E.T.s are indeed utilizing this energy, we have to understand their methods."

Lisa, another team member, chimed in as she scrolled through the data on her tablet. "The readings show fluctuations that correlate with the water flow. It's as if they're tapping into the river's energy to communicate or transmit information."

"And what about the minerals found in the water? Could they be enhancing the conductivity?" Dr. Patel added, her curiosity piqued.

"If that's the case, we need to analyze the composition immediately," Sam interjected. "The more we know, the better we can prepare."

Just then, Dr. Orrington entered the lab, his presence commanding. He quickly surveyed the scene, sensing the urgency among his team. "What's the latest?"

Dr. Patel gestured to the monitor. "We've captured footage of the charged river. The interaction with the energy fields is unlike anything we've seen."

"Excellent. But we need to move fast," Dr. Orrington replied, his voice firm. "I want a full analysis of that water. Every mineral, every trace element could hold the key to understanding how these species operate."

"I can coordinate with the geochemistry lab to expedite the analysis," Lisa volunteered, already typing notes into her tablet.

"I'll prepare a team to head to the site," Dr. Thomas said, determination in his tone. "We need to gather samples and document everything."

Dr. Orrington nodded, satisfied with the plan. "Let's get to work. Time is of the essence."

The scientists gathered around a large table, data scattered before them. Dr. Orrington stood at the front, addressing the team. "We have a unique opportunity here. The charged river could be a communication conduit for interdimensional species. We need to devise a strategy to study it without disrupting its natural state."

"Agreed," Dr. Patel said. "But how do we approach this without alerting them? We don't know how they might react."

"Stealth is key," Sam suggested. "We should use drones to collect samples from a distance."

"Drones might work, but we must ensure they are equipped to handle potential energy fluctuations," Dr. Thomas added, his brow furrowed in thought.

"What about using sound waves?" Lisa proposed. "We could send out low-frequency signals to interact with the energy without disturbing the river itself."

Dr. Orrington nodded appreciatively. "That's a solid idea, Lisa. Let's explore the sound wave concept further. But we'll need to conduct tests to determine the best frequencies to use."

"I can run simulations on that," Sam said, his enthusiasm growing. "If we can find the right parameters, we might be able to establish a baseline for our interactions."

Dr. Patel interjected, "And what about the potential risks? We need to be prepared for any unforeseen consequences."

Dr. Orrington raised a hand, silencing the room. "We must proceed with caution. I want a thorough risk assessment before we begin any experimental work."

"I'll draft a protocol for our research plan," Lisa offered, her fingers flying over her tablet as she noted down the details.

"Excellent. Let's reconvene in two days to review our findings and next steps," Dr. Orrington concluded. The team nodded, their expressions excitement and concern.

The atmosphere was tense as the team reconvened. Dr. Orrington leaned against the table, reviewing the data on the screen. "What have we learned?"

Lisa looked up from her tablet, her voice steady. "The simulations indicate that low-frequency sound waves between 10 to 20 Hz could resonate with the energy field of the charged river."

Dr. Patel chimed in, "And we're also seeing signs of mineral conductivity enhancing the energy's intensity. If we can harness that, we might amplify our signals."

Sam leaned in, excitement bubbling in his voice. "This could be groundbreaking! If we can communicate effectively, we might gain insights into their technology and intentions."

Dr. Thomas crossed his arms, skepticism evident. "But we have to remember the risks. We're not just poking at a scientific mystery; we're potentially inviting a response from an unknown entity."

"What if they don't respond?" Lisa asked, her brow furrowing. "What if they're not even aware of our presence?"

Dr. Orrington considered this. "It's a possibility. But the chance of disrupting their environment is real, and we can't underestimate their capacity for reaction."

"I'll ensure we have a solid contingency plan," Dr. Patel said. "We should prepare for both peaceful and hostile outcomes."

"I'll set up a protocol for extraction and evacuation, just in case," Sam added, his mind racing with possibilities.

"Good. Now, let's discuss our next steps," Dr. Orrington said, the weight of responsibility evident in his tone.

The team gathered around a table strewn with maps and data. Dr. Orrington pointed at a section of the map. "This is where the charged river is located. We'll set up our monitoring station here and establish a perimeter to ensure safety."

Dr. Patel nodded, studying the map. "We should deploy our drones from this vantage point. It gives us a clear line of sight and minimizes our exposure."

Sam raised his hand, a hint of uncertainty in his voice. "What if the energy levels spike while we're out there? Are we sure the drones can handle that?"

"Good point," Dr. Thomas said, rubbing his chin thoughtfully. "We need to account for potential fluctuations. I recommend we have backup drones on standby."

"And what about our communication? If something goes wrong, we need a quick way to alert the team," Lisa suggested.

"I can set up a direct line to the monitoring station," Dr. Orrington replied. "Let's ensure we have multiple channels of communication."

As the team continued to discuss logistics, the atmosphere shifted from apprehension to determination. They knew they were on the brink of something monumental, and each decision carried the weight of that reality.

The lab was dimly lit, the hum of equipment the only sound as the team prepared for their expedition. Dr. Orrington stood at the front, rallying the team. "Tonight, we stand at the precipice of discovery. What we uncover could change everything we know about interdimensional life and their interactions with our world."

"Let's not forget, we're doing this for the future," Dr. Patel added, her eyes shining with purpose.

Sam grinned, the excitement palpable. "And if we succeed, we'll be pioneers in a field no one has dared to explore."

Dr. Thomas glanced around the room, his demeanor serious. "Let's ensure we're vigilant. Our safety is paramount, and the last thing we want is to provoke something we can't control."

The team nodded, a shared understanding passing among them. They were venturing into the unknown, but together, they would face whatever lay ahead.

The countdown clock ticked down as they prepared to launch the drones. Lisa sat at the control panel, her fingers poised over the keyboard. "Ready when you are."

Dr. Orrington took a deep breath, steadying himself. "Initiate launch sequence."

As the drones soared into the night sky, the tension was palpable. Each member of the team held their breath, hoping for success.

The screen lit up with data from the drones as they approached the charged river. The team watched in awe, the energy fluctuations dancing before their eyes.

"Look at that!" Sam exclaimed, pointing at the screen. "The energy levels are increasing."

"Prepare to send out the sound waves," Dr. Orrington instructed, his voice steady. "Let's see if we can establish a connection."

Lisa activated the sound transmission, her heart racing. "Sending now."

The team waited in suspense, eyes glued to the monitors. Suddenly, a pulse of energy flickered on the screen, followed by a series of rapid fluctuations.

"What's happening?" Dr. Patel asked, her voice tinged with concern.

"Looks like a response," Sam said, his eyes wide. "The energy is reacting to our sound waves!"

Dr. Orrington leaned closer to the screen, his focus unwavering. "Keep monitoring. We need to decipher their response."

Suddenly, the monitors flickered, and a wave of energy surged, momentarily overwhelming the system. Alarms blared, and the room erupted into chaos.

"Shut it down! Shut it down!" Dr. Thomas shouted, scrambling to regain control.

Lisa frantically typed at her keyboard, trying to stabilize the system. "I can't! The energy levels are too high.

Chapter 71

The camera panned over a glowing, charged river flowing beneath the surface. The water shimmered with an unnatural energy, casting an otherworldly light in the darkness.

Dr. Orrington stood at the riverbank, his gaze fixed on the luminescent water. He turned to his team, who were gathered around him, their expressions awe and concern.

"Water can store data, have memory, and send signals," he said, his voice steady yet filled with urgency. "This has been scientifically validated by Nobel Prize winner Professor Luc Montagnier. We need to understand how this river operates."

Dr. Patel, a physicist in the group, leaned closer to the river's edge, mesmerized. "It's beautiful, but how can something so simple as water hold such complex properties?"

Dr. Thomas, the head of the research team, adjusted his glasses, his brow furrowing. "It's not just beautiful. It's dangerous if we don't approach it with caution. We don't know what we're dealing with."

Lisa, a junior researcher, pulled out her tablet, quickly scrolling through data. "We have to consider the implications. If water can transmit signals, what kind of information is being communicated here? And who is receiving it?"

"Exactly," Dr. Orrington agreed, crossing his arms as he studied the river. "If interdimensional beings are using this river as a conduit, we could be standing on the brink of a monumental discovery."

Sam, a junior researcher known for his skepticism, scoffed lightly. "Or we could be making a huge mistake. We're assuming a lot based on pretty lights and theories. What if it's just a natural phenomenon?"

Dr. Patel shot Sam a sharp look. "You can't deny the research supporting the memory of water. We need to explore this further, not dismiss it."

Dr. Orrington nodded in agreement. "Let's not forget the potential consequences. We need a thorough analysis. Sam, you and Lisa will take samples from the river. Be careful. Stay within the safety parameters."

"Understood," Lisa replied, her determination palpable. "We'll gather what we can without disturbing the flow."

Dr. Thomas interjected, "Make sure to document everything. The last thing we want is to overlook crucial data."

As they prepared to collect samples, the team's excitement was palpable, but so was the tension in the air. Dr. Orrington glanced at his watch, realizing they were running out of time.

"We need to work quickly," he said. "The energy levels fluctuate, and we may only have a short window to gather information."

Sam looked at the river, then back at Dr. Orrington. "What's our plan if we encounter something unusual? We can't just assume everything will go smoothly."

Dr. Orrington took a deep breath, meeting Sam's gaze. "We'll have contingency measures in place. If anything goes wrong, we'll retreat immediately. Our safety is paramount."

The team set to work, carefully collecting water samples and recording data. Lisa crouched by the river, her hands steady as she filled a vial with the shimmering liquid.

"This is incredible," she said, looking up at Sam. "Can you believe this is happening?"

Sam shrugged, still wary. "It's impressive, sure. But we need to keep our heads in the game. We can't let excitement cloud our judgment."

Dr. Patel joined them, holding her own sample container. "You're right to be cautious, Sam. But look at this. The energy signature from the water samples we've collected already suggests something is happening beneath the surface."

As they continued collecting samples, a low hum resonated through the air. The team exchanged glances, uncertainty creeping in.

"Did you hear that?" Lisa asked, her voice barely above a whisper.

Dr. Orrington straightened, his eyes scanning the surroundings. "Yes, I did. Stay alert."

The humming grew louder, reverberating through the ground. Sam's eyes widened as he took a step back. "What do you think it is?"

"Could be the energy from the river," Dr. Patel speculated, her expression focused. "We should analyze the frequencies."

"Let's move away from the river," Dr. Thomas suggested, glancing around nervously. "We don't want to risk getting too close to whatever that is."

They retreated to a safer distance, gathering near the trees lining the riverbank. The hum intensified, vibrating through the air and sending shivers down their spines.

"I've never heard anything like this," Sam said, his skepticism fading. "What if it's a warning?"

Dr. Orrington frowned, his eyes narrowing as he concentrated on the sound. "A warning? From whom?"

"I don't know," Sam replied. "But we should consider the possibility that we're not alone here."

Dr. Patel shook her head, dismissing Sam's concerns. "This is science, not fiction. We're here to gather data, not to jump to conclusions."

"Let's focus on the task at hand," Dr. Orrington interjected, trying to regain control of the situation. "We need to collect more data and analyze these frequencies before drawing any conclusions."

The humming persisted, pulsating rhythmically as the team worked to set up their equipment. They positioned microphones and sensors near the riverbank, hoping to capture the strange energy resonating from the water.

"Okay, let's see if we can isolate the frequency," Lisa said, her fingers flying over the controls of the monitoring device. "I'll adjust the settings to capture the data."

The monitor lit up, displaying graphs and waveforms as Lisa adjusted the settings. "There it is! The frequency is fluctuating."

Dr. Orrington leaned closer, his excitement growing. "Can we amplify it? We need to understand what's causing these changes."

"I'll try," Lisa replied, concentrating on the controls. "Just a moment…"

As she worked, the humming transformed into a series of distinct tones, each one resonating with the charged river. The atmosphere in the group shifted, anticipation and apprehension swirling among them.

"Listen to that!" Dr. Patel exclaimed, her eyes wide. "It's like the river is communicating with us."

Sam's skepticism returned. "Or it could be a warning. We have no idea what we're messing with."

"Now's not the time to back down," Dr. Orrington urged, his voice steady. "If this is a form of communication, we have to engage with it. We might be able to learn something significant."

"What if it's not friendly?" Sam retorted. "We don't know what these signals mean. We could be inviting trouble."

"Look, we're here for a reason," Dr. Patel argued. "Science demands that we explore the unknown. We can't let fear dictate our actions."

Dr. Thomas interjected, "We need to establish a protocol for interaction. If we're going to engage, we should have a plan."

"Agreed," Dr. Orrington said, nodding. "Let's develop a framework for how we'll respond to the signals."

Lisa was still focused on the monitor, adjusting the settings as the waves continued to shift. "I'm trying to isolate the different frequencies. If we can pinpoint them, we might be able to send something back."

"Something back?" Sam echoed, incredulous. "You mean, respond to whatever this is?"

"Why not?" Dr. Patel replied. "If they're sending us signals, there might be an opportunity for communication."

"Let's not jump to conclusions," Dr. Thomas warned. "We have to proceed with caution."

The atmosphere grew tense as they debated the best course of action. Dr. Orrington weighed their options, his mind racing with the possibilities.

"Okay, let's take a step back. We'll run some simulations first, see how the signals respond to different frequencies. If we establish a baseline, we can attempt a response."

Lisa nodded, determination etched on her face. "I can work on that immediately."

"Sam, I want you to assist her," Dr. Orrington instructed. "Keep an eye on the energy levels, and let me know if anything changes."

"Fine," Sam relented, still wary. "But we have to be careful. This could go sideways quickly."

The team worked in concert, each member focused on their tasks. As the energy around them pulsed and hummed, they felt the weight of the unknown pressing in.

A few minutes later, Lisa turned to the group, her excitement palpable. "I've managed to isolate several frequencies. If we can amplify this one," she pointed to the screen, "it might resonate with the energy patterns from the river."

"Let's try it," Dr. Orrington said, heart pounding with anticipation. "Set up the transmission equipment."

Sam connected the transmission device while Lisa fine-tuned the frequency. "Okay, we're ready to transmit."

Dr. Orrington took a deep breath, glancing at the river. "Send it."

The sound echoed through the air, a low tone pulsing from their equipment towards the river. The team held their breath, waiting for a response.

For a moment, silence enveloped them, and then the humming returned, louder and more intense. The river seemed to react, its shimmering surface shifting in rhythm with the sound.

"Look! It's responding!" Dr. Patel exclaimed, pointing at the river.

The water glowed brighter, swirling as if alive, and the team exchanged incredulous looks.

"What does it mean?" Sam asked, his skepticism replaced with wonder.

"I don't know," Dr. Orrington replied, his eyes fixed on the display. "But whatever it is, it's significant."

The energy intensified, rippling through the air as the river pulsed in response to their transmission. They watched in awe as new patterns emerged.

Chapter 72

Dr. Orrington stood in his study, the soft glow of his desk lamp illuminating the pages of a large, well-worn book. He carefully opened it, revealing the title, "Harnessing The Power of Water: A Revolutionary Approach To Achieve Success." He held it up to the camera, a glint of determination in his eyes.

"Water absorbs energy waves across the entire spectrum, indicating its propensity to consume and utilize energy," he explained, his tone serious. "This understanding is pivotal. It reshapes everything we know about both water and energy."

The camera zoomed in on the book, its pages filled with intricate diagrams and notes. Dr. Orrington flipped through the chapters, pausing at a page with bold headings.

"Researchers have shown that water can store information and even communicate," he continued, the weight of his words sinking in. "This isn't just theoretical; it has practical implications for our future, especially in how we interact with our environment."

He closed the book and looked directly into the camera, a sense of urgency in his demeanor. "We need to harness this knowledge. The discoveries we're making could change the course of humanity."

As he set the book down, the camera panned out, revealing a cluttered desk filled with papers, notes, and models of molecular structures. It conveyed the chaotic brilliance of a mind constantly seeking answers.

Dr. Orrington took a step back, allowing the camera to capture his thoughtful expression. "Every interaction we have with water is part of a larger conversation—a conversation we have yet to fully understand."

He walked over to a large whiteboard filled with equations and diagrams. With a marker in hand, he began to sketch out a flowchart. "If we can learn to interpret the signals from water, we can unlock new methods of energy consumption, communication, and possibly even healing."

As he spoke, the camera followed his movements, capturing the fervor with which he illustrated his ideas. "Imagine a world where we can use water as a means of storing and transmitting energy—like a supercomputer, but for natural resources."

The door creaked opcn, and Dr. Patel stepped inside, her expression curious. "What are you working on, Dr. Orrington?"

He gestured toward the whiteboard, enthusiasm shining in his eyes. "I'm outlining our next steps in understanding how water can be manipulated for energy storage. It's more than just absorption; it's about learning to communicate with it."

Dr. Patel raised an eyebrow. "Communicate with water? How does that work?"

"Think about it," he replied, pacing back and forth. "If water can absorb energy across the spectrum, what if we could send specific frequencies to influence its behavior? What if we could create a feedback loop that enhances its capacity to store energy?"

She crossed her arms, considering his words. "That's ambitious. But how would we test that hypothesis?"

Dr. Orrington stopped pacing and faced her, a spark of inspiration lighting up his expression. "We'll need to conduct experiments in controlled environments. Create specific conditions and analyze the results. If we can harness the right frequencies, we may unlock something extraordinary."

"Sounds like we'll need a lot of data," Dr. Patel replied. "And a solid team to help with the experiments."

"Absolutely," he agreed. "I want to bring everyone together. We can hold a meeting tomorrow to outline our research plan and delegate tasks."

"I'll prepare the materials we need," she said, her enthusiasm matching his. "This could be groundbreaking."

As Dr. Patel left the room, Dr. Orrington returned to the whiteboard, jotting down ideas and equations. The energy in the room crackled with potential as he envisioned the possibilities ahead.

The next day, the team gathered around a large conference table, the atmosphere buzzing with anticipation.

"Thank you all for coming," Dr. Orrington began, his voice steady. "We're at a pivotal moment in our research. Today, I want to discuss how we can harness the properties of water for energy storage and communication."

Lisa leaned forward, excitement evident in her demeanor. "What's the first step?"

"We need to establish a baseline for our experiments," Dr. Orrington explained. "I want each of you to focus on different aspects—frequency analysis, energy absorption, and data collection. We'll converge our findings to form a comprehensive understanding."

Sam raised a hand, skepticism still evident. "And what if we can't replicate the effects we observed? What if it's just an anomaly?"

Dr. Patel interjected, "That's why we need to approach this methodically. If we document everything, we can rule out variables and narrow down what works."

"Exactly," Dr. Orrington agreed. "We'll run a series of experiments under controlled conditions. I want everyone to collaborate closely, sharing data and insights."

Dr. Thomas nodded, a hint of excitement breaking through his usually stoic demeanor. "Let's get to work then. We need to gather as much data as possible."

The team dispersed, each member taking on their assigned tasks. As they worked, conversations flowed around the lab, excitement mingling with the air of uncertainty.

Lisa and Sam set up their equipment in one corner, preparing to analyze the energy absorption rates of different water samples.

"Think we'll find anything significant?" Sam asked, pouring a vial of water into a testing chamber.

"Definitely," Lisa replied, her eyes shining. "If water has memory and can transmit signals, we have to find a way to tap into that. It's a game changer."

"Just remember to keep your expectations grounded," Sam cautioned, glancing at the readouts. "We can't let our excitement get ahead of the data."

She chuckled, shaking her head. "You sound like a science teacher."

"Better safe than sorry," he said with a smirk, adjusting the settings on the monitor. "Let's see what the numbers say."

Meanwhile, Dr. Orrington and Dr. Patel reviewed the data collected from the previous experiments.

"This is promising," Dr. Patel said, pointing at a series of charts. "The energy levels are fluctuating more than we expected."

"Exactly," Dr. Orrington replied, enthusiasm bubbling in his voice. "It means we're on the right track. We just need to refine our approach."

As they continued their analysis, Sam called out from the testing area. "Hey, you guys should come see this!"

The two rushed over, curiosity piqued.

"What is it?" Dr. Patel asked, peering over Sam's shoulder.

"Look at this," he said, gesturing to the monitor. "The energy absorption is off the charts. It's like the water is reacting to the frequencies we've been testing."

Dr. Orrington's eyes widened in disbelief. "Can you isolate the frequency?"

"I'm trying," Sam replied, his fingers flying over the controls. "There's a spike here—"

Just then, the monitor emitted a series of sharp tones, echoing through the lab. The team exchanged excited glances.

"Is that what I think it is?" Lisa asked, her breath hitching in her throat.

Dr. Orrington leaned closer, his heart racing. "Yes! It's responding! The water is communicating back!"

Sam adjusted the settings further, excitement and anxiety in his expression. "I can amplify the signal. If this works, we might be able to establish a two-way communication."

"Do it," Dr. Orrington urged, his pulse quickening. "This could be the breakthrough we've been waiting for."

With a deep breath, Sam amplified the signal, and the lab was filled with the resonant hum of the water's response. It was a sound that seemed to vibrate through their bones, sending waves of anticipation rippling through the team.

"What happens now?" Lisa asked, her eyes wide with wonder.

Dr. Orrington stepped back, taking in the moment. "Now, we listen. We need to analyze these frequencies and understand what they're trying to tell us. This is just the beginning."

As the team worked together, piecing together the puzzle before them, they knew they were standing at the precipice of a monumental discovery. Each sound, each vibration was a whisper of the unknown, beckoning them to dive deeper into the mysteries of water and the universe.

Dr. Orrington's voice broke through the anticipation. "Let's keep our minds open and our spirits high. The journey ahead will be challenging, but together, we can unlock the secrets of this river."

Chapter 73

Dr. Orrington leaned over his desk, a stack of papers and open books surrounding him. "I've developed a technique to harness the power of a star," he said, his voice steady but filled with urgency. "It's all detailed in my book. The researchers believe they are presenting humanity with an unprecedented scientific discovery."

Dr. Patel, who had been sitting across from him, raised an eyebrow. "Harnessing the power of a star? That's quite a bold claim, Dr. Orrington. What makes you think we can achieve that?"

"The energy output of stars is incredible," he explained, leaning back in his chair. "If we can replicate their processes here on Earth, we can create limitless energy. The technology already exists; we just need to adapt it to our needs. The key lies in understanding the fundamental principles of astrophysics and translating them into practical applications."

"And the implications?" Dr. Patel pressed. "What would that mean for society?"

"Imagine a world where energy is no longer a commodity but a freely available resource," he replied, a glimmer of excitement in his eyes. "We could eliminate poverty, reduce conflict over resources, and revolutionize transportation and technology."

"But at what cost?" she questioned, her brow furrowing. "The dangers of manipulating such powerful forces could be catastrophic if we don't fully understand them."

Dr. Orrington sighed, running a hand through his hair. "That's why I'm gathering a team. We need a multidisciplinary approach to tackle the ethical implications and safety protocols before proceeding."

He glanced out the window, the stars twinkling against the night sky, and took a deep breath. "We have to act quickly. Other factions are interested in similar technologies, and we can't let them beat us to it."

The camera panned up to the night sky, where an opening appeared, revealing a swirling mass of stars and energy. A blue orb emerged, gliding silently through the atmosphere, tracking something below among the trees. The scene felt mysterious and eerie, casting an otherworldly glow over the landscape.

As the orb hovered, a low humming filled the air, resonating with an intensity that seemed to vibrate through the very ground. Below, a group of researchers were setting up equipment for their experiments, unaware of the phenomenon unfolding above them.

"Did you hear that?" Lisa asked, glancing around nervously as she tightened a bolt on a piece of machinery.

"Hear what?" Sam replied, focused on calibrating the sensors. "I didn't hear anything."

She shook her head, trying to shake off the unease that had settled in her stomach. "It sounded like a… humming. Like something is watching us."

"Probably just the equipment acting up," Sam said dismissively. "We're in the middle of a forest, after all. Weird sounds happen."

"Yeah, but this feels different," Lisa insisted, scanning the treetops. "Like it's alive."

Just then, Dr. Orrington and Dr. Patel arrived, their expressions serious. "What's going on?" Dr. Orrington asked, noticing the tension in the air.

"Lisa thinks she heard something," Sam replied, shrugging it off.

Dr. Patel frowned, looking up at the sky. "We need to stay focused. Whatever it is, we can't let it distract us from our work."

"But what if it's related to our research?" Lisa pressed. "What if it's connected to the energy fluctuations we've been observing?"

"Let's not jump to conclusions," Dr. Orrington interjected. "We'll keep monitoring the readings, but we can't lose sight of our goals. We need to gather more data before making assumptions."

The blue orb continued to hover silently above them, its glow casting an ethereal light on the ground. As the researchers resumed their tasks, the orb began to pulse, sending waves of energy downward.

Lisa shivered as the vibrations intensified. "It's getting stronger," she said, her voice barely above a whisper.

"Focus on the readings!" Dr. Orrington instructed, eyes locked on the instruments. "We need to document everything."

Suddenly, the humming escalated, and a surge of energy erupted from the orb, illuminating the entire area in a blinding flash. The researchers shielded their eyes, and the ground trembled beneath them.

"Get the data!" Dr. Patel shouted, frantically scribbling notes. "This could be the breakthrough we've been waiting for!"

As the light dimmed, the researchers blinked in disbelief. The readings on their monitors had skyrocketed. "What just happened?" Sam exclaimed, eyes wide.

"I don't know," Dr. Orrington admitted, staring at the instruments in awe. "But whatever that was, it's unlike anything we've ever encountered."

Lisa checked the data. "The energy levels are off the charts! This is incredible!"

The orb hovered closer, its glow pulsating rhythmically as if responding to the excitement in the air. "We need to get a closer look," Dr. Patel urged.

"This could be our chance to understand its properties."

"But what if it's dangerous?" Lisa protested, fear creeping into her voice.

"We'll take precautions," Dr. Orrington reassured her. "But this is a once-in-a-lifetime opportunity. We can't let fear hold us back."

With a shared glance of determination, the team gathered their equipment and moved closer to the orb. The air was thick with anticipation as they approached the source of the energy.

"Keep your distance, but get the readings!" Dr. Orrington instructed, adjusting his own device to capture the data.

As they drew nearer, the orb began to emit a series of harmonious tones, echoing through the trees. It was a sound unlike any they had ever heard, a blend of frequencies that seemed to resonate with their very being.

"What is it doing?" Sam asked, mesmerized by the spectacle.

"I think it's communicating," Dr. Patel suggested, her voice filled with wonder. "Maybe it's trying to establish a connection."

"Connection?" Lisa echoed, unsure of what that meant.

Dr. Orrington frowned, processing the implications. "If it is indeed communicating, we need to determine the nature of that connection. This could lead to groundbreaking advancements in our understanding of energy and communication."

With careful precision, they continued to monitor the orb, gathering data and notes as it hovered above them. The harmonious tones shifted, forming a melody that wrapped around them, urging them to listen closer.

"Can you feel that?" Lisa asked, captivated by the sound.

"It's almost... alive," Sam breathed, entranced by the orb's rhythm. "Like it's trying to tell us something."

The orb pulsed brighter, the tones intensifying as if responding to their thoughts. Dr. Orrington felt a shiver run down his spine, a strange sense of recognition washing over him.

"It's not just energy," he murmured, realization dawning. "It's information."

"What do you mean?" Dr. Patel asked, looking at him with intrigue.

"Water can store data, communicate through vibrations. What if this orb is using similar principles? What if it's an entity that understands how to transmit energy in a way we've never comprehended?" he explained, his voice steady but filled with excitement.

The researchers exchanged glances, a mixture of awe and uncertainty settling in.

"Are we really ready for this?" Lisa questioned, her heart racing. "What if we're not equipped to handle the consequences?"

Dr. Orrington placed a reassuring hand on her shoulder. "We've trained for this. We're scientists, and discovery often comes with risks. But if we can harness this knowledge, it could change everything."

As the orb hovered closer, they felt the weight of its presence, the potential of their discovery resonating in the air around them. The melody reached a crescendo, wrapping them in an embrace of energy and sound.

In that moment, they understood: they stood on the precipice of a new era, where the boundaries of science and the mysteries of the universe intertwined.

"We need to document everything," Dr. Patel urged, her pen racing across the pages. "This could redefine everything we know about energy."

"Yes," Dr. Orrington agreed, eyes shining with determination. "And we must proceed with caution. Let's ensure our safety and keep communication open. We don't know what this entity is capable of."

As the team set to work, their excitement mingled with trepidation, knowing they were stepping into uncharted territory. The orb pulsed above them, a beacon of hope and possibility, whispering secrets of the cosmos yet to be unveiled.

Chapter 74

Dr. Orrington's voice echoed through the dimly lit room as he recounted the details of the extraordinary event. "In Season Two, Episode Ten, an eyewitness reported seeing an opening in the sky and a blue orb tracking something in the trees. This observation supports the theory that extraterrestrial beings utilize advanced mechanical spacecraft for interdimensional travel."

Dr. Patel leaned forward, intrigued. "You really think that's what they're doing? Interdimensional travel?"

"Absolutely," Dr. Orrington replied, tapping a finger on the desk. "The consistency of sightings across various locations and their patterns suggest a purpose beyond mere observation. These crafts are engineered for something more than just crossing space."

"Like gathering data?" Sam interjected, glancing at his notes. "Or maybe even harvesting resources?"

"Exactly," Dr. Orrington affirmed. "If they're capable of traversing dimensions, they likely possess technology that could manipulate energy and matter in ways we can only begin to comprehend."

Lisa shifted uneasily in her chair. "But what if their intentions aren't peaceful? If they're capable of such advanced technology, what's to stop them from exploiting our resources or worse?"

Dr. Patel shook her head. "We can't jump to conclusions. We need to gather evidence and understand their motives before making assumptions. Fear can cloud our judgment."

Dr. Orrington nodded, recognizing the concern in Lisa's eyes. "That's why we need to be vigilant. Our understanding of these phenomena must be rooted in science and rational inquiry, not fear."

A hush fell over the room as the weight of their discussion sank in. The implications of what they were theorizing felt monumental.

"Let's take a step back," Sam suggested, trying to redirect the conversation. "What do we know about the technology these orbs might be using? Is there any way we could study it?"

Dr. Orrington smiled slightly, appreciating Sam's initiative. "Great question. We have some preliminary data from previous sightings. I propose we analyze it further. We can look for patterns and see if there's a correlation with electromagnetic fluctuations."

"I can start compiling the data," Lisa said, her fingers itching to get to work. "We should also cross-reference it with known scientific phenomena to see if any theories hold water."

"Good idea," Dr. Patel agreed. "If we can identify a signature or frequency that these orbs emit, it could lead us to a better understanding of their technology."

The room buzzed with energy as they began to discuss their next steps, bouncing ideas off one another.

"Let's also reach out to other research teams," Dr. Orrington suggested. "Collaboration could yield valuable insights. The more data we gather, the clearer the picture will become."

As they formulated a plan, a soft light flickered from the corner of the room, drawing their attention. The blue orb hovered just outside the window, casting an ethereal glow over their discussion.

"Is that—?" Lisa began, her voice trailing off in disbelief.

"Stay calm," Dr. Orrington instructed, moving toward the window. "Let's observe it before making any sudden moves."

The orb pulsated, its light shifting from blue to a deeper hue, almost as if it were responding to their presence. The humming sound returned, vibrating in the air around them.

"What does it want?" Sam asked, a mixture of awe and fear in his voice.

"I think it's trying to communicate," Dr. Patel replied, her eyes wide. "We should document this."

Dr. Orrington nodded, his gaze fixed on the orb. "Everyone, get your equipment ready. This could be a critical moment in our research."

As they scrambled to gather their tools, the orb began to emit a series of tones, harmonizing in a way that felt almost melodic. The sound resonated deep within them, stirring something primal and ancient.

"Can you hear that?" Lisa whispered, entranced by the sound.

"It's beautiful," Sam breathed, captivated by the otherworldly music.

"Let's not get lost in the moment," Dr. Orrington cautioned, focused on setting up the recording devices. "We need to analyze the frequency and amplitude."

As they recorded the sounds, Dr. Patel pointed out the fluctuation in the orb's light. "The energy output is increasing. It's like it's feeding off our excitement."

"Or responding to it," Dr. Orrington mused, adjusting the settings on his device. "This could be a breakthrough in understanding how these entities interact with us."

With the orb hovering closer, the atmosphere shifted, a palpable tension filling the room. They all felt it— the weight of discovery and the uncertainty of what lay ahead.

"What if it's dangerous?" Lisa voiced her concern again, her brow furrowing.

"Danger often accompanies discovery," Dr. Orrington replied, his tone steady. "But we are prepared. We'll proceed with caution."

The orb pulsed again, sending ripples of energy through the air. The harmonious tones shifted, creating a pattern that seemed to correspond with their heartbeats. It was as if the orb was attuned to their very beings.

"I think it wants to show us something," Sam said, glancing back at Dr. Orrington. "Maybe it's trying to connect with us."

"Connection is the key," Dr. Patel added, her eyes sparkling with inspiration. "What if we can establish a two-way communication? If we can respond in a way it understands, we might unlock new avenues of research."

"Let's try," Dr. Orrington said, excitement igniting in his voice. "Everyone, focus on the orb. We need to create a response. Use your devices to emit sound waves at similar frequencies."

As they aligned their equipment, the orb shimmered with anticipation. The humming intensified, echoing through the room like a call to the wild.

"On three," Dr. Orrington instructed, his heart racing. "One, two, three!"

They all activated their devices simultaneously, sending a wave of sound toward the orb. The response was immediate—the orb pulsed and emitted a brilliant flash of light, enveloping them in an aura of energy.

"What just happened?" Lisa gasped, her eyes wide with amazement.

"I don't know, but I think it's working," Dr. Orrington exclaimed, barely containing his excitement. "Keep going! Adjust your frequencies!"

As they continued to manipulate the sound waves, the orb responded, shifting its color and light with every pulse. It felt as if they were engaged in a dance, the boundaries of communication expanding beyond spoken words.

Suddenly, the orb projected a holographic image above them—a vibrant display of interdimensional landscapes filled with swirling colors and geometric patterns.

"Is that…?" Sam started, mesmerized by the sight.

"Dimensions," Dr. Patel breathed, captivated by the visual representation. "These are different realms!"

The realization washed over them. This orb wasn't just a vessel; it was a gateway—a link to other worlds, other possibilities.

"Document everything!" Dr. Orrington urged, adrenaline surging through him. "This is our chance to witness the unimaginable."

As they recorded the unfolding spectacle, the orb continued to illuminate their surroundings, the display becoming more intricate. Each dimension shown was a testament to the vastness of existence.

"Look at that," Lisa pointed. "Is that water? It looks alive."

"Water in another form," Dr. Patel noted, her scientific mind racing. "It could hold the key to understanding energy and life itself."

The team stood in awe, realizing they were no longer just observers; they were participants in something far greater than themselves. This experience was a culmination of their research, their passion, and their commitment to uncovering the unknown.

As the images faded, the orb began to pulse gently, its energy calming.

"Thank you," Dr. Orrington whispered, feeling a sense of gratitude wash over him.

The orb dimmed slightly, and the hum transformed into a soothing melody, as if the entity acknowledged their appreciation.

"What now?" Sam asked, looking to Dr. Orrington.

"We continue our work," he said firmly. "We share this knowledge and prepare for what comes next. This is only the beginning."

With renewed determination, they gathered their equipment, eager to analyze the data and explore the new possibilities that lay ahead. The orb lingered for a moment longer, then slowly retreated into the night sky, leaving them with a sense of wonder and purpose.

In that moment, they knew they were on the cusp of a monumental shift in understanding the universe, where science and the mysteries of existence intertwined. They were not just witnesses to a phenomenon; they were pioneers, ready to navigate the uncharted territories of knowledge and discovery.

Chapter 75

Researchers huddled around an array of high-tech monitors, their faces illuminated by the glow of the screens. The atmosphere was thick with tension and anticipation as they analyzed footage captured by the state-of-the-art cameras, focusing on the mysterious blue orb and the inexplicable opening in the sky.

Dr. Orrington's voice resonated through the room, his tone serious and commanding. "The importance of cameras is evident in situations where human visual perception is limited. Advanced mechanical aircraft used by interdimensional species surpass the capabilities of the human eye."

Dr. Patel leaned closer to one of the screens, squinting at the footage. "Look at that!" she exclaimed, pointing at a section of the clip where the orb pulsed in sync with the fluctuations of light around it. "You can see the energy waves emanating from it. This might be the key to understanding their technology."

"Can we enhance that section?" Sam, the tech specialist, asked, his fingers already flying over the keyboard. "If we can isolate those energy patterns, we might find a frequency to communicate with it."

"Do it," Dr. Orrington instructed, crossing his arms as he watched the screen intently. "We need to understand how this technology operates, especially if we are to establish any form of communication."

As Sam worked on the enhancement, Lisa reviewed the accompanying data on her tablet. "The orb seems to emit a variety of frequencies. I've noticed some spikes correlate with electromagnetic disturbances recorded in the area."

"Interesting," Dr. Patel said, her brow furrowed in thought. "This could mean they're using those disturbances to cloak their presence. We might not even be seeing the full picture."

The room buzzed with excitement, each researcher feeding off the collective energy. Sam turned back to the group, his eyes wide with discovery. "I've isolated the energy wave patterns. They seem to vary based on the orb's activity. It's like it's responding to external stimuli."

"Could you replicate that?" Dr. Orrington asked, intrigued. "If we could mimic the frequencies, we might just lure it back or even gain its attention."

"Yes, I think so," Sam replied, a hint of a grin forming on his lips. "If I can generate those frequencies, we could test how the orb reacts."

"Let's do it," Dr. Orrington said, his determination evident. "We can't waste any time. This could be our best chance to connect with them."

As Sam set up the equipment to generate the frequencies, Lisa monitored the data streams, ensuring everything was in sync.

"Keep an eye on the output," Dr. Patel instructed. "If anything spikes or shifts, we need to be ready to adapt."

Moments later, Sam turned to face them, his hands hovering over the control panel. "I'm ready. On my count—three… two… one!"

He activated the system, and a series of harmonic tones filled the room, each one meticulously designed to match the orb's energy patterns. The sound resonated through the high-tech observation room, vibrating in the air.

"Is it working?" Lisa asked, her heart racing with anticipation.

"I'm not sure yet," Sam said, watching the readings closely. Suddenly, the monitors flickered, and the orb's image appeared on the main screen, pulsing rhythmically to the tones.

"It's responding!" Dr. Orrington shouted, his eyes gleaming with excitement. "Look at that!"

The orb's light brightened, illuminating the room with an ethereal glow. The pulsing intensified, syncing perfectly with the frequencies they were generating.

"Adjust the tones," Dr. Patel urged, her voice laced with urgency. "We need to find the sweet spot!"

Sam quickly manipulated the controls, shifting the frequencies higher and lower until they found a perfect match. The orb expanded in size, and an audible hum resonated through the room, creating a surreal atmosphere.

"It's almost like it's trying to communicate," Lisa said, awe-struck. "I can feel it in my chest."

"Keep it going!" Dr. Orrington commanded, watching the orb's transformation with fear and excitement. "We're on the brink of something monumental."

As they maintained the frequency, the orb emitted a series of lights—blue, green, and violet—creating a mesmerizing display. The patterns morphed into complex geometric shapes, almost as if they were conveying a message.

"What does it mean?" Sam asked, entranced by the visual spectacle.

"I'm not sure," Dr. Patel replied, her eyes locked on the screen. "But we need to record everything. This could hold the key to understanding their intent."

The lights danced across the monitors, creating a tapestry of color that filled the room. The orb pulsated with energy, its movements synchronizing with their harmonic tones, suggesting a deeper connection between them.

"I think it's trying to show us something," Lisa said, her voice barely above a whisper.

Suddenly, the orb released a brilliant flash, and the footage froze on a single frame—a moment captured that depicted the orb radiating energy toward the camera.

"Did you see that?" Sam exclaimed, eyes wide with excitement. "It's like it's projecting something!"

"Let's enhance that frame," Dr. Orrington ordered, barely able to contain his enthusiasm. "We need to analyze it closely."

As Sam worked to enhance the image, Lisa's fingers danced over her tablet, compiling the data from the experiment. "I'll prepare a report on our findings, just in case we need to present this later," she said, her focus unwavering.

"Good thinking," Dr. Patel replied, glancing between the screens and the data. "This is going to be groundbreaking."

The energy in the room was electric as they worked, the orb's presence inspiring their determination. Sam finally isolated the enhanced image, and they gathered around the screen to view the details.

"Look at the patterns!" he exclaimed, excitement bubbling over. "It's almost like a blueprint of sorts."

"Exactly," Dr. Orrington said, analyzing the intricate designs. "These shapes could represent a language or a code."

"What if it's a navigation system?" Lisa suggested, her eyes sparkling with possibility. "They might be mapping out their travel routes or energy pathways."

"That's a fascinating hypothesis," Dr. Patel agreed, her mind racing. "If we can decipher this, it might lead us to their origins, or even their intentions."

"We need to share this information with the broader scientific community," Dr. Orrington stated firmly. "The implications are vast. We can't keep this to ourselves."

Sam nodded, his focus shifting back to the orb. "But first, let's see if we can maintain the connection. If we can keep it here longer, we might get even more data."

The orb's glow flickered, and they could sense a shift in energy.

"Stay focused," Dr. Orrington reminded them. "We've come too far to lose this connection now."

As they maintained their frequencies, the orb vibrated, and another wave of energy pulsed outward, sending ripples through the air.

"I can feel it!" Lisa gasped, her heart racing as the hum resonated through her. "It's almost like it's alive."

Dr. Patel closed her eyes for a moment, tuning into the frequencies. "There's something profound about this interaction. It feels like we're not just observers; we're participants in a greater narrative."

The orb continued to react, its light shifting in response to their tones.

"What do you think they want from us?" Sam asked, a hint of concern creeping into his voice.

"I don't know," Dr. Orrington admitted, a frown creasing his brow. "But we need to be cautious. If they're capable of this technology, they might not have our best interests at heart."

"Or they might be trying to warn us," Lisa suggested. "What if this is their way of reaching out?"

"Let's not jump to conclusions," Dr. Patel interjected. "We need to gather more evidence before making assumptions about their intentions."

As they continued their work, the orb emitted another series of lights, transforming the atmosphere into a vibrant display. The walls seemed to pulse with energy, and a sense of unity filled the room.

"We're connected," Sam said softly, awed by the experience. "It's like we're sharing a moment in time."

Dr. Orrington smiled, feeling a sense of hope wash over him. "This could be the beginning of a new era of understanding. We're on the precipice of discovery."

With renewed determination, they focused on the orb, eager to unravel the mysteries it held. As the night wore on, the lines between science and the extraordinary blurred, and they found themselves part of a cosmic dance—a journey into the unknown, guided by the light of the orb above.

Chapter 76

Dr. Orrington leaned over the sprawling map of the ranch, his brow furrowed in concentration as he marked various points of interest with a red marker. The soft glow of the desk lamp illuminated his focused expression, revealing the determination etched on his face.

"This isn't just a hunch," he murmured to himself, underlining a particular spot marked 'Energy Anomaly.' "The data analyzed confirms a remarkable discovery: extraterrestrial life exists right here on Earth, not in outer space. This ranch has been identified as a special and dangerous location where all answers are likely to be found."

A soft knock on the door interrupted his thoughts. It swung open to reveal Dr. Patel, her face curiosity and concern.

"What are you working on, Orrington?" she asked, stepping into the study.

He gestured toward the map, excitement lighting up his features. "I've been piecing together the data we've collected from the recent sightings and energy readings. It's all connected to this place."

She approached the map, scanning the points he'd marked. "Are you suggesting that the ranch is a hotspot for extraterrestrial activity?"

"Exactly," he replied, tapping on the map. "Look here and here—these coordinates correspond with the energy spikes we've recorded over the last month. It's more than coincidence."

Dr. Patel crossed her arms, absorbing the information. "But we need to be careful. If this place truly is dangerous, we can't afford to make reckless moves."

"I agree," Dr. Orrington said, his tone turning serious. "But we need to investigate. The ranch could hold secrets that are crucial to understanding their presence."

"What do you propose?" she asked, raising an eyebrow.

"We organize a field expedition," he suggested, his voice steady. "We'll bring our best equipment and a small team. We need to gather firsthand evidence and see if we can make contact."

Dr. Patel hesitated, weighing the risks. "It could be dangerous, but if what you're saying is true, it could change everything. We have to prepare for the unknown."

"Exactly," he said, nodding in agreement. "I'll draft a proposal for the team, and we can discuss it in the morning."

Just as they were settling into their plans, a sudden loud crash echoed from outside the study, causing both scientists to jump.

"What was that?" Dr. Patel exclaimed, eyes wide.

"I don't know," Dr. Orrington replied, his heart racing. "Let's check it out."

They hurried out of the study, moving cautiously toward the source of the noise. As they reached the front door, they spotted Sam, the tech specialist, sprawled on the ground with equipment scattered around him.

"Sam! What happened?" Dr. Orrington rushed over to help him up.

"I tripped over the cables while bringing in the new sensor," Sam said sheepishly, brushing himself off. "But I think I caught something on the surveillance feed. You need to see this."

Dr. Patel's interest piqued. "What did you find?"

Sam pointed toward the laptop he had managed to set up despite the chaos. "I was running an analysis of the area when I saw something on the feed— something moving near the edge of the ranch."

Dr. Orrington peered over Sam's shoulder as he pulled up the footage. A grainy image flickered on the screen, revealing a dark shape darting through the trees, illuminated by the moonlight.

"Is that…?" Dr. Patel started, her voice trailing off.

"Looks like something, doesn't it?" Sam replied, his excitement bubbling over. "I was able to enhance the image a bit. Look at this."

The image sharpened, revealing a faint outline of a creature that seemed to shimmer, almost as if it were bending light around it.

"That's incredible!" Dr. Orrington said, leaning closer. "It's definitely not a known animal."

"We need to gather more evidence," Dr. Patel said, her analytical mind racing. "If this is what we think it is, we might finally have proof of extraterrestrial life right here."

Sam nodded, his eyes alight with enthusiasm. "We should head out there now. I can set up a camera trap to capture more footage, and maybe we can track it down."

Dr. Orrington shared a look with Dr. Patel, both weighing the potential risks against the promise of discovery.

"We need to be cautious," Dr. Patel cautioned, though the thrill of the unknown tugged at her. "We don't know what we're dealing with."

"That's why we go prepared," Dr. Orrington insisted. "If we can make contact, we can learn so much more."

After a brief discussion, they quickly gathered their gear. Sam equipped himself with the camera and various sensors, while Dr. Orrington and Dr. Patel prepared their field notebooks, ready to document whatever they encountered.

As they stepped outside, the cool night air hit them, mingling with the scent of pine and earth. The ranch was eerily quiet, but anticipation hung in the air.

"Stick close together," Dr. Orrington instructed, leading the way down a narrow path toward the edge of the woods where the figure had been spotted. "We don't want to lose anyone in the dark."

"Got it," Sam replied, clutching the camera tightly, his eyes scanning the shadows.

Dr. Patel followed closely behind, her senses heightened. "I can't shake the feeling that we're being watched," she whispered.

"Just keep your eyes open," Dr. Orrington said, his voice steady but firm. "Stay focused on the task at hand."

They approached the area where the footage had captured the figure, the trees looming overhead like ancient sentinels. The ground was littered with fallen leaves and branches, the sound of their footsteps muffled by the soft earth.

"Set up the camera here," Dr. Orrington instructed as they reached a small clearing. "This should give us a good vantage point."

Sam quickly got to work, securing the camera in place and connecting it to a power source. "If anything moves in this area, we'll capture it," he said, his fingers deftly adjusting the settings.

"Now what?" Dr. Patel asked, glancing around uneasily.

"We wait," Dr. Orrington replied, pulling out his notebook. "Keep an eye on the surroundings while I document everything."

As they settled into their positions, the tension in the air thickened. The forest around them felt alive, each rustle of leaves and snap of twigs heightened their senses. Minutes stretched into what felt like hours as they remained vigilant, watching for any sign of movement.

Then, suddenly, a low hum filled the air, vibrating through the ground beneath their feet.

"What is that?" Sam whispered, eyes wide.

"I don't know," Dr. Patel replied, scanning the trees. "It's coming from over there!"

Dr. Orrington quickly turned, his heart racing. "Stay together! Let's move cautiously toward the sound."

They crept forward, the hum growing louder with each step, an almost musical resonance that seemed to draw them in. As they approached the source, the trees parted to reveal a small clearing bathed in an otherworldly light.

In the center stood a figure—tall and ethereal, its form shifting as if made of light itself. The hum intensified, wrapping around them like a warm embrace.

"What is that?" Sam gasped, unable to tear his eyes away from the sight.

"I don't know," Dr. Orrington breathed, captivated. "But it's beautiful."

"Is it... communicating with us?" Dr. Patel asked, taking a cautious step forward.

As if sensing their presence, the figure turned toward them. The hum transformed into a series of melodic tones, resonating deep within their chests. Each note seemed to vibrate with meaning, a language they instinctively felt rather than heard.

"What do we do?" Sam asked, torn between awe and fear.

"Let it come to us," Dr. Orrington instructed, raising a hand in a gesture of peace. "We mean no harm."

The figure paused, its shimmering form pulsating in rhythm with the melody. Slowly, it began to move toward them, the air around it shimmering as it drew closer.

"Stay calm," Dr. Patel whispered, her eyes locked on the being. "This is it—the moment we've been waiting for."

As the figure approached, the hum transformed into distinct notes, weaving together in a harmony that resonated with the very fabric of their being. It was as if the figure was sharing something profound, something that transcended words.

Dr. Orrington felt a surge of emotion, an overwhelming sense of connection that he couldn't fully explain. "I believe it wants us to understand," he said softly, watching as the figure extended a hand—a gesture of invitation.

"What does it want to show us?" Sam murmured, captivated by the unfolding spectacle.

"I think it's revealing its essence," Dr. Patel replied, her voice barely above a whisper. "It's showing us its truth."

The atmosphere thickened with anticipation, and in that moment, they knew they stood on the brink of an extraordinary revelation—a bridge between their world and the unknown, a glimpse into a reality that defied comprehension.

Chapter 77

The moon cast an eerie glow over the sprawling ranch, its vast fields stretching into the night, the atmosphere thick with mystery. Shadows danced across the ground, and the faint rustle of leaves hinted at something unseen moving just beyond the edge of their perception.

Dr. Orrington stood at the edge of the ranch, staring into the distance, lost in thought. His mind raced with the possibilities of what they might discover here— answers that could change everything they knew about the universe.

"This place," he said, his voice low and contemplative, "it holds the key to unlocking the mysteries of these interdimensional species."

Dr. Patel stood beside him, arms crossed as she glanced around warily. "The phenomena we've observed here… it's unlike anything else. But are we really prepared for what we might uncover?"

"Prepared or not," Dr. Orrington replied, his eyes still fixed on the ranch, "we have no choice. Its unique properties and the events recorded here are critical to our understanding. If we're going to unlock the secrets of these beings, it starts here."

Sam adjusted the camera strapped to his shoulder, looking between them. "I've heard rumors about this place for years. People say the ranch is cursed, that strange things happen here all the time."

"Those rumors might be more fact than fiction," Dr. Patel murmured. "There's something about this land… something that defies logic."

Dr. Orrington nodded, his expression resolute. "That's exactly why we need to investigate. The ranch might be the focal point for the activities we've been tracking. If we can uncover the truth, it could be the breakthrough we've been waiting for."

Suddenly, a strange sound echoed across the ranch— an unsettling hum that vibrated through the air. The team stiffened, exchanging uneasy glances.

"Did you hear that?" Sam asked, gripping his equipment tighter.

Dr. Orrington motioned for them to follow him. "Stay close. We need to see where that sound is coming from."

They moved cautiously through the ranch, the tall grass brushing against their legs as they ventured deeper into the unknown. The hum grew louder, more distinct, pulsating with an unnatural energy.

"It's coming from up ahead," Dr. Orrington whispered, leading them toward a cluster of trees near the edge of the property.

As they approached, the hum intensified, and the air around them seemed to shimmer with an otherworldly glow. Just beyond the trees, a faint blue light flickered, casting an eerie glow across the landscape.

"Do you see that?" Sam asked, his voice barely audible.

Dr. Patel nodded, her eyes wide with awe. "It's just like the sightings we've recorded—an orb of light."

Dr. Orrington's heart raced as they drew closer. The blue orb hovered in the air, its form shifting and pulsating as if it were alive. It seemed to be watching them, studying their every move.

"This is it," Dr. Orrington said softly. "This is what we came for."

The orb flickered, then began to move, slowly drifting away from them. Without hesitation, Dr. Orrington signaled for the others to follow.

They trailed the orb through the trees, the hum growing louder with every step. The atmosphere around them felt charged with energy, as if the very air was alive with possibility.

"Do you think it's leading us somewhere?" Dr. Patel asked, her voice tinged with excitement.

"Perhaps," Dr. Orrington replied, keeping his eyes fixed on the glowing orb. "Or it's testing us, seeing how far we're willing to go."

The orb led them deeper into the woods until they reached a small clearing. In the center of the clearing stood a strange structure—an ancient-looking stone circle, its surface etched with symbols that seemed to pulse with the same energy as the orb.

"What is this place?" Sam asked, stepping closer to the stone circle.

Dr. Orrington studied the markings, his mind racing. "It looks like some kind of gateway… a connection point between dimensions."

Dr. Patel knelt beside the stones, running her fingers over the symbols. "These markings… they're not of human origin. This is alien technology."

The orb hovered above the stones, its glow intensifying. The hum reached a fever pitch, vibrating through their bodies as if resonating with the very essence of their being.

"Whatever this is," Dr. Orrington said, his voice filled with awe, "we're standing on the threshold of something extraordinary."

Suddenly, the orb pulsed with a bright flash of light, and the hum stopped abruptly, leaving an eerie silence in its wake.

For a moment, the team stood frozen, unsure of what to do next.

"Did… did it activate something?" Sam asked, glancing nervously at the stone circle.

Before anyone could answer, the ground beneath their feet began to vibrate. The stones in the circle started to glow, their symbols lighting up one by one.

Dr. Patel stepped back, her eyes wide with alarm. "Something's happening!"

The air around them crackled with energy, and a low, rumbling sound filled the clearing. The stone circle began to spin, slowly at first, then faster, until it was a blur of light and motion.

"This isn't possible," Dr. Orrington muttered, his eyes locked on the spinning stones. "We're witnessing a dimensional shift… a gateway opening."

The orb floated to the center of the circle, its glow merging with the light from the stones. The hum returned, louder and more intense than before, vibrating through their very bones.

Dr. Patel took a step back, her voice trembling. "What do we do now?"

"We wait," Dr. Orrington replied, his gaze never leaving the orb. "We watch and learn."

As they stood there, watching the orb and the stone circle, the light grew brighter and the hum more powerful. The air seemed to shimmer and distort, bending the very fabric of reality.

Then, without warning, the light exploded outward in a blinding flash, and everything went silent.

When the light faded, the orb was gone, and the stone circle stood still, its glow extinguished.

"What… just happened?" Sam asked, his voice barely above a whisper.

Dr. Orrington let out a slow breath, his mind struggling to process what they had just witnessed. "We've just seen a gateway open… and close. We've witnessed interdimensional travel."

Dr. Patel stared at the stone circle in disbelief. "This changes everything."

"It does," Dr. Orrington agreed, a sense of awe and wonder washing over him. "We've just taken the first step toward understanding a reality far beyond our own."

As they stood in the clearing, the weight of what they had witnessed settled over them. The ranch, with all its mysteries and dangers, had revealed its secrets to them—but those secrets only raised more questions.

And the answers, they knew, were still out there, waiting to be discovered.

Chapter 78

Dr. Orrington leaned back in his chair, his fingers steepled in thought as the faint glow of his desk lamp cast shadows across the room. His expression was intense, his mind replaying the events of the night over and over again. He finally broke the silence.

"We must continue to investigate," he said, his voice quiet but resolute. "The phenomena we've witnessed… it's undeniable. The evidence points to something far greater than we ever imagined— extraterrestrial life, advanced technology, not from distant stars, but here, right under our noses."

Dr. Patel, seated across from him, nodded slowly, still processing everything they had seen. "The ranch… the orb… the gateway," she murmured, almost to herself. "This changes everything."

"It does," Orrington agreed, his gaze unwavering. "We've barely scratched the surface, but this could redefine our understanding of reality. These entities, these beings—they're not bound by the limitations we know. Their technology, their knowledge—it's beyond anything we've ever seen."

Sam, still shaken from the encounter at the ranch, shifted in his seat. "But what are they doing here? Why Earth? And why that ranch of all places?"

Dr. Orrington took a deep breath, his mind racing as he spoke. "That ranch is special—there's something about the land, the energy there. We've seen portals open, interdimensional entities crossing over… it's like a focal point, a bridge between realities. The question isn't just why, but how."

Dr. Patel leaned forward, her eyes gleaming with curiosity. "The stone circle, the symbols… it's alien technology, isn't it? They've been here before, maybe for centuries. We've just never had the means to detect them."

Orrington nodded. "Exactly. We've been blind to their presence, but now we're beginning to understand. Water, energy, sound waves—all of it is connected. We're only just beginning to comprehend how they manipulate the very fabric of our reality."

Sam frowned, his brow furrowed in thought. "And what about the orb? It was almost like it was… watching us, leading us somewhere."

Dr. Orrington's expression darkened. "The orb was intelligent, in some way. It's not just a machine; it's a part of something bigger. I believe it was testing us, seeing if we were capable of understanding what it showed us. These beings—if they wanted to harm us, they could have. But they haven't. Not yet, anyway."

"So what do we do now?" Dr. Patel asked, her voice tinged with both excitement and concern.

"We keep pushing forward," Dr. Orrington replied. "This journey we're on is crucial—not just for us, but for humanity as a whole. If we can understand these beings and their technology, we can protect ourselves from whatever may come next. We need to explore further, gather more evidence, and unlock the secrets of that ranch."

"And if we can't?" Sam asked, his voice barely above a whisper.

Dr. Orrington's gaze was sharp, his determination palpable. "Failure isn't an option. What we're dealing with here could reshape our understanding of the universe and our place in it. We must continue to investigate, to push the boundaries of what we know. The future of our world depends on it."

The room fell into silence once again, each of them contemplating the enormity of what lay ahead. Outside, the night stretched on, quiet and still, but within the walls of Dr. Orrington's study, the gravity of their discoveries weighed heavy.

After a long pause, Dr. Patel broke the silence. "There's no turning back, is there?"

Dr. Orrington shook his head. "No. We've opened a door that can't be closed. Now, we need to understand what lies beyond."

Sam shifted uneasily in his seat. "And the government? Do we involve them in this? There's no way they haven't noticed the things happening at that ranch."

"They know more than they let on," Dr. Orrington said grimly. "But they've kept it hidden—perhaps for good reason. What we've discovered could cause widespread panic if handled incorrectly. That's why we need to control the narrative, gather irrefutable evidence before we make any moves."

Dr. Patel glanced at Sam, then back at Orrington. "We're walking a fine line. One wrong step and everything could fall apart."

"That's why we have to be careful, methodical," Orrington replied, his tone steady. "The truth will come out, but it needs to be on our terms. We're not just uncovering scientific facts; we're dealing with the future of humanity."

Sam let out a long breath, his hands tightening around the armrests of his chair. "And what if these beings don't want to be understood? What if they see us as a threat?"

Dr. Orrington's gaze hardened. "Then we need to be ready. We're not dealing with simple extraterrestrial encounters—we're dealing with a potential shift in power, a challenge to the dominance of human beings on this planet. If they view us as a threat, we need to find a way to protect ourselves."

Dr. Patel folded her arms across her chest, her expression thoughtful. "So it's a race against time, then? We have to learn as much as we can before they make their next move?"

"Precisely," Orrington confirmed. "They've shown us a glimpse of what they're capable of, but we don't know their endgame. We need to be proactive, to stay ahead of whatever they're planning."

The weight of his words hung heavy in the air. Each of them understood the stakes—the unknown dangers, the unprecedented challenges ahead. Yet despite the fear, there was a sense of excitement, of possibility. They were standing at the edge of discovery, on the cusp of something extraordinary.

"Tomorrow," Orrington said finally, breaking the silence, "we return to the ranch. We need to examine every inch of that land, find out what else is hidden there. This is just the beginning."

Dr. Patel and Sam nodded, their expressions resolute.

"Agreed," Dr. Patel said. "If that ranch is the key, we need to unlock every secret it holds."

"And we will," Orrington replied, his eyes blazing with determination. "But we need to be prepared for whatever comes next. This isn't just about science anymore—it's about survival."

As the night wore on, the three of them sat in the study, planning, strategizing, preparing for the journey ahead. They knew that the path they had chosen was fraught with danger, but there was no turning back now.

The world as they knew it was about to change, and they would be at the forefront of that change. Whatever awaited them at the ranch—answers, threats, or something far more unimaginable—they were ready to face it head-on.

"Tomorrow," Orrington repeated, his voice firm. "We uncover the truth."

Chapter 79

Dr. Orrington sat back in his chair, eyes darting across the scattered papers and screens flickering with surveillance footage. He exhaled sharply, rubbing his temples. The weight of what he'd uncovered sat heavy on his shoulders.

"They're watching us," he muttered, almost to himself. He turned toward the monitor, where a small blue orb floated through the trees on the screen. "They've always been here. We just weren't looking close enough."

The door creaked open, and Dr. Patel stepped into the dimly lit study. She glanced at the footage before meeting Dr. Orrington's eyes. "Any progress?"

Orrington gestured to the screen. "This... this orb is their method of watching us. We've only scratched the surface of what they're capable of." He paused, turning to face her fully. "They manipulate everything around us, even the water. Remember Montagnier's theory on water memory?"

Dr. Patel nodded. "You've mentioned it before. Water as a conduit for energy waves, holding memory, transmitting information. But do you really think it's connected to them?"

Orrington leaned forward, his fingers tapping the desk impatiently. "I'm certain. The data shows these interdimensional beings have a way of harnessing energy from water itself. The ranch is just the beginning."

Patel's brow furrowed as she leaned over the desk, examining the data. "But if this is true, why haven't we seen more evidence? More physical proof?"

Orrington let out a frustrated sigh. "Because they're far more advanced than we are. They control what we can and cannot see. Look at this." He pointed to the footage of the blue orb. "This was captured using a high-frequency infrared camera. To the naked eye, that orb was invisible."

Patel crossed her arms. "So, what now? We can't just keep chasing these shadows without a plan."

Orrington stood, his movements sharp. "We don't have time for second-guessing. The ranch holds the key. The energy fluctuations, the strange anomalies—it all centers around that location. We need to go there, gather more data, and find out what they're hiding."

Patel hesitated. "But the last team that went there... didn't they report strange disturbances? Equipment failures? Even physical sickness?"

Orrington's jaw tightened. "Yes, but that's exactly why we need to go back. Whatever is happening there, it's beyond anything we've seen before. And I'm convinced it's all connected to the interdimensional species we've been tracking."

Patel looked uncertain, but there was a spark of curiosity in her eyes. "Alright. But we need more than just the two of us. If we're going back to the ranch, we'll need backup."

Orrington nodded. "I've already contacted a team. They'll meet us there tomorrow night. We go in, we observe, and we record everything we can. No mistakes this time."

Patel glanced at the footage one last time before turning toward the door. "I'll gather my equipment. This might be the breakthrough we've been waiting for."

As Patel left the room, Orrington sat back down, staring at the blue orb on the screen. His thoughts raced, the weight of the mission bearing down on him. He reached for a notebook, flipping it open to the page where he'd jotted down notes on the ranch's peculiar energy readings.

"This is it," he whispered to himself. "This is where we find the truth."

The night seemed to stretch on as Orrington poured over the data, the silence of his study broken only by the hum of the monitors. He couldn't shake the feeling that they were being watched—not just by the orbs, but by something much larger, much more dangerous.

The next evening, Orrington and Patel arrived at the ranch. The sky was clear, a vast expanse of stars stretching out above them, but the air felt thick with tension. Orrington adjusted the strap of his camera bag, his eyes scanning the horizon.

Patel glanced around uneasily. "It feels different here. Like the air is... charged."

Orrington nodded. "That's the energy I've been tracking. It's stronger here than anywhere else. Stay close."

As they made their way toward the center of the ranch, the ground beneath them seemed to vibrate, a low hum that grew louder the closer they got. Orrington stopped suddenly, pulling out his infrared camera and holding it up to his eye.

"There," he said, pointing ahead. "The orb. It's here."

Patel squinted into the darkness. "I can't see anything."

"Exactly," Orrington muttered, snapping a picture with the camera. "But it's there. Just like the others."

Patel frowned. "If they're watching us, what do they want? Why this place?"

Orrington's eyes narrowed. "The ranch is a hotspot. A convergence point for different energy fields. It's the perfect place for them to observe us—and possibly more."

They continued walking, the hum growing louder. Orrington stopped again, his attention drawn to a large patch of ground. "This is where the energy readings spiked."

Patel knelt down, pulling out a small device from her bag. She switched it on, and the screen immediately began to flash, the readings jumping off the chart.

"These levels are off the scale," she said, her voice filled with awe. "Whatever's causing this... it's not natural."

Orrington crouched beside her, his hand hovering over the ground. "It's them. They're here, right beneath our feet."

Patel stood up, her face pale. "What are we dealing with, Orrington?"

He didn't answer at first, his gaze fixed on the flashing lights of her device. Finally, he stood, his expression grim. "We're dealing with something beyond our understanding. Something that defies the laws of physics as we know them."

Patel's voice shook slightly. "And what happens if we dig too deep? What if we provoke them?"

Orrington met her eyes. "Then we find out what they're really capable of."

Suddenly, the ground beneath them rumbled, and a bright flash of light lit up the sky. Orrington instinctively grabbed Patel's arm, pulling her back as the earth shook violently.

"What the hell was that?" Patel gasped, stumbling backward.

Orrington's eyes widened as he stared at the spot where the light had come from. "They're opening a portal."

Patel's hand trembled as she gripped her device. "We need to get out of here. Now."

Orrington shook his head. "No. We need to record this. This could be the proof we've been searching for."

The light grew brighter, pulsating in the distance. Orrington raised his camera, focusing on the center of the disturbance. As the shutter clicked, the outline of a large figure began to take shape in the glow.

"It's them," Orrington whispered. "They're coming through."

Patel's breath caught in her throat. "Orrington, we have to go. This is way beyond what we expected."

But Orrington was transfixed, his eyes locked on the figure emerging from the portal. "This is what we came for, Patel. This is our chance to understand them."

The figure stepped forward, its form humanoid but towering over them. Its skin shimmered with a metallic sheen, and its eyes glowed a deep, unnatural blue.

Patel took a step back, her voice barely above a whisper. "Orrington... we're not prepared for this."

Orrington lowered the camera, his heart pounding in his chest. "We'll never be prepared. But we need to know. We need to see."

The figure stood motionless, watching them. Orrington could feel its gaze piercing through him, like it was studying every fiber of his being.

Without warning, the portal snapped shut, and the figure vanished, leaving only the eerie silence of the night behind.

Chapter 80

Dr. Orrington sat at his desk, surrounded by a chaotic arrangement of documents, notes, and scientific equipment. The gravity of the situation weighed heavily on him, and his brow furrowed with concern. He focused intently, ready to convey vital information.

"Understanding these tactics and technologies is crucial for addressing the threats posed by these organizations and interdimensional species," he said, his voice steady but urgent. "The evidence is mounting, and our awareness must grow in tandem."

Across the room, Patel, his assistant, shuffled through a pile of papers, her expression mirroring his seriousness. "Dr. Orrington, we can't ignore the implications of this. If the UAPs are using a specific frequency for communication, that means they have a method of organizing, strategizing."

Dr. Orrington nodded, tapping a pen against the desk thoughtfully. "Exactly. In the third episode of Season Three, we witnessed a fascinating and troubling demonstration of the influence of extraterrestrials and unidentified aerial phenomena on living organisms."

Patel glanced up, intrigued. "What exactly did the research team uncover?"

"The team identified a 1.6 GHz frequency, which they suspected to be a communication channel used by UAPs," Dr. Orrington explained, leaning back in his chair. "They observed changes in local wildlife behaviors coinciding with the frequency's transmission."

"What kind of changes?" Patel asked, her curiosity piqued.

"Unexplained migration patterns, altered feeding habits, even signs of distress in certain species," he replied, gesturing to a series of graphs on the wall. "It's as if the UAPs are exerting some form of control over these organisms."

Patel frowned, clearly concerned. "That sounds alarming. If they can manipulate wildlife, what's stopping them from influencing humans?"

Dr. Orrington's expression hardened. "That's precisely the point. We need to understand the full scope of their capabilities. We can't afford to underestimate them."

Patel shifted uneasily in her seat. "What do you propose we do next?"

"We need to gather more data," he said decisively. "I want you to reach out to our contacts in the field. See if they've noticed anything unusual regarding animal behaviors near known UAP hotspots."

"On it," Patel replied, already jotting down notes. "I'll also check in with the tech team about enhancing our monitoring equipment."

Dr. Orrington watched her with a mixture of admiration and concern. "Be careful, Patel. We don't know how far-reaching their influence is. Keep me updated on any findings."

Patel gave him a reassuring nod before stepping out of the study. Alone again, Dr. Orrington stared at the array of documents before him. The evidence was growing more concerning by the day, and he couldn't shake the feeling that time was running out.

The following day, Patel returned with a new sense of urgency. "Dr. Orrington, you need to see this," she said, her voice barely concealing her excitement.

"What have you found?" he asked, leaning forward.

"I contacted several researchers in the field, and one of them reported an unusual event in a nearby national park," Patel explained. "They observed a flock of birds behaving erratically just before a UAP was sighted."

Dr. Orrington raised an eyebrow, intrigued. "What exactly did they see?"

"The birds flew in chaotic patterns, almost as if they were being directed by something unseen. It happened right before the UAP descended," she elaborated, her eyes shining with enthusiasm.

"That's a critical observation," he replied, rubbing his chin thoughtfully. "It suggests a connection between the UAPs and the wildlife."

"Exactly! They even managed to record some of it on video," Patel said, pulling out her tablet and scrolling through files. "Here it is."

Dr. Orrington leaned closer as Patel played the video. The footage showed a dense cluster of birds darting across the sky, their movements erratic and frantic. In the background, a glimmering object descended, cloaked in mystery.

"Remarkable," he murmured, transfixed. "If we can link this behavior to the UAP's presence, it could change everything we know about their influence."

Patel paused the video, her finger hovering over the screen. "What do we do with this information?"

"We need to analyze the data further," he said, determination flooding his voice. "Can you arrange for a team to investigate the area where this occurred?"

"Absolutely," she replied, her enthusiasm infectious. "I'll start organizing a field team immediately."

As she prepared to leave, Dr. Orrington added, "And Patel, make sure they approach with caution. We still don't fully understand the risks involved."

"Understood, Dr. Orrington," she said with a nod, already focused on her task.

Days passed, and the field team reported back with significant findings. Patel excitedly burst into the study. "Dr. Orrington! You won't believe what we discovered!"

"What is it?" he asked, looking up from his notes, anticipation buzzing in the air.

"The wildlife is exhibiting more strange behaviors, and we found evidence of potential UAP activity in the area," she explained, her voice animated. "We've documented changes in both predator and prey species."

Dr. Orrington's eyes widened. "This is groundbreaking. What else did you learn?"

"The team collected samples of the soil and vegetation in areas where the anomalous behavior was recorded. They're still analyzing it, but initial results show unusual chemical signatures," Patel said, flipping through her notes.

"What do you mean by unusual?" he probed, leaning forward.

"Substances not typically found in the environment. We think they may be linked to the UAPs," she clarified. "If we can prove a direct correlation, it could be a major breakthrough in our understanding."

"Let's convene the team. I want everyone's input on how we can expand our research," Dr. Orrington said, his mind racing with possibilities.

Patel quickly organized a meeting, gathering the research team in the study. As they settled in, Dr. Orrington stood at the head of the table, his expression serious.

"Thank you all for coming on such short notice," he began. "Patel has shared some critical findings regarding the influence of UAPs on wildlife, and I believe it's imperative that we strategize our next steps carefully."

The room buzzed with murmurs of interest as the team leaned in.

"Can you summarize the findings for us, Patel?" one of the researchers asked, eager for details.

"Certainly," she said, her voice steady. "We've observed erratic behavior in several species near UAP sightings, along with unusual chemical signatures in soil and vegetation samples."

Dr. Orrington interjected, "These findings suggest a direct influence that these UAPs may have on local ecosystems. If we can establish a pattern, it may lead us to understanding their communication methods and intentions."

"What's our first step?" another researcher asked, glancing around the table.

"I propose we conduct further field studies in areas with known UAP activity, focusing on both wildlife behavior and environmental samples," Dr. Orrington replied, his eyes scanning the room.

"And what about the risks? We need to consider the potential for exposure," one of the researchers voiced, concern etched on her face.

Patel nodded in agreement. "We need to ensure we're taking all necessary precautions to protect ourselves and our data."

Dr. Orrington held up his hands to calm the growing apprehension. "I understand the concerns, and I assure you that safety will be our top priority. We will approach these investigations with the utmost caution and preparedness."

The room fell silent as the team processed his words.

"Let's break into smaller groups," Patel suggested. "We can cover more ground that way and gather more data."

"Agreed," Dr. Orrington said, looking at each team member. "Let's split up into two groups: one focusing on wildlife observation and the other on environmental sampling. We'll reconvene in a week to share our findings."

The team nodded in unison, their determination rekindled.

As they dispersed, Patel caught Dr. Orrington's eye. "You really think we're on the brink of something significant?"

"I do," he replied, a flicker of hope igniting within him. "But we must remain vigilant. There's still much we don't know about these entities and their intentions."

Patel smiled, her resolve strengthening. "Then let's uncover the truth."

The next week brought a flurry of activity as the teams ventured into the field. They observed animal behaviors, collected samples, and shared insights, each passing day heightening their sense of urgency and purpose.

When the team reconvened, the atmosphere in the study was electric. Dr. Orrington stood at the head of the table, ready to hear their findings.

"Let's start with the wildlife observations," he said, looking around the room.

A researcher named Foster spoke up. "We witnessed several species displaying heightened stress responses. They were skittish, and some were even moving in erratic patterns. It's as if they sensed something we couldn't."

Patel nodded. "That aligns with what we've seen in previous cases. We need to analyze how their behaviors correlate with UAP sightings."

"Exactly. I believe we're onto something," Dr. Orrington replied, jotting down notes. "What about the environmental samples?"

Another team member, Lena, chimed in. "The samples showed elevated levels of certain chemicals, particularly heavy metals and unknown compounds.

They're unlike anything we've encountered in this region before."

Dr. Orrington's interest piqued. "Could these be residuals from UAP activity?"

"It's possible," Lena confirmed. "We're still analyzing the data, but the preliminary findings suggest a connection."

Chapter 81

The research lab hummed with the low buzz of machinery, the atmosphere thick with anticipation as the team monitored their equipment. Dr. Orrington paced back and forth, glancing at the numerous screens displaying various frequencies. Suddenly, the familiar tone of the 1.6 GHz frequency activated, cutting through the air with an unexpected clarity.

"What just happened?" Patel, his assistant, asked, her eyes darting to the nearest monitor.

Dr. Orrington narrowed his eyes at the flickering screen. "It shouldn't be active right now. We're not transmitting anything."

A ripple of confusion swept through the team, each researcher exchanging uncertain glances. "Could it be a glitch?" one of the technicians suggested, frowning at the equipment.

"No, this frequency has been stable all day," Dr. Orrington replied. "This is different. Let's check the logs."

As the team scrambled to pull up the data, a sudden, shocking sound echoed in the lab: their own voices, clear as day, echoed over the speakers.

"Did you hear that?" Patel gasped, stepping back. "That's us!"

"Wait, what?" Foster, another team member, looked up from his monitor, disbelief etched on his face. "How is that even possible?"

Dr. Orrington leaned closer to the speakers, his brow furrowed with concentration. "We're not transmitting anything. There are no visible devices here that could be broadcasting our voices."

Patel shook her head, trying to make sense of the situation. "This doesn't make any sense. We confirmed there were no listening devices on us or any equipment capable of transmitting our voices."

"Maybe it's a malfunction in the equipment," Foster suggested, crossing his arms skeptically. "How can we rule that out?"

Dr. Orrington turned sharply, his gaze piercing. "No, this is something more significant. We need to investigate further. If we're picking up our own voices on this frequency, it could mean—"

"—that something or someone is listening to us," Patel finished, her voice barely above a whisper.

"Exactly," Dr. Orrington confirmed, turning back to the screens. "I want a full diagnostic on every piece of equipment. If there's a way our voices are being transmitted, we need to find it."

The team sprang into action, fingers flying over keyboards as they checked every connection, every piece of hardware. The tension in the room escalated, urgency and anxiety hanging in the air.

"Dr. Orrington," one of the technicians called out, glancing up from his station. "I'm seeing some unusual spikes in the data logs. It's like the frequency is fluctuating unexpectedly."

"Fluctuating? In what way?" Dr. Orrington asked, stepping closer.

"Right before we heard our voices, the frequency jumped," the technician explained, pointing at the screen. "Look at these readings."

"Interesting," Dr. Orrington mused, leaning over the monitor. "We need to find out if there's a pattern to these fluctuations."

Patel watched the exchange, her brow furrowing deeper. "If there's a pattern, that means it's not random. Someone or something could be orchestrating it."

"Exactly. We need to determine whether this is a natural phenomenon or if we're dealing with something intentional," Dr. Orrington said, his mind racing with possibilities. "What about the location of the frequency? Can we track its origin?"

Foster piped up, "We should be able to triangulate the signal if we access the satellite feeds."

"Good idea. Let's do it," Dr. Orrington ordered, his eyes narrowing with determination. "I want everyone on this. We can't let this slip away."

As the team continued to analyze the data, tension hung thick in the air. Patel glanced at Dr. Orrington, her voice low. "What if this isn't just about surveillance? What if it's a warning or even a form of communication?"

Dr. Orrington met her gaze, the gravity of her words sinking in. "If it is a form of communication, it changes everything. We need to approach this carefully. I don't want to provoke whatever is out there."

"Right," Patel agreed. "But we can't ignore it either. This could be the breakthrough we've been waiting for."

"Let's focus on gathering more data first," Dr. Orrington said, straightening up. "We need to understand what we're dealing with before we make any decisions."

As they worked through the next hours, the atmosphere in the lab oscillated between excitement and anxiety. The data streamed in, revealing patterns that hinted at the mysterious nature of the frequency.

Finally, Foster called out, his voice ringing with excitement. "I think I've got something! The frequency's fluctuations seem to align with specific times of the day."

"Show me," Dr. Orrington commanded, moving to Foster's station. The technician pulled up a series of graphs, each one indicating a corresponding spike in activity.

Patel leaned in, her eyes widening. "That's around the same time sightings have been reported in the area."

"Exactly," Foster said, enthusiasm radiating from him. "It's almost like the UAPs are responding to something. If we can determine what's triggering these spikes, we might be able to understand their behavior better."

Dr. Orrington nodded, his mind racing. "We need to cross-reference these times with local reports of UAP activity. If there's a correlation, it could lead us to a deeper understanding of their communication methods."

The team worked tirelessly, pulling in data from various sources, piecing together the puzzle.

"Dr. Orrington," Patel said suddenly, interrupting the focused atmosphere. "I think we should reach out to the other research teams who've encountered these frequencies. They might have additional insights."

"Good thinking, Patel. Let's do it," Dr. Orrington agreed. "They might have faced similar phenomena. We can compare notes."

The team began sending messages to their colleagues at different institutions, hoping to gather more evidence and experiences related to the frequency. As they waited, the lab continued to buzz with energy, each member eager to uncover the truth.

Days passed, and the team received responses from various research teams.

"Dr. Orrington!" Patel called excitedly, rushing over to his desk. "Look at this! One of the teams reported similar occurrences of their voices being transmitted, but they also mentioned experiencing strange electromagnetic disturbances around the same time."

"Electromagnetic disturbances?" Dr. Orrington repeated, intrigued. "That could be a significant lead. If there's a connection between these disturbances and the frequency…"

"Exactly! It's almost like they're connected to the UAPs in some way," Patel concluded, her excitement contagious.

Dr. Orrington tapped his pen against the desk, deep in thought. "We need to find out if these disturbances can be measured or if they correspond to the spikes we've observed."

Patel nodded, her mind racing. "I can arrange for a team to head to the sites where those disturbances were reported. We can set up monitoring equipment to gather data."

"Do it. I want every detail analyzed," Dr. Orrington ordered, a sense of urgency driving his words. "We need to understand the implications of these findings before we proceed any further."

As Patel organized the field team, Dr. Orrington gathered the rest of the researchers to discuss their next steps.

"Everyone, listen up!" he called, drawing their attention. "We've made some significant progress, but we're still in the early stages of this investigation. I want us to remain vigilant and ready to adapt as we uncover more information."

Foster raised his hand. "What about the electromagnetic disturbances? Shouldn't we prioritize investigating those?"

"That's a valid point," Dr. Orrington replied. "We can't afford to overlook any potential connections. We'll need to approach this investigation from multiple angles. Patel will lead the team monitoring the disturbances while we continue analyzing our data here."

"Got it," Patel affirmed, already jotting down her plans. "I'll make sure the field team is equipped with everything they need."

"Great. Let's stay focused, team," Dr. Orrington said, instilling a sense of purpose in the room. "We're on the brink of something important, but we must remain cautious."

As the team dispersed, the atmosphere crackled with determination and anticipation. Everyone understood the significance of their work and the potential consequences of their findings.

In the following days, the field team ventured out to investigate the electromagnetic disturbances, while Dr. Orrington and Patel stayed behind to analyze the data and follow up with their colleagues.

"Patel, I want to review all the previous studies on UAPs and their electromagnetic signatures," Dr.

Orrington instructed. "There might be historical data that can shed light on what we're experiencing."

"On it," Patel replied, her fingers flying over the keyboard. "I'll compile everything relevant to our current research."

As the hours ticked by, the tension in the lab mounted.

Then, just as Patel was about to lose herself in a mountain of data, a notification pinged on her computer. "Dr. Orrington, I just got an alert from the field team. They're reporting strange readings."

"What kind of readings?" he asked, leaning in closer.

"Electromagnetic fields spiking at irregular intervals," Patel said, her heart racing. "And they're seeing UAPs in the area as well."

"Let's get them on the line," Dr. Orrington commanded, his focus sharp. "I want to hear exactly what they're seeing."

Patel quickly dialed in, connecting the field team to their communication system.

"Field team, this is Dr. Orrington. Can you hear me?" he spoke firmly.

Chapter 82

The sun hung high in the sky as the team at the research facility buzzed with excitement and trepidation. Outside, the air was alive with sounds of nature—a faint rustle of leaves, birds chirping, and the distant hum of vehicles. Inside, however, the atmosphere was charged with the weight of recent discoveries. Dr. Orrington's team had been grappling with an anomaly that had the potential to reshape their understanding of communication and UAPs.

"Alright, everyone," Patel called out, gathering the team around the entrance. "We need to see if this broadcasting phenomenon holds true outside. Let's take it to the field."

The team members exchanged glances, some looking skeptical, others eager for the challenge. "You really think our voices will carry out there?" Foster asked, a hint of doubt in his tone.

Patel shrugged. "We have to test it, right? We've seen what happens inside. Why not see if it's the same outside?"

"Good point," Dr. Orrington chimed in, stepping forward. "Let's conduct a few simple tests. Everyone grab a piece of equipment to monitor the frequency. We'll keep the communication lines open."

With that, the group filed outside, excitement building with every step. They found a quiet area near the edge of the facility, where the trees swayed gently in the breeze.

"Okay, let's see if our voices are still transmitted," Patel instructed, her voice steady. "Everyone, just talk normally. I'll start the monitoring."

As the team began to chatter amongst themselves, their voices floated into the air, unimpeded by the surrounding nature. Patel's equipment crackled, capturing their words with startling clarity.

"Hey, did you see the latest data?" Foster asked, his voice ringing out. "I can't believe we're still picking it up out here."

"Yeah, it's bizarre!" another team member, Jenna, replied. "It's like we're broadcasting on some cosmic radio station or something."

The group laughed, but there was an underlying tension in the air. Patel checked her equipment, her brow furrowing as she reviewed the readings. "The frequency is still active. It's just as strong out here as it was indoors."

"Are you serious?" Foster exclaimed, looking incredulous. "How is that even possible?"

Dr. Orrington, observing closely, interjected. "We need to consider all possible factors. Let's think about what could be carrying the signal."

"What do you mean?" Jenna asked, glancing at him curiously.

Dr. Orrington turned to face the team, his expression serious. "Let's consider an overlooked aspect: the water vapor expelled every time we breathe or talk. It could be a carrier wave for our voices, allowing them to be transmitted over the UAP frequency."

A moment of silence fell over the group as they processed his words. "So you're saying every time we exhale, we might be broadcasting?" Patel asked, her eyes widening.

"Exactly," Dr. Orrington replied, nodding. "This water vapor could be collecting and carrying our voices, making it possible for them to be picked up by the frequency."

"Wow, that's wild," Foster said, shaking his head in disbelief. "It's like we're walking microphones."

"Let's get some visual data to support this," Dr. Orrington suggested, his mind racing. "Patel, can you create a visual representation of how this water vapor works in relation to the frequency?"

"Absolutely. I'll get right on it," she affirmed, her fingers already moving over her tablet.

As Patel began working, the rest of the team continued talking, their voices excitement and confusion. Dr. Orrington observed them, his mind whirling with possibilities.

"Okay, how about this?" Jenna proposed, breaking into the conversation. "What if we try to manipulate the way we speak? Like, if we change our tones or speeds, would that affect the broadcast?"

Dr. Orrington considered this for a moment. "That could yield interesting results. Let's try it. Speak at varying volumes and speeds. We'll monitor to see if there are changes in the frequency output."

The team agreed, and as they shifted into their experimental phase, they began to alter their speech. Some shouted, others whispered, while a few chose to speak in rapid bursts. Patel's equipment hummed, capturing the shifts in their voices.

"Can you hear me?" Foster shouted dramatically, his voice echoing through the trees. "Testing, testing! One, two, three!"

Patel laughed, her eyes glued to the screen. "We've got it! The frequency is fluctuating with your volume, Foster!"

"Really?" Foster replied, grinning. "I feel like a radio DJ!"

"Alright, now let's try something different," Dr. Orrington said, his eyes sparkling with excitement. "Let's see if emotional tone affects the transmission. Try speaking with different emotions—anger, joy, sadness."

The team exchanged looks but nodded in agreement. "I can do angry!" Jenna proclaimed, crossing her arms and glaring at Foster. "I can't believe you didn't back up the data!"

"Whoa, calm down, it's just data!" Foster laughed, pretending to flinch.

The laughter in the air eased the tension, but everyone was aware of the significance of their experiment. As they continued to experiment with different emotional tones, Patel's readings showed significant spikes and fluctuations in the frequency.

"Dr. Orrington, look at this!" Patel exclaimed, excitement bubbling in her voice. "The emotional tone is absolutely affecting the transmission. This could open up a whole new avenue for understanding how we communicate!"

Dr. Orrington's eyes gleamed with a mixture of awe and determination. "This is groundbreaking. If we can understand how emotional tone and water vapor affect communication with UAPs, we might uncover a method of reaching out to them."

"What do you mean?" Foster asked, his interest piqued.

"Think about it," Dr. Orrington said, gesturing animatedly. "If we can manipulate our voices in a way that enhances our transmission through the water vapor, we may be able to establish some form of communication with these entities."

The team fell silent, the weight of his words settling in. "So, you're saying we could actually talk to them?" Jenna asked, her voice barely above a whisper.

"Exactly," Dr. Orrington affirmed, his passion shining through. "But we need to be careful. Communication isn't just about broadcasting our voices; it's about understanding the language they might be using as well."

"Alright, so what's the plan?" Patel asked, her determination mirroring his. "How do we proceed from here?"

"First, we gather all the data from today's experiments and analyze it," Dr. Orrington replied, his voice steady. "We'll look for patterns in the fluctuations and correlations with our emotional tones. Then, we can create a protocol for future communication attempts."

"Got it," Patel said, already scribbling notes. "I'll compile all the readings and document everything we've learned today."

As the team wrapped up their outdoor experiments, they couldn't shake the excitement coursing through them. The potential implications of their discoveries loomed large.

Back inside the facility, Dr. Orrington gathered everyone around a central table laden with laptops and data sheets. "Let's go over what we have. We need to create a cohesive plan moving forward."

"Here's what we know so far," Patel began, her voice confident. "The 1.6 GHz frequency is consistently active, regardless of location. Our voices are being transmitted through water vapor, and emotional tone significantly impacts the frequency output."

Foster chimed in, "And we might be able to manipulate our voices to enhance communication with UAPs."

"Yes," Dr. Orrington said, nodding. "But we must remember that we're venturing into uncharted territory. We need to approach this scientifically and cautiously."

Jenna raised her hand. "What about the visual representation of water vapor? Can we use that to illustrate our findings?"

"That's an excellent idea," Dr. Orrington replied. "Patel, I'd like you to create visual data to accompany our findings. It could be crucial in presenting our research to the scientific community."

"Will do," Patel said, her enthusiasm palpable. "I'll get started right away."

As the team continued discussing their next steps, the camaraderie and shared sense of purpose deepened. They were united by their curiosity and determination to uncover the truth behind the phenomena they were experiencing.

Hours turned into days as the team delved deeper into their research. They meticulously analyzed data, conducted experiments, and developed new methods for communication.

One evening, as the sun dipped below the horizon, painting the sky in hues of orange and pink, the team gathered once more in Dr. Orrington's study.

"I think we're ready to share our findings," Dr. Orrington announced, his voice filled with confidence. "We need to reach out to the broader scientific community and start discussing our results."

"But what if they don't believe us?" Jenna asked, concern etched on her face. "This is groundbreaking, but it's also a lot to digest."

"We'll present our data clearly and concisely," Dr. Orrington assured her. "We've backed our findings with empirical evidence, and we'll invite scrutiny. That's how science works."

The team nodded in agreement, their resolve strengthening. They were ready to share what they had discovered, knowing the significance of their work could potentially change the course of research into UAPs and communication.

"Let's finalize our presentation and set a date to share our findings," Patel said, determination shining in her eyes.

Chapter 83

The buzz of anticipation filled the room as Dr. Orrington gathered his team for another meeting. Their discoveries over the past few weeks had raised more questions than answers, and he was eager to dive into the latest findings.

"Alright, team," he began, leaning against the table strewn with data sheets and equipment. "Let's talk about what we learned from the previous experiments. The implications of our discoveries could be monumental."

Foster, sitting at the edge of his seat, chimed in. "So, are we saying that every word we say is actually being heard by extraterrestrial beings? That sounds almost too fantastic to believe."

"Fantastic, yes," Dr. Orrington replied, "but it's grounded in our research. Nobel Prize winner Prof. Luc Montagnier demonstrated that all water is interconnected. Water transmits signals, receives them, and stores information. This understanding of water changes our perception entirely."

"So, you're saying that water vapor in the air acts like a medium for our voices?" Patel asked, furrowing her brow in thought.

"Exactly," Dr. Orrington affirmed. "And this brings us to our next point. It is well documented that highly charged subterranean water is found near planetary orbits. Consequently, every word we utter is transmitted through the air's water vapor, which then broadcasts the signal to E.T. and UAPs. They hear everything in real time."

Jenna, who had been silent up to that point, raised her hand. "So, does that mean we're essentially broadcasting a message to them every time we speak? What if they're responding?"

A wave of excitement rippled through the team. "That's a possibility we need to explore," Dr. Orrington said, his eyes glinting with determination. "If we can learn to modulate our voices and use our emotional tones effectively, we could establish a form of communication."

"Isn't that risky?" Foster interjected. "What if they don't want to communicate? Or worse, what if they misinterpret our intentions?"

"We have to approach this with caution," Dr. Orrington agreed. "But the potential for groundbreaking discoveries far outweighs the risks. We owe it to ourselves and to science to pursue this."

"Okay, so what's the next step?" Patel asked, her voice eager.

Dr. Orrington smiled. "I want us to refine our techniques for modulating our voices. Let's gather data on different emotional tones and their effects on the transmission. Then we'll try to create a structured communication protocol."

Jenna nodded, enthusiasm bubbling in her. "I'll start working on a guide for emotional expression in our speech. We can create categories and test how each affects the frequency output."

"Perfect," Dr. Orrington replied. "And I'll compile the research on water's communicative properties. If we can present a compelling case for this connection, we can gain more credibility in the scientific community."

As the team dispersed to tackle their tasks, the energy in the room was palpable. They were pioneers on the brink of a significant breakthrough, and the potential for discovery hung in the air.

Days turned into a whirlwind of research, discussions, and experiments. The team worked late into the night, fueled by coffee and excitement as they honed their methods.

One afternoon, as they gathered in the lab, Foster leaned back in his chair, looking contemplative. "You know, I keep thinking about what we discussed last week. If E.T.s are indeed hearing us, what do you think they're thinking?"

Jenna chuckled. "Probably wondering why we're so obsessed with them! Or they might be confused about why we keep shouting into the void."

"Or maybe they're laughing at us," Patel added with a smirk. "Imagine a bunch of aliens listening to our mundane conversations."

Dr. Orrington interjected, a serious tone creeping into his voice. "We have to remember that our approach matters. Every word we speak carries weight. If they're listening, we need to ensure we're sending a message of curiosity and openness, not fear or aggression."

Foster nodded slowly. "You're right. It's not just about transmitting information; it's about understanding the nature of communication itself."

"Exactly," Dr. Orrington said. "And the more we understand about our own communication, the better equipped we'll be to engage with them."

That evening, Patel brought her findings to the table, ready to share her thoughts. "I've been analyzing emotional tones and how they affect our frequency output. Here's what I've come up with."

She clicked a button on her laptop, and a graph appeared on the screen, illustrating the relationship between emotional expression and frequency modulation. "This shows that positive emotions like joy and excitement produce a higher frequency output, while negative emotions like anger lower it significantly."

"Interesting," Foster commented, leaning closer to the screen. "So, if we want to reach out to E.T.s, we should focus on speaking positively?"

"Yes, but it's more nuanced than that," Patel continued. "We also need to consider the context.

How we frame our questions and statements can impact how our messages are received."

"Let's test this," Jenna suggested, her enthusiasm bubbling over. "We can set up a series of recordings where we vary our emotional tones and see how the frequency changes. Then we can analyze the results."

"Good idea," Dr. Orrington said, nodding. "Let's schedule a session for tomorrow. I want everyone to be prepared to express a range of emotions as we record."

As the team prepared for the next day's experiments, excitement buzzed in the air. They were no longer just researchers; they were communication pioneers.

The following morning, the team gathered in the lab, ready to put their plans into action. Dr. Orrington set up the recording equipment, ensuring everything was in place for their experiment.

"Okay, let's get started," he said, his voice firm but encouraging. "Remember, we're focusing on a variety of emotional tones. We want to capture how each affects our transmission."

Foster stepped forward, a mischievous glint in his eye. "I'll go first. How about I try excitement?"

"Go for it!" Patel encouraged.

Foster took a deep breath and exclaimed, "I can't believe we're doing this! This is going to be amazing!"

Dr. Orrington monitored the readings as Foster spoke, nodding approvingly. "Great energy, Foster. Let's see how that translates."

Next, Patel stepped up, preparing to express sadness. "I just feel like we're on the brink of something incredible, but there's always a part of me that worries about what lies ahead."

Jenna recorded the output while Dr. Orrington watched the data stream. "Interesting. There's a noticeable drop in frequency. We'll want to analyze that further."

As the recording session continued, they moved through various emotional tones—anger, joy, curiosity, fear. Each time, Dr. Orrington monitored the frequency output, noting the fluctuations that resulted from their emotional expressions.

Finally, they reached the end of their session. "That was enlightening," Jenna said, her eyes sparkling with enthusiasm. "I can't wait to see the analysis!"

"Me too," Dr. Orrington agreed. "The data we've gathered today could help us understand not only how we communicate but also how we might effectively reach out to potential extraterrestrial listeners."

The team spent the next few days analyzing their recordings, pouring over the data to discern patterns and insights. As they reviewed the findings, the excitement continued to build.

One afternoon, as they gathered to discuss their results, Patel looked up from her laptop, her expression thoughtful. "What if we combined our findings with the theory of interconnected water? We could theorize that not only are our voices transmitted, but the emotional tones we use might resonate with similar frequencies in the water vapor around us."

"Like a cosmic echo?" Foster suggested, his eyes widening with intrigue.

"Exactly!" Patel replied. "If we're all connected through this medium, then it stands to reason that our emotional expressions could influence the way E.T.s perceive us."

"Let's outline a plan to present this theory," Dr. Orrington said, a sense of urgency creeping into his tone. "This could be the breakthrough we've been waiting for."

As they delved into the nuances of their findings, a sense of purpose filled the room. They were no longer just researchers chasing vague leads; they were on the cusp of a revolutionary discovery.

Over the next week, they refined their presentation, preparing to share their findings with the scientific community. As they rehearsed their pitch, the excitement among the team continued to build.

"Alright, team," Dr. Orrington said, his voice steady as they gathered for their final rehearsal. "Let's run through this one last time. Remember, we're not just sharing data; we're presenting a vision for the future of communication."

As they practiced, the energy in the room shifted from nervousness to confidence. They had worked hard, and their discoveries held the potential to change the conversation about extraterrestrial life forever.

Finally, the day arrived for their presentation. As they stood in front of a packed auditorium filled with scientists, researchers, and journalists, Dr. Orrington took a deep breath.

"Thank you all for being here today," he began, his voice firm. "What we are about to share with you may challenge the way you think about communication, both on Earth and beyond."

As he launched into their presentation, the room fell silent, captivated by the possibility of what lay ahead. And as Dr. Orrington spoke, the weight of their research—the countless hours of experimentation and collaboration—hung in the air like an unspoken promise.

"Let's not just talk about our findings," he concluded, looking out over the audience. "Let's open the doors to new ways of understanding not just ourselves.

Chapter 84

Dr. Orrington's study was a cacophony of papers and books, a fortress of knowledge nestled among artifacts that seemed to hum with energy. He leaned closer to the camera, his brow furrowed with intensity.

"Water is not a simple substance. It has unique properties essential for various processes. This understanding is crucial as interdimensional species are capable of monitoring us through the water in our atmosphere."

The camera captured his unwavering gaze, a silent plea for his audience to grasp the gravity of his words.

"Did you know," he continued, "that a recent documentary on the History Channel discussed how UAPs disabled nuclear missiles? It was compelling, despite the skepticism surrounding it."

The scene shifted to the documentary footage. Military personnel, stone-faced, watched UAPs hover ominously over missile silos.

"Initial disbelief crumbled," Dr. Orrington's voice echoed, "when it became evident these unidentified aerial phenomena could render our most powerful weapons useless."

Back in his study, Dr. Orrington's expression was one of mounting frustration.

"Numerous experiments have failed due to equipment malfunctions," he stated. "E.T. and UAPs can interfere with all technology—computers, robots, cell phones, GPS. This interference is a stark reminder that all communication on Earth originates from water, and Earth itself was formed from water."

He paused, visibly struggling with the weight of his message.

"Based on my experiences," he continued, "interdimensional species can control weather patterns. This control further underscores the need to understand and address these phenomena."

Cut to the tumultuous storm outside, wind howling and rain lashing against the windows. Dr. Orrington's voice remained steady against the backdrop of chaos.

"We are constantly under surveillance, with no defense against E.T. and UAPs. Understanding their methods and the role of water in their surveillance is essential for our survival and awareness."

Dr. Orrington leaned back in his chair, hands steepled as he contemplated the camera. "In the ninth episode of Season Three, a breakthrough was revealed. Researchers drilling in the Mesa region discovered a metal with superconducting properties—artificially manufactured and used for cloaking purposes."

Footage of the Mesa region showed the drilling operation, machines whirring and workers surveying the terrain. The camera panned to reveal glimmering metal samples being extracted.

"This metal's application in cloaking technology is a crucial component of extraterrestrial and interdimensional species' surveillance methods," Dr. Orrington narrated, his tone unwavering. "In the ninth episode, a translucent metallic object orbiting the Earth was barely visible to the naked eye but enhanced through a camera."

Cut to the documentary series, where the cloaked object flickered against the night sky, a ghostly presence that sent shivers down the spine.

"This illustrates the power of extraterrestrial technology," Dr. Orrington continued, "and their capability for long-term observation. These cloaked machines monitor specific subjects from above."

The footage shifted, displaying military personnel deploying aerial surveillance techniques, their focus palpable.

"You will witness how the military conducts surveillance, highlighting the necessity of protecting oneself from aerial threats," Dr. Orrington urged. "I have developed several scientific systems for personal protection against such threats."

He paused, visibly concerned. "Interdimensional species consume significant amounts of water and employ various communication methods. The key to understanding how they interact with water lies in the signals they receive."

The camera shifted to Dr. Orrington in a laboratory, arranging bottles of distilled water under the sun with Bob Marley music playing softly in the background.

"I urge you to drink only distilled water. Expose it to two hours of sunlight with Bob Marley music," he instructed. "Follow this regimen for 30 days, and you will perceive the answer beyond mere words. It is a signal you must experience firsthand."

Scenes of people sipping distilled water in serene outdoor settings played alongside his voiceover.

"The answer you seek is not expressed in words but in the experience itself," he reiterated. "It is a signal that will become clear through personal insight and observation."

In his study, Dr. Orrington gazed earnestly into the camera. "Remember, understanding E.T. and UAP activities requires more than study—it demands personal experience and a deeper connection with the fundamental elements of our world."

Dr. Orrington's intensity heightened as he spoke of the wonders he had witnessed. "In the tenth episode of Season Four, we observed a stone mountain behaving like water. This sight reinforces our understanding of water as a supercomputer, a collective consciousness program designed for harmony and interaction."

Footage of the mountain undulating like water captivated the viewers, its majestic presence awe-inspiring.

"This observation supports the idea that water is more than just a substance," he continued. "It acts as a conduit for interdimensional entities to create organic computer programs, blending past and future energy lifeforms with organic matter."

He held up a DVD case of "War Games," eyes gleaming with passion. "For a deeper understanding of water's objectives, watch this film. It will provide insights into the concept of water as a supercomputer with specific goals and functions, much like supercomputers have their own objectives."

In a scientific lab, researchers conducted experiments, carefully observing water's responses.

"To replenish water effectively, we must embrace periods of inactivity. This approach will not only benefit us but also help us receive extraordinary gifts."

Dr. Orrington placed a hand on his heart, eyes filled with hope. "One such gift is the capacity to merge any energy lifeform, whether from the past or future, with organic matter. This ability allows for the healing of all flesh, facilitated by specific frequencies of energy waves."

Outside, a serene landscape unfolded, sunlight filtering through the trees and a gentle stream babbling nearby.

"We have witnessed how UAPs can hear everything through water at their 1.6 GHz frequency," Dr. Orrington's voice echoed. "By putting our environment first, we show our commitment to this universal balance."

He stood by the window, gazing out into the starry night, his voice shifting to a contemplative tone. "We are presented with a golden opportunity to achieve what no ancient society ever could. By embracing stillness and allowing the water to replenish, we align ourselves with the cosmic order."

The night sky sparkled with possibilities as Dr. Orrington's voice reverberated through the silence. "Remember, time is not linear. Our actions, when aligned with the natural rhythms of water, can lead us to a profound victory. We come from water and return to it, absorbing the electric spirit that guides us."

Turning back to the camera, he spoke with quiet determination. "So, I implore you: let us all sit still, respect the water, and embrace this opportunity. Together, we can win the game. Be well, my friend."

***

The early Sunday morning light gently filled Dr. Orrington's family room, illuminating the chaos of his notes sprawled across the coffee table.

A soft wind brushed against the windows, creating a soothing atmosphere.

Dr. Orrington reclined in his favorite armchair, eyes scanning the jumbled pages. "I need to find a way to communicate this," he murmured to himself.

Just then, a strange occurrence began to unfold. A large white cloud seeped through the walls, moving like a wisp of fog. He blinked, captivated rather than frightened, as the ethereal cloud danced around the room.

"What is this?" he whispered, leaning closer, curiosity piqued.

The cloud hovered at the center of the room, shimmering with life. Dr. Orrington's heart raced as the remarkable phenomenon unfolded before him.

Minutes slipped by as he observed, completely entranced. Suddenly, from the heart of the cloud, a radiant Golden Drop emerged, glowing softly, shimmering with an unearthly light.

As the Golden Drop descended, it was accompanied by four smaller clear drops, orbiting around it like loyal satellites.

His eyes widened in disbelief as the Golden Drop hovered right in front of him. "I had read about moments like this," he thought. "But never could I have imagined…"

The Golden Drop paused, hanging in the air for a moment, then touched Dr. Orrington's chest. A wave of golden energy radiated outward, enveloping him in warmth.

***

Time seemed to stretch as he experienced a profound shift.

Knowledge cascaded into him, immersive and eternal. "I felt it. The pulse of energy. I understood. I truly understood all things," he thought, overwhelmed by the surge of realization.

Visions flashed before his eyes—an expansive universe filled with flowing water, interdimensional beings cloaked in radiant light watching over Earth, the intricate web of life united by water and energy.

His fingers gripped the armrest of his chair, the energy coursing through him. Tears brimmed in his eyes, rolling down his cheek. "I see... I see it all now."

The cloud began to dissipate, the light of dawn brightening the room.

Dr. Orrington sat in silence, eyes closed, breathing deeply as he embraced the newfound clarity. "Now... now I understand everything. The answers were always in the water. In the waves. In the pulse."

www.ingramcontent.com/pod-product-compliance
Lightning Source LLC
Chambersburg PA
CBHW070046030426
42335CB00016B/1810